• Federalism and Environmental Policy •

American Governance and Public Policy series

Series Editor: Barry Rabe, University of Michigan

How Governments Privatize: The Politics of Divestment in the United States and Germany
Mark Cassell

Improving Governance: A New Logic for Empirical Research
Laurence E. Lynn, Jr., Carolyn J. Heinrich, and Carolyn J. Hill

Justice and Nature: Kantian Philosophy, Environmental Policy, and the Law
John Martin Gillroy

Lobbying Together: Interest Group Coalitions in Legislative Politics
Kevin Hula

Pluralism by the Rules: Conflict and Cooperation in Environmental Regulation
Edward P. Weber

Policy Entrepreneurs and School Choice
Michael Mintrom

The Politics of Automobile Insurance Reform: Ideas, Institutions, and Public Policy in North America
Edward L. Lascher, Jr.

The Politics of Ideas and the Spread of Enterprise Zones
Karen Mossberger

The Politics of Unfunded Mandates: Whither Federalism?
Paul L. Posner

Preserving Public Lands for the Future: The Politics of Intergenerational Goods
William R. Lowry

Virtual Inequality: Beyond the Digital Divide
Karen Mossberger, Caroline J. Tolbert, and Mary Stansbury

Welfare Policymaking in the States: The Devil in Devolution
Pamela Winston

Federalism and Environmental Policy

Trust and the

Politics of Implementation

Second Edition
Revised and Updated

Denise Scheberle

Georgetown University Press / Washington, D.C.

Georgetown University Press, Washington, D.C.
© 2004 by Georgetown University Press. All rights reserved.
Printed in the United States of America

10 9 8 7 6 5 4 3 2 1 2004

This book is printed on acid-free paper meeting
the requirements of the American National Standard
for Permanence in Paper for Printed Library Materials.

Library of Congress Cataloging-in-Publication Data
Scheberle, Denise.
Federalism and environmental policy : trust and the politics of
implementation / Denise Scheberle. — 2nd ed. rev. and updated.
    p.   cm. — (American governance and public policy)
Includes bibliographical references and index.
ISBN 1-58901-100-7 (pbk. : alk. paper)
1. Environmental policy—United States.
2. Federal government—United States.
3. Environmental protection—United States—Case studies.
I. Title.   II. Series.
HC110.E5S387   2004
354.3′28′0973—dc22
2003019466

To Steve,

my husband and best friend

In memory of my father Deane Jewell,

the bravest, smartest, best person I have ever known

Contents

• 1 •

Environmental Federalism and Federal–State Working Relationships   1

• 2 •

Implementing Environmental Laws   32

• 3 •

Unintended Consequences, Policy Retreat, and Refocusing Events in Asbestos Policy   55

List of Tables

List of Figures

Preface

When I first looked at environmental programs twelve years ago, my hope was to better understand the way these programs ran (or failed to run). I quickly began to understand two things. First, each policy was unique and told its own fascinating implementation story. Each program evolved differently, with individual political, economic, logistical, and technical constraints. I discovered that even though they were different, the programs I studied could be viewed through the lens of a policy implementation framework. The framework that I designed for the first edition of this book, which was based upon the work of previous implementation scholars, seemed versatile enough to help explain the rate and process of implementation for environmental programs as diverse as radon and coal mining.

My second understanding came from dozens of conversations with state and federal employees over the years, most of whom were responsible for overseeing a particular environmental program. Put simply, my understanding was that working relationships matter, and matter a lot. Intergovernmental relationships are so important that implementation often depends upon them. Environmental laws are almost always based on the premise that states will do the on-the-ground work to implement and maintain the program while their federal counterparts oversee state efforts. However, this premise may be sorely tested when working relationships are strained.

The conversations I had with state and federal officials did more than help me understand how important intergovernmental working relationships were to implementing effective environmental programs. They led to my attempt to characterize these relationships based on mutual trust and the "right" kind of involvement of federal headquarters, regional, and state staffs. The typology of working relationships that I created for the first edition of this book represented my fledgling attempt to describe the reality presented to me by people who actually do the work of implementing programs.

In the years since the first edition, the operating principles of oversight have undergone dramatic shifts. In a way reminiscent of the song that asks "can't we all just get along," federal and state environmental officials have looked for better and more collaborative ways to run effective environmental programs. The National Environmental Performance Partnership System

(NEPPS) Agreement signed by the U.S. Environmental Protection Agency and state officials in 1995 offered the promise of increased flexibility for state environmental programs, with mutually agreed-on performance measures and the ability to prioritize state environmental efforts according to state environmental goals. A similar mindset emerged within coal-mining regulatory efforts. And the U.S. Department of the Interior's Office of Surface Mining reorganized its field offices and adopted what is known as the REG 8 Directive, which is designed to give more flexibility to state environmental officials.

Moreover, changes also have occurred in some of the programs I reviewed. For example, my review of the Safe Drinking Water Act came before Congress passed legislation in 1996 addressing many of the obstacles that had challenged the law's implementation in previous years. Costly new health-based standards for arsenic, radium, and radon in drinking water have raised the ire of many state and local government officials. Thus, a new "chapter" in this policy story needed to be written. Asbestos lawsuits have escalated, and the discovery of asbestos-related deaths in Libby, Montana, has focused even more attention on national asbestos policy. New discussions about indoor air quality have changed federal and state official orientations toward radon, with the result that radon is now seen as just one of many indoor pollutants, such as second-hand tobacco smoke and mold. Meanwhile, the mountaintop removal of coal has prompted a firestorm of protest in West Virginia and other Appalachian states.

In political arenas, things have changed as well. First, the language of devolution resurfaced in the mid-1990s, offering the prospect that additional duties in policy areas such as welfare and environmental protection would be shifted from Washington to state and local governments. Devolution in environmental arenas spurred the growth of community-based environmental protection, watershed management, and more state and local collaboration. Add to this the preference of George W. Bush's administration to hold the line on many environmental standards and programs and to not deal with global warming (as indicated by the Senate's failing to approve the Kyoto Protocol and the president's notable absence from the UN conference on global warming), and policymakers and practitioners face potentially very different political constraints.

As is true of virtually every policy area, the politics of implementing national environmental laws now includes considerably more discussion of national security since the terrorist attacks of September 11, 2001. Seven years ago, there were few political discussions about protecting America's public water supplies from terrorist attacks. But since September 11, these discussions have moved front and center in many debates about environmental laws, including the Safe Drinking Water Act. And asbestos emerged as an issue in cleaning up the World Trade Center site and surrounding office buildings and homes.

The new emphasis on national security and the war on terrorism since September 11 has also affected the budgets of environmental programs. And it has increased, prolonged, and deepened the economic recession, which in turn has affected state budgets. Increasing federal budget deficits mean that the federal government is less likely to increase its contribution to environmental protection efforts—unless that protection is in the interest of "national security." At the time of this writing, nearly every state is facing a budget deficit, and many states are contemplating some kind of budget reduction for environmental programs.

I have written this second edition for three reasons. First, I want to explore whether these apparently major shifts in policy related to federal oversight have changed federal–state working relationships (as perceived by front-line implementers). Second, I want to look at how major changes in the political landscape have changed the ways environmental policy is implemented. In this, my goal is to tell a deeper and richer story of policy implementation than in the first edition. Third, I want to modify and more closely describe the implementation model and the working relationship typology.

This new edition is more than just an update—it is an attempt to see whether federal–state relationships really have changed in the face of new policies and to recast the analyses of the programs reviewed before in the light of dramatic changes in the political arena. In doing so, the introductory chapter describes environmental federalism (and its evolution during the past decade) as well as the new federal–state working relationship programs (i.e., NEPPS and REG 8). Much more attention is given to chronicling the policy stories of the environmental programs reviewed in the first edition. Although the focus of this edition is the same as the first, I hope readers will find a more meaty treatment of each program—asbestos, radon, drinking water and surface mining—and perhaps learn a few new things along the way. I know that through my conversations with state and federal officials and key stakeholders, I certainly did. For that, I am deeply grateful.

Acknowledgments

Countless people contributed to the completion of this book, and I am deeply grateful for their assistance. I am especially indebted to the many hard-working staff members of the U.S. Environmental Protection Agency, the Office of Surface Mining of the U.S. Department of the Interior, state environmental and public health agencies, and professional and environmental organizations. These individuals graciously gave their time to talk with me, often for an hour or more, about the implementation of their programs. They wrote to me by e-mail; they added pages of notes to the surveys. Without their generosity, this study would not have been possible.

Many people were exceptionally generous in helping me understand the nature of environmental policy. I would like to mention a few by name: Ed Antz, Everett Bishop, Richard Bryson, Carmen Caldwell, David Chase, Greg Conrad, Tom Fitzpatrick, Charles Gasque, Ken Hechler, Jeanne Herb, Tom Hogan, Phil King, my old friend Milt Lammering, Linda Martin, Chuck Meyers, Kristy Miller, Lon Hesla, Mark Thompson, John Podolinsky, Vivian Stockman, and Larry Tessier. Each one was a storehouse of information and a fount of wisdom and insight. Several of these dedicated professionals also reviewed and provided comments on draft versions of the book. Nonetheless, any errors in the book are mine.

My deep appreciation also goes to two unsung heroes at the University of Wisconsin–Green Bay, Pam Schoen and Chris Terrien, for all their efforts on my behalf. Thanks are also due to the university and to its Research Council for supporting the copying and mailing costs associated with the research.

This book would not have been written but for the encouragement and astute comments of Gail Grella, the associate director and acquisitions editor, and Barry Rabe, the editor of the American Government Series, at Georgetown University Press. They were instrumental in helping me formulate my ideas and in providing guidance and direction; but most of all, they are terrific colleagues. Finally, my deepest thanks go to my husband Steve, who let me commandeer the kitchen table for several months with seemingly endless stacks of government reports, books, and articles, and who was an invaluable ally in fighting computer glitches, and to my daughter Jenni, who kept telling me that I really could do it.

Abbreviations

ACM	asbestos-containing material
AHERA	Asbestos Hazard and Emergency Response Act
CO	cessation order
DWSRF	Drinking Water State Revolving Fund
ECOS	Environmental Council of the States
EPA	U.S. Environmental Protection Agency
FTACO	failure-to-abate cessation order
FTE	full-time equivalent
GAO	U.S. General Accounting Office
GPRA	Government Performance and Results Act
IRAA	Indoor Radon Abatement Act
LEA	local education agencies
MCL	maximum contaminant levels
MCLG	maximum contaminant level goal
NAS	National Academy of Sciences
NEPPS	National Environmental Performance Partnership System
NESHAP	National Emission Standards for Hazardous Air Pollutants
NOV	notice of violation
NPDWR	National Primary Drinking Water Regulations
OSM	Office of Surface Mining, U.S. Department of the Interior
pCi/L	picocuries per liter
ppb	parts per billion
PPA	Performance Partnership Agreement
PPG	Performance Partnership Grant
PWS	public water system
SAB	Science Advisory Board
SDWA	Safe Drinking Water Act
SIRG	State Indoor Radon Abatement Grant
SMCRA	Surface Mining Control and Reclamation Act
TDN	ten-day notice
TSCA	Toxic Substances Control Act
UMRA	Unfunded Mandates Reform Act

· 1 ·

Environmental Federalism and Federal–State Working Relationships

This book explores two premises. The first is that positive relationships between federal and state officials facilitate implementation of environmental programs. To put it another way, in an ideal working relationship, federal and state officials "pull together." Pulling together suggests that state and federal personnel involved in the implementation of a program work cooperatively, regarding each other with mutual trust, respect, and a shared sense of program goals. Similarly, poor working relationships among federal and state officials may inhibit progress in environmental programs. In these cases, relationships are "coming apart." State and federal officials may have little or no respect for each other, exhibit frustration, lack a common vision, and not fully trust the actions of officials from the other agency. Working relationships that have come apart contain hidden agendas; little or no effective communication; and, at worst, open hostility. Effective implementation, I argue, could hardly be the result of such interactions.

The environmentalist may challenge the connection between effective programs and good intergovernmental working relationships, arguing that Congress passed environmental laws because state governments were reluctant to get into the business of environmental protection. Thus, without the strong arm of the federal government, environmental programs in the United States would not be as far along as they are today. Indeed, no fewer than twenty-four states have passed laws that prevent their own environmental agencies from promulgating regulations that are more stringent than federal baselines.[1] Moreover, they might argue, a continued strong federal presence, one that closely monitors the actions of state officials, is the only guarantee that environmental programs are effective. In other words, the danger in going too far down the road of harmonious federal–state interaction is that nothing will be accomplished. Regulatory provisions will fall by the wayside as federal officials try to provide maximum flexibility and autonomy to state implementers.

However, this first premise of this book takes as a given that environmental programs need the "federal gorilla in the closet," in the words of William

1

Ruckelshaus, former administrator of the U.S. Environmental Protection Agency (EPA).[2] The book assumes that the intergovernmental implementation of environmental programs with a national base level of protection constitutes a system that is not likely to disappear, nor one that should disappear. Nevertheless, within the system of federal oversight rest opportunities for collaborative working relationships. Finally, the book argues that most state and federal agency staff (not always the politicians, but the people with on-the-ground implementation responsibilities) share a common desire: to protect human health and the environment.

The second premise of the book is that the implementation of environmental policy is a story of high-stakes politics—a story as rich with contextual factors as the time the policy was formulated. The best understanding of this story can be gained by looking at an array of national- and state-level political forces. It also is gained by examining statutory and regulatory language and court decisions. The nature of the group targeted for behavioral change also adds rich detail to the story. Equally important are the cast of characters and the strategies they employ to make implementation unfold on their terms. This includes state and federal agency officials and staff. Within this process, however, are "implementation energizers," people who—often despite political or bureaucratic forces to the contrary—continue to fight for effective and efficient environmental programs. At the risk of too many metaphors, these energizers are the spark plugs of policy implementation. Finally, as is illustrated below in analyzing cases on environmental law, implementation may change due to refocusing events. The second premise is described in chapter 2.

The book explores both premises by examining four environmental laws: the Asbestos Hazard and Emergency Response Act (chapter 3), the Indoor Radon Abatement Act (chapter 4), the Safe Drinking Water Act (chapter 5), and the Surface Mining Control and Reclamation Act (chapter 6). The next sections of this chapter describe the evolution of federal–state working relationships, concepts of environmental federalism, new approaches to working relationships, and a typology for a working relationship.

Responses to Intergovernmental Working Relationships in the 1990s

Intergovernmental cooperation is often at the heart of the process of implementing laws. Sometimes these relationships become so rocky that they capture the attention of executives and legislators. In the 1990s, a collective light bulb in federal environmental agencies came on, illuminating the importance of positive working relationships. Evidence of this light of understanding about intergovernmental relationships has taken several forms. At the national level, efforts to understand, redirect, and rethink the construction of federal-state relationships began in the 1990s. EPA established the State/EPA Capacity Steering Committee in 1993 to lead a federal–state dialogue on creating and maintaining an environmental "partnership" between state and federal officials. Because of this effort, EPA administrator Carol Browner and several state officials signed a Joint Commitment to Reform Oversight and Create the National Environmental Performance Partnership System on May 17, 1995.[3] Moreover, many of the media-specific programs within EPA, such as the drinking water program, made improving relationships with state officials a primary programmatic goal in the mid-1990s.[4]

In 1993, state officials—unhappy with the pace of change in federal–state relationships and displeased with what they viewed as the heavy-handedness of EPA—formed the Environmental Council of the States (ECOS) to lobby for greater flexibility. Mary Gade, director of the Illinois Environmental Protection Agency, quipped, "State environmental leaders could no longer stand by and let EPA take the lead. States were, quite simply, 'Fed up.'"[5] ECOS became a major player advocating change in federal–state working relationships.

Federal–state interactions in environmental programs were also the focus of activity by the U.S. Congress and its audit, evaluation, and investigative arm, the U.S. General Accounting Office (GAO). At the request of the U.S. Senate Committee on Governmental Affairs, GAO examined the quality of EPA–state relationships. In its April 1995 report, *EPA and the States: Environmental Challenges Require a Better Working Relationship*, GAO confirmed that intergovernmental relationships were important and noted opportunities for improvement.[6] According to the report, the largest obstacle to running environmental programs was the lack of sufficient resources. EPA and state officials both agreed that federal funding has not kept pace with new environmental demands on state governments. However, other factors also contributed to less than stellar federal–state working relationships, including inconsistent EPA oversight across EPA regional offices; tendency of EPA staff to micromanage state programs; lack of involvement of state staff in major EPA decisions affecting state programs; and the need for EPA to provide technical support for increasingly complex program requirements.[7]

A 1995 report by the National Academy of Public Administration (NAPA) suggested that a key part of a new direction for EPA and for sustained progress in protecting the environment rests with the ability of EPA and of Congress to hand more responsibility and decision-making authority to the states. According to NAPA, "A new partnership needs to be formed, one based on 'accountable devolution' of national programs and on a reduction in EPA oversight when it is not needed."[8]

Earlier, Bill Clinton's administration had indicated its commitment to reforming the federal bureaucracy to make it less top-heavy, more decentralized, and more committed to serving "customer" interests. President Clinton released the first report of the National Performance Review headed by Vice President Al Gore on September 7, 1993. Among the 384 major recommendations for improving performance were many for enhancing intergovernmental relationships and building federal–state partnerships.[9]

It was with the backdrop of the National Performance Review that the Clinton administration expressed its desire to enhance the cooperative nature of federal–state relationships in environmental programs.[10] Central to the administration's reinvention strategy for EPA was the need to "partner" with state, local, and tribal governments. To this end, the administration asked EPA to "vigorously pursue" performance-based grants, which allowed states increased flexibility in using environmental grant monies. EPA should employ consensus-based rule making, enlisting the early participation of state and local governments in developing regulations; and a 25 percent reduction in paperwork, including reporting requirements for states.[11] These actions illustrated that federal oversight should shift away from highly prescriptive, command-and-control orientations toward states and move toward more cooperative, "pulling together" approaches.

Even the Science Advisory Board (SAB), an independent group of scientists, engineers, and other professionals who provide technical advice to EPA, recognized the importance of agencies in state and national governments to pull together. SAB believed that EPA must "expand its current capabilities and look beyond near-term problems to long-term environmental protection."[12] However, the enormity of future environmental challenges suggested that EPA cannot address them alone and, therefore, intergovernmental cooperative efforts would be "even more important" in the future.[13]

Other federal agencies charged with implementing environmental programs did not ignore the charge to improve working relationships. The U.S. Department of the Interior's Office of Surface Mining (OSM), reviewed in chapter 6, is a case in point. In his 1995 testimony before Congress, Robert Uram, then OSM's director, stated, "The key to improving this program lies in building a positive working relationship among all who are interested in the national surface mining program. Over the last eighteen months, everything we've done has been devoted to building that positive relationship [with primacy states and the tribes]."[14]

Thus, it appeared that the dialogue of intergovernmental cooperation, devolution of responsibility to state governments and federal–state partnerships was under way in nearly every arena: the administration, executive agencies, Congress, state and local governmental associations, and various research institutions. Because most environmental programs had been around for twenty years or more, why was there a crescendo of concern about federal–state relationships in environmental policy in the 1990s?

Perhaps one reason is that few policy areas placed greater and more diverse demands on states than environmental programs. After the environmental decade began in 1970, the federal government pressed state governments to do more—maintain National Ambient Air Quality Standards, preserve wetlands, address nonpoint-source water pollution, supply safe drinking water, control hazardous wastes, encourage recycling, and even test schools for radon. Congress's intent was to capitalize on the strengths of each level of government. State and local governments would be the front-line delivery agents of environmental programs. Federal agencies, in turn, would set strong health or technology based environmental standards and monitor state performance within environmental programs. Like the old Nike ads, state and local governments were told to "just do it." During the 1970s and 1980s, federal assertion into previous state policy territory reached its zenith, with preemptions more than doubling after 1969. Indeed, more than half of the federal mandates enacted since 1789 were passed in the 1970s and 1980s, and many of these preemptions dealt with environmental protection.[15]

Yet much to the chagrin of subnational governments, the national impetus for environmental action often occurred without sufficient (or any) funding. For example, the 1986 amendments to the Safe Drinking Water Act required states to implement wellhead protection programs and authorized $35 million in federal funds, but subsequently appropriated nothing. However, even $35 million was chickenfeed, given the requirements in the same law to test and treat for various contaminants in drinking water. Complying with drinking water regulations threatened to cost public water suppliers billions of dollars (see chapter 5). The combination of continuing demands on state governments coupled with unfunded or underfunded environmental mandates put state and local governments in an implementation bind.

As the concern over costly environmental mandates increased, state and local governments began a politically adroit campaign against what they viewed as the unfunded mandate problem. The International City/County Management Association created an Environmental Mandates Task Force in 1992, providing local governments with more opportunities to respond to federal and state environmental requirements.[16] Intergovernmental groups including the National League of Cities, U.S. Conference of Mayors, National Association of Counties, International City/County Management Association, and the National Governors Association sponsored National Unfunded Mandate Day on October 26, 1993, to highlight a host of studies that revealed sharply increased mandate burdens on state and local governments. According to these studies, counties would spend $870 million and cities would spend $8.6 billion for fiscal years 1994 through 1998 to comply with existing requirements of the Safe Drinking Water Act alone.[17] Considered with other environmental laws such as the Clean Water Act, costs of complying with mandates were daunting. These reports, together with intense lobbying by state and local government organizations, focused governmental and public attention on the cumulative effect of federal environmental mandates and increasingly tense intergovernmental relations under environmental laws.[18]

Politicians soon sought to champion the views of state and local governments. President Clinton declared that the "era of big government was over" in his 1994 State of the Union Address. Mandate relief was one of the ten planks in the Republicans' Contract with America. In 1995, it became the first plank to become law when Congress passed the Unfunded Mandates Reform Act (UMRA).[19] UMRA signaled that Congress and the president had finally recognized the concern of subnational governments about increasing national mandates. Senator Dirk Kempthorne (Idaho), a sponsor of the unfunded mandates legislation, epitomized the devolution rhetoric that accompanied the new law: "You'll get better decisions, because they [state officials] are closer to the problem. Washington, D.C., does not corner the market on wisdom."[20]

UMRA required Congress and the administration to gauge the potential effects of unfunded mandates before imposing them on states or businesses. Under the law, the Congressional Budget Office reviews bills for the presence of federal mandates on state and local governments costing more than $50 million annually. Once an unfunded mandate is identified, Congress must approve it in a separate vote, a process that creates both political and legislative hurdles for imposing the mandate. Although some analysts believe that this may defer the pace of national demands on state governments, it was not clear that this law would do much (if anything) to help the current situation of limited federal funding, particularly because the law deals only with future, not existing, mandates.[21] Indeed, Congress finds it difficult not to impose unfunded mandates on state and local governments. The Congressional Budget Office estimates that 12 percent of the bills reported out of committee between 1996 and 2001 had unfunded intergovernmental mandates.[22]

State and local governments also increasingly challenged federal intrusion on what they viewed as subnational issues. The zeal to address environmental concerns from the national level was viewed by state and local governments as "micromanaging" their programs, especially when those programs had long histories of what state officials viewed to be compliance with federal demands. In the twenty or so years since national environmental laws had been passed, state agencies had grown into their role as stewards of the environment. Many scholars observed that states enhanced their capacity to deal with environmental problems by enlarging staff, increasing the expertise and technical understanding of state-level implementers, and adding state sources of funding.[23] To put it simply, states were better prepared in the mid-1990s to implement environmental programs than they had been twenty years earlier.

Finally, the increased focus on intergovernmental relationships coincided with reassessments of future directions for environmental protection. Environmental policy analysts agreed that the third and fourth generations of environmental efforts required new approaches if the United States wanted to protect ecosystems. Most notably, these new approaches included increased reliance on grassroots participation and less reliance on command-and-control regulation—or what DeWitt John refers to as "civic environmentalism."[24] Civic environmentalism was necessary because the unfinished business of environmental protection (e.g., restoration of ecosystem health, combating nonpoint-source pollution, prompting individual behavioral change) required the use of new tools and techniques. According to John, "The central idea animating civic environmentalism is that in some cases, communities and states will organize on their own to protect the environment, without being forced to do so by the federal government. . . . Civic environmentalism is fundamentally a bottom-up approach to environmental protection."[25]

In its 1996 report, the President's Council on Sustainable Development pointed to the need for sustainable communities and the involvement of citizens in environmental protection.[26] Sustainable communities are only possible when citizens make environmentally sensitive choices about land-use controls, the protection of biodiversity, watershed management, and other important actions in the province of state or local control. Citizen actions thus are preventative, valuing the natural resource in a way that the federal government cannot mandate.

In short, it is not surprising that the 1990s brought to a head concern about the nature and quality of intergovernmental relationships and the connection of those relationships to effective environmental protection programs. Programs were costly and activities were proliferating; states were gaining expertise while experiencing increasing demands for environmental improvement from their citizens. Meanwhile, federal policymakers and officials within federal agencies recognized that all was not well in the implementation phases of many environmental efforts.

Concepts of Federalism

Federalism, which has been defined by Thomas Anton as "the system of rules for the division of public policy responsibilities" among national and state governments, has prompted as much debate as perhaps any constitutional principle.[27] John Donahue referred to federalism as "America's endless argument," while historian Richard Hofstadter famously quipped that government was "a harmonious system of mutual frustration."[28] Debates over the appropriate scope and division of power, responsibilities, and authority among the federal and state governments are certainly not over, and especially not for environmental federalism. When Congress passed a series of environmental laws three decades ago, lawmakers envisioned federalism and intergovernmental relations in environmental governance changing in dramatic and permanent ways, but they had no idea at the outset how complicated and contentious intergovernmental relations would become.

Students of federalism have long hoped for collegial approaches between federal and state officials in solving public problems. The term "marble-cake federalism" was popularized by Morton Grodzins, who suggested that public responsibilities could not be precisely defined but were nonetheless shared by federal, state, and local officials.[29] This functional sharing promoted patterns of cooperative and collaborative behavior, behavior negotiated among intergovernmental actors.[30] Terry Sanford used a metaphor of a rowboat to describe the interdependency of federal, state, and local officials: "The governments are all in the same boat, tossed by the same waves and dependent upon each other's paddles. When any one fails to row, they all move more slowly, and the waves become more dangerous for all."[31]

Most often, when state and federal officials become partners, they do it within the context of a legal relationship. Several types of federal–state legal relationships exist in environmental laws. The prevailing national pattern for environmental policy was to write strong statutory language that relied on command-and-control regulatory schemes and an initial preemption of state laws, then permit devolution of responsibility back to state and local governments.[32] Under this partial-preemption legislative strategy, Congress requires the federal oversight agency (usually EPA) to set national environmental quality standards and then allows the agency to delegate day-to-day programmatic responsibilities to states with approved programs. Each environmental law establishes activities the states must undertake to receive delegated authority. This always includes a determination by the federal oversight agency that state laws and regulations be at least as strict as federal requirements. The principle of primacy preserves a state's right to pass requirements more stringent than those found under national law and regulations. Two laws examined in this book, the Safe Drinking Water Act and the Surface Mining Control and Reclamation Act, contain primacy provisions.

This partial-preemption regulatory approach represents a middle ground in the implementation of a national regulatory policy. Federalism scholar Joseph Zimmerman observed that partial-preemption statutes have not only increased the complexity of the federal system but have raised accountability issues as well.[33] Unlike total preemption, complete with federal mandates requiring state performance according to federal prescription, partial preemption allows states certain flexibility in program design. States have leeway to implement their laws and design their enforcement strategies, provided these laws are at least as stringent as the applicable federal statute. Furthermore, states can opt not to go along. If state officials choose not to shoulder the implementation responsibility for the regulatory program, the federal government remains the regulatory agent. If approved state programs prove inadequate in enforcing national standards, the federal government reserves the right to "preempt" state authority and reassume primacy. Thus, the states' acceptance of primacy for a national regulatory program is not, in theory at least, an abdication of national control.

Though most states have pursued delegated authority, states sometimes decide it is not in their best interest. As of 1998, 74 percent of all environmental programs were delegated to the states, up from 41 percent in 1993.[34] Complicating primacy further, states may have authority for one section of a law but not others. For example, only Michigan and New Jersey have approval to operate the federal wetlands permitting program under Section 404 of the Clean Water Act. However, forty-four states are authorized to run the National Pollutant Discharge Elimination System permitting program for point-source dischargers, the most important component of the same law.[35]

Sometimes, environmental laws do not provide for complete delegated authority, which would include both the inspection and enforcement components of a regulatory program. Rather, states can receive a waiver to operate the inspection, outreach, and informational components of an environmental program. States can also enter into cooperative agreements with EPA to operate some aspects of the program, such as enforcement activities under the Toxic Substances Control Act. However, enforcement responsibilities reside with the federal oversight agency. The implementation of the Asbestos Hazard and Emergency Response Act is an example of this type of approach, as is described in chapter 3.

A second way states become involved in implementing environmental laws is through a direct statutory order. In this case, congressional architects of environmental laws oblige the states to perform certain tasks. For example, Congress mandated that states conduct source water assessments under the 1996 amendments to the Safe Drinking Water Act. Absent state activity, the federal agency would not assume responsibility for implementation. States can opt not to comply, but they may face sanctions in other programs. Also, with no federal assumption of programmatic responsibilities (e.g., as provided for under the partial-preemption approach), states that ignore the mandate may be compelled under court order to perform their duties—provided, however, that national requirements do not represent a constitutional encroachment on state sovereignty. The Supreme Court has recently shown some willingness to limit the use of the Commerce Clause, the primary constitutional vehicle through which Congress has passed many environmental laws.[36]

A third approach to federal–state interactions in environmental programs is to establish principally voluntary relationships and rely on grant monies as incentives for state participation. The Indoor Radon Abatement Act, for example, provided matching funds for states to conduct residential radon surveys. As is typical of this approach, federal grant awards are matched with state funds. As state programs get under way, the federal match may decrease in future grant years. Under the radon program, states had a federal allotment of 75 percent the first year, 60 percent the second year, and 50 percent in subsequent years. One law may contain multiple approaches, and many environmental programs provide some level of federal funding to facilitate state implementation.

These statutory relationships define one level of federal–state interaction. Equally important, however, are the ongoing working relationships that develop between federal and state officials. These working relationships include informal and formal contact that occurs between state and federal personnel in operating any intergovernmental program. To return to Sanford's rowboat metaphor, federal and state actors may be in the boat together but certainly not agree about which direction to head.

NEPPS and the REG 8 Directive

"Endless arguments" and "a harmonious system of mutual frustration" describe federalism, but they may also describe the day-to-day interactions of federal and state staffs. Here, the most salient issues for devolving environmental responsibilities include the extent of federal "micromanagement" of state programs and the degree to which states are given flexibility to set policy priorities reflecting problems of local importance. As was mentioned above, the major solution for strained federal–state relationships under EPA's auspices was the National Environmental Performance Partnership System (NEPPS).

As described in the 1995 ECOS/EPA *Joint Commitment to Reform Oversight and Create a National Environmental Performance Partnership* System, NEPPS was created to "strengthen our protection of public health and the environmental by directing scarce public resources toward improving environmental results, allowing states greater flexibility to achieve those results, and enhancing our accountability to the public and taxpayers."[37] The Joint Commitment laid out seven principal components of the federal-state partnership: increased use of environmental indicators, a new approach to program assessment by states, Performance Partnership Agreements (PPAs), differential oversight, performance leadership programs, public outreach and involvement, and joint system evaluation.[38]

When these components are considered, NEPPS clearly represents a significant realignment of federal-state relationships under environmental laws implemented by the EPA. Indeed, the Environmental Law Institute referred to NEPPS as the "most substantial nationwide reform in EPA-state relationships since those relationships were first established over twenty-five years ago."[39] Of particular note was the change in oversight orientation by the EPA. As noted in the agreement:

> We have learned that better decisions result from a collaborative process with people working together, rather than from an adversarial one that pits them against each other. . . . The states should serve as the primary front-line delivery agent, managing their own programs, adapting to local conditions, and testing new approaches for delivering more environmental protection for less.[40]

Implicit in that language was an understanding that the EPA would maximize state flexibility in "partnering" with states. The cornerstone of NEPPS was the PPA, which maximized oversight flexibility by greatly increasing the role of states in determining what the EPA would oversee. As envisioned in the original commitment, a PPA would come from joint planning and priority-setting dialogue between the state and its corresponding EPA regional office, and from public involvement. Part of this involvement was included in a state's self-assessment, designed to establish a baseline of environmental conditions on the ground, but also to identify environmental issues of greatest state priority. EPA and state officials would then agree on the appropriate environmental goals and program performance indicators. Rather than states submitting work plans program-by-program, EPA regional and state officials would agree on the work states would do as part of the PPA, including any necessary disinvestments due to limits on available resources.

States and EPA incorporated outcome measures into PPAs, which would then form the basis for measuring state performance. Initially, the 1995 agreement called for EPA to develop Core Performance Measures (CPMs), or a "limited number of program and multi-media performance measures on which each state shall report."[41] ECOS and EPA envisioned that CPMs would be a uniform suite of environmental and programmatic measures of progress for all states participating in the NEPPS program.

Performance measures became controversial almost before the ink was dry on the first agreements. At issue was the ability of states to incorporate core performance measures selectively into their PPAs. In response, ECOS and EPA further refined the set of core performance measures in late 1998 for implementation in fiscal year 2000. In 1999, ECOS asked its members to approve the set of core performance measures as a mandatory requirement for states participating in NEPPS.[42] Many state officials objected to this wholesale adoption of core performance measures, for at least three reasons.

First, a mandatory, "one-size-fits-all" requirement was not in line with the spirit of NEPPS, designed to maximize state flexibility. Moreover, some states were ahead of the EPA in developing strategic planning documents for environmental management and had other indicators in place. Second, the report requirements often were in addition to other operational reporting requirements under regulatory programs. In rejecting CPMs in 1999, Stephan Adams, Florida Department of Environmental Protection spokesperson, commented: "In our view, the ECOS reporting system is being imposed on states by the EPA without any concurrent reduction in the beans we are counting, and we want to go our own way because we in Florida know our priorities better than the federal government."[43]

Third, some state officials felt that EPA was tailoring the NEPPS performance measure to conform to the environmental outcome measures under the Government Performance and Results Act of 1993 (GPRA), rather than on what states wanted to measure. Indeed, EPA, with a new "results-based" reporting burden of its own, had a stake in closely aligning performance measures under NEPPS with its own requirements under GPRA. EPA was to begin reporting progress toward environmental outcomes in 1997.

In response to state concerns about core performance measures, ECOS and EPA added an addendum to the 1997 *Joint Statement on Measuring Progress under NEPPS*.[44] The addendum clarified that states were not directly responsible for fulfilling EPA reporting requirements under the GRPA. (However, many CPMs are closely aligned or identical to what EPA must report under the GRPA.) Most important, states could modify, substitute, or eliminate a core performance measure, with EPA approval. Members of ECOS subsequently adopted a resolution approving the core performance measures for fiscal year 2000 and beyond with the acknowledgment that such adoption would "not bind individual States to adopt any or all of the core performance measures."[45]

If PPAs were the building blocks for providing programmatic flexibility to states, performance partnership grants (PPGs) potentially did the same for funding flexibility. Authorized by Congress in 1996, PPGs permitted states to consolidate up to sixteen categorical environmental grants into one block grant. Now, for the first time in the history of U.S. environmental law, states could spend federal grant dollars according to state priorities. Providing states with a single, therefore more flexible, grant under NEPPS in theory, at least, would be a strong tool for improving federal-state relationships. Categorical grants eligible for inclusion in a PPG include sections of the Clean Air Act, Clean Water Act, Safe Drinking Water Act, Toxic Substance Control Act and Solid Waste Disposal Act.

From 1997 to 2000, the average number of grants combined in a PPG has remained at about seven, with the most frequently combined grants being water pollution control, hazardous waste management, air pollution control, and pesticide enforcement and applicator certification.[46] The total number of grants increased from 175 in 1997 to 248 in 2000. However, that represented less than a third of the total number of grants eligible for consolidation by states with PPGs.[47] States consolidated only $217 million of the $745 million in state environmental program grants available in 1998. While that represented an increase of 28 percent from the previous year, it still meant that states were not taking full advantage of PPGs.[48]

Though participation is voluntary, most states have opted into the NEPPS process. State participation grew from six states in the initial year (1996) to 38 states by the end of 2001.[49] States do not have to have an approved PPA in place to receive a PPG, nor is a PPG required as part of a PPA. In fiscal year 2000, 28 states had both a PPA and PPG; 6 had only a PPG; 4 had only a PPA.[50] State participation in NEPPS also varies by EPA region. All of the states in EPA Regions 1 and 8 are participating in NEPPS, and have both PPAs and PPGs in place. In contrast, only one state in Region 9 (Arizona) is participating in NEPPS, and Arizona's participation is limited to a PPG. According to the most recent EPA data available, environmental agencies in California, Pennsylvania, Virginia, West Virginia, Florida, Alabama, Michigan, Ohio, and the District of Columbia have chosen not to participate in NEPPS.[51]

However, changing oversight in intergovernmental relations is no easy task. On paper, federal–state relationships under NEPPS were changing. Nevertheless, a series of reviews by analysts inside and outside government presented a mixed picture of success. In its 1997 review, GAO noted several barriers to attempts to promote innovation in the federal–state relationship.[52] GAO observed that EPA struggled to get buy-in from its rank and file, many of whom had grown accustomed to the regulatory structure. EPA and state officials disagreed over issues of state flexibility and the extent to which external stakeholders should be part of negotiations. Federal–state tensions came to a head in February 1997, when EPA withdrew from discussions about an EPA–ECOS joint proposal to promote and implement regulatory reinvention efforts.[53] Though EPA eventually came back to the table with ECOS, more than a year would pass before EPA officials signed the agreement.

Two widely cited studies by NAPA also found that NEPPS had not yet lived up to its expectations. Barriers to NEPPS goals included the single-medium culture at EPA and state agencies; the extent to which PPAs had become "ruling documents" for state commitments and deliverables; competing visions of oversight and enforcement; and a lack of adequate or appropriate data on which to conduct performance-based assessment.[54] GAO and NAPA studies found that most state officials believed participation in NEPPS had not brought significant reductions in reporting and other oversight activities by EPA staff. Researchers pointed to bureaucratic norms and EPA agency culture, and they predicted that "EPA is unlikely to be able to efficiently and effectively maintain two distinct and separate systems of program oversight and management. If NEPPS is to continue to make progress toward its original vision, states and regions operating under NEPPS cannot simultaneously meet the requirements of both NEPPS and the traditional system."[55] EPA officials themselves observed, "Some EPA oversight practices resulted in duplication of effort, burdensome reporting and unproductive relationships."[56]

The arrangement of EPA, with a single headquarters and ten regional offices, complicates efforts to "get the word out" to all frontline regional staff. However, more than geographic distance seems to exist between EPA headquarters and regional officials. EPA regional officials identified ongoing compliance problems in state programs that necessitated greater oversight. EPA regulators were reluctant to reduce oversight without measures in place to ensure that environmental programs were maintained. The difficulty in resolving disagreements over the extent to which states could exercise regulatory flexibility was clearly a setback for NEPPS.

Even at EPA headquarters, offices divided sharply on the level of state oversight. The Office of Enforcement and Compliance Assurance was particularly vocal in support of pre-NEPPS oversight system to ensure adequate enforcement. Officials felt that EPA's vigilance is a key factor in motivating state action, even in states with strong programs. The EPA's Office of the Inspector General issued reports critical of state enforcement practices. One report, criticizing enforcement in Pennsylvania, led that state's environmental agency to call off its preparations to participate in NEPPS.[57]

Challenges remain with performance measures. In addition to the challenge of developing appropriate indicators of environmental results and making those commensurate with program requirements (a Herculean task), CPMs are not the only kind of accountability faced by state environmental agencies. As William Gormley notes, CPMs were "grafted onto other systems of accountability, including state-level systems that sought to make state environmental agencies—as well as other state agencies—more accountable to state politicians."[58] Thus, CPMs overlay state strategic plans, existing data and reporting systems and political climates, as well as existing federal-state reporting requirements.

In 1996, OSM adopted the REG 8 Directive, which applied to states that had primacy to implement surface mining programs. (Directives are the policies, guidelines, or procedures that OSM establishes to provide implementation direction to the staff.) This directive compares in many ways to NEPPS. First, it was the product of a federal–state oversight team. Second, it represents fundamental change in OSM's oversight approach. Third, it contains the language of "shared commitment," a term very close to the "partnership" term of NEPPS. Fourth, it incorporates a commitment to performance-based evaluation of state programs and the use of indicators.

However, the directive went farther than NEPPS in its willingness to forgo previous requirements for states. OSM, promising that "oversight will not be process-driven," instead would focus on "on-the-ground/end-result success."[59] Most important, the directive established a system that discouraged micromanagement and focused on the success or failure of state programs rather than on the activities of states.[60] Heretofore, previous oversight directives had concentrated on state agency outputs, such as the number of inspections or notices of violation issued. For example, a 1988 version of oversight policy stated that the oversight approach is to "measure directly whether state inspectors are citing all violations." It further directed OSM inspectors to "document the state's reasons for failing to cite violations."[61] In contrast, the new REG 8 Directive was so oriented toward flexible oversight that it provided a flowchart for its oversight personnel to follow, one that allowed numerous opportunities for state–federal consultations in program implementation (see figure 6.4).

Like NEPPS, primacy states work with OSM officials to create annual performance agreements. Performance agreements should foster mutual respect, assure that oversight topics reflect OSM/state priorities and consider the impacts on state resources, and use on-the-ground results as the principle measure of state performance.[62]

Unlike NEPPS, however, each agreement contains only three broad measures of state performance. The first required states to measure off-site impacts from mining operations. Simply put, states were to report anything resulting from a surface coal mining and reclamation activity or operation that caused a negative effect on resources (people, land, water, structures), with the expectation that states, through regulating mining operations, would minimize any negative impacts. A second is reclamation success. Under this measure, OSM would evaluate the effectiveness of the state program in ensuring successful reclamation on lands affected by surface coal mining operations. The third element was customer service. OSM evaluates the effectiveness of customer service provided by the state by monitoring the state's responses to complaints and requests for assistance and services. To accomplish this, OSM reviews the timeliness, accuracy, completeness, and appropriateness of state actions in handling of citizen complaints, permitting actions, bond releases, or other administrative activities.[63]

Beyond these three categories, the Directive stressed the importance of developing state-specific evaluation plans tailored to the unique conditions of each state's surface mining program. These evaluation plans may be part of the performance agreement or they may stand alone. By design, REG 8 provides wide latitude for each OSM field office to work with states in directing oversight resources to fit state conditions. The only requirement is that the plans or agreements contain the three national measurements described above.

The Clinton administration seemed pleased with this new direction in federal–state relations. In 1997, the OSM Oversight Team received the Hammer Award from Vice President Al Gore, recognizing REG 8 as a model of reinventing government and embracing the ideals of the NPR.[64]

REG 8 has not been the subject of much scholarly, GAO, or NAPA attention. In an internal review, the OSM Oversight Outreach Team found that OSM regulatory staff members embrace REG 8, if not with open arms, at least with tacit acceptance.[65] The report noted that most OSM field staff believes that performance agreements help to resolve some of the long-standing animosity between the OSM and states. However, some interagency tensions remain. OSM inspectors do not believe that they should perform fewer oversight activities, only that the oversight might be more effective under the more flexible, results-oriented approach of REG 8. Some OSM staff worry that the agency's credibility has diminished in the eyes of external stakeholders who perceive a decrease in the agency's independence in conducting enforcement actions. As discussed below, most state officials are satisfied with the new oversight direction of the OSM.

Chapters 3, 4, 5, and 6 explore the implementation and working relationships within four environmental programs. Because NEPPS and REG 8 potentially affect working relationships, EPA regional and state program managers, along with OSM and state surface mining directors, were asked their perceptions about these new oversight arrangements through surveys and telephone interviews. (See the appendix to this book for a description of the study design.) In addition, surveys were sent to ten NEPPS coordinators (one in each region). This exploratory research with EPA, OSM, and state officials provides anecdotal observations about how well NEPPS and REG 8 are working.

Five out of ten NEPPS coordinators in EPA regional offices provided opinions about NEPPS. None of the five believed that NEPPS was operating perfectly, or even well. This is somewhat surprising, because these coordinators were implementing NEPPS at the regional level. Many of their comments reflect the studies conducted by NAPA and GAO. One official commented, "The greatest struggle has been to try (unsuccessfully) to make EPA headquarters understand that NEPPS is a voluntary program, and its greatest value is its flexibility. Headquarters 'NEPPSters' are being driven . . . to write rules and regulations that will formalize, standardize, and ossify NEPPS to the point where it will be just 'one more program.' It's not a program; it's a way of doing business."

Another official echoed the concern that EPA was ignoring the spirit of NEPPS: "I wish I could magically make program managers more interested in the planning aspects of the PPAs. Headquarters should better define what NEPPS is and is not. Stop spending so much time with ECOS and more with the regions working directly with the states." Still another official put it this way: "The greatest struggle has been in determining what makes a PPA really worthwhile. Initially thought to be a streamlining approach, it can take a high level of coordination and involvement that would not have to happen [under the traditional approach]. NEPPS takes a lot of energy, and people are generally more comfortable to leave things in place." One NEPPS coordinator lamented, "Headquarters should stop acting like NEPPS is a silver bullet. It is one tool in the box. They also need to realize that we [states and EPA regions] were engaged in joint planning and priority setting long before NEPPS. Partnerships flow out of mutual respect—not mandates. Headquarters should disabuse itself of any notion that making NEPPS mandatory is a solution to anything."

Also intriguing are the perceptions these coordinators have about the influence of NEPPS on working relationships. None of the five respondents agreed that states with PPAs have more effective environmental programs than states without them. Only half of the respondents agreed that the process of developing PPAs has improved federal–state working relationships. Finally, every coordinator who responded to the survey disagreed that EPA regional project officers were enthusiastic about NEPPS, and only one coordinator felt that state environmental managers were enthusiastic.

Taken collectively, these statements provide some evidence that all is not well with NEPPS implementation, at least as perceived by some persons tasked with implementing NEPPS in EPA regions. When thirteen EPA regional officials running radon, drinking water, or asbestos programs were asked about NEPPS, only two spoke positively and confidently about the program. Most were indifferent to NEPPS, calling it just one more "management program." One hoped NEPPS would just "go away."

Two officials were much more strident in their criticism, noting issues of accountability and control. One EPA project officer suggested that "NEPPS is a nightmare. It is like driving up to a state line with bags of money, dropping them off and not having a say in what states do with the money. We have lost our ability to influence state activities. At least with a single grant, we have some say about what the states do and what they report." Another noted: "NEPPS is a huge issue for our program. NEPPS minimizes reporting requirements for states, yet the kind of data required by EPA headquarters for our program accountability was counter to what states were going to report under PPAs. The message from states in our region is that you can't ask for all of this, so we were caught between what headquarters wanted and what NEPPS required."

Several EPA project officers worried that the NEPPS made the state programs more vulnerable. One regional staff member summed it up this way: "I think the real threat of NEPPS is that state programs will fade into obscurity. The concept of NEPPS is great, but now there's no way to tell if the money we give to the states is really being used to address the environmental goals in our specific program."

Interestingly, many state officials agreed. In the drinking water program, state administrators knew about NEPPS, PPAs, and PPGs. However, three-fourths of drinking water officials in states that had PPAs in place had a neutral or negative opinion about the agreements. When asked how the adoption of PPAs had changed their state drinking water programs, comments ranged from "not much" and "not that noticeable" to "we anticipate a deleterious effect—primarily through funds transferred to other areas" and "it allowed the [state] administration to take funds intended for drinking water and apply them to higher priority programs." Only a few drinking water officials noted that the PPAs had given them more programmatic or funding flexibility.

Most state radon officials did not know whether or not their state had adopted PPAs, nor had they heard of NEPPS. Of the seven who knew that their state had PPAs, opinions were divided. One state official observed that "the PPA has required the program to focus on long-range goals and milestones more than it had prior to the PPA." Another supported the PPA: "It's given us better quality assurance and a better planning process." A third noted that the radon program received "a little better funding." Those that had neutral or negative opinions pointed to reporting requirements. "Since the NEPPS, we have to do double reporting," commented one official. Another, in frustration, offered, "Our region requires a separate grant application to be done and submitted. The EPA regional radon coordinator does not understand the goal of PPAs or PPGs."

Like radon officials, most state asbestos officials were not aware of PPAs or were not involved with the process. Of the six who knew their states had PPAs, only two offered an opinion. Speaking of PPGs, one stated: "The adoption of a PPG has actually increased our workload, as it has increased some of the paperwork for the program. It has also 'muddied the waters,' because there are less clear-cut deliverables [i.e., the number of inspections] in the PPG, but they are still required at the program level. On the plus side, managing the money through the PPG has been easier and less work." Another observed that the PPA has "allowed some streamlining of the grant application."

Perhaps one state official put it best when he observed, "Program people at the EPA have a need to understand the finite details. Regional [EPA] people still want [agency] outputs. On the other hand, environmental administrators need a broad-brush measure of outcomes. NEPPS is, in a sense, touchy-feely where programs are nuts and bolts."

In sum, anecdotal evidence from state, EPA regional project officers, and even EPA regional NEPPS coordinators suggests that they do not embrace NEPPS with open arms. This is not hard to imagine, because EPA regional staff are accountable for quantitative measures of program success. However, project officers in the much larger programs, such as those dealing with air, water, and hazardous wastes, may have a much more optimistic view of NEPPS. Still, it appears that more work needs to be done to make NEPPS the most substantial and successful nationwide reform in EPA–state relationships in twenty-five years, as suggested by the Environmental Law Institute.

A more optimistic picture emerges with the REG 8 Directive, based upon the perspectives of state and federal surface mining directors. Though it is more fully discussed in chapters 6 and 7, some comments are worth mentioning here. Because the surface mining program is the only program administered by OSM, comparisons with EPA's large number of programs are a bit unfair. OSM deals with one grant, one program, and twenty-four states. The level of intergovernmental and programmatic complexity is not nearly the same as at EPA. However, the OSM–state working relationships are infamous for their highly contentious nature. REG 8 was designed to remedy the federal–state brawl, and it appears to have been successful, at least from the perspective of most state officials.

Fifty percent of state officials responding to the survey agree that working relationships are better since REG 8. Only 22 percent of state officials believe that REG 8 has not improved working relationships. As one official observed, "Since REG 8, our state and the local OSM office have worked closely and in a team environment to scope how oversight will be conducted each year. We meet and discuss issues of mutual concern and work out any differences in developing an oversight plan. Reports and analyses are jointly prepared with the goal of obtaining real programmatic improvement. Since the state and OSM are both owners of the performance agreement, we feel it is a means to show not only that the state is meeting its regulatory responsibilities, but also a tool to effect continuous overall program improvement." Another comment compared oversight before and since REG 8: "Prior to REG 8, OSM would draft an oversight plan and let us know what parts of the program would be subject to oversight that year. The state had very little involvement."

Although not all OSM field office staff embrace the much more accommodating posture of the REG 8 Directive, it appears that most do. Working relationships within surface mining seem less confrontational than when the program was reviewed in the study done six years ago. However, environmental groups are not pleased with such a dramatic realignment of OSM's oversight style. In a letter to William J. Kovacic, director of OSM's Lexington Field Office, the Kentucky Resources Council called REG 8 a "grossly inadequate" evaluative tool. The council blasted OSM for abdicating its enforcement of the Surface Mining Control and Reclamation Act, saying that the agency had "ceased to be an independent regulatory agency performing the oversight function intended by Congress, and has instead granted to the states the right to 'negotiate' the terms of how their performance will be evaluated."[66]

No doubt, the context for federal–state relationships has changed. Both EPA and OSM created dramatic new approaches to oversight with NEPPS and REG 8. NEPPS promised more than it has yet delivered, according to NAPA and GAO studies and anecdotal evidence in this section. OSM made REG 8 the cornerstone of its oversight posture, sometimes to the chagrin of citizens' groups. The next section presents a framework for looking at federal–state working relationships.

A Typology of Working Relationships

The role orientations of federal actors can dramatically affect working relationships and implementation patterns. Many scholars note the error of federal overseers leaning too vigorously on their state counterparts in order to secure compliance with federal goals.[67] If one agrees that coercion may not be the best approach for federal oversight officials to adopt, what conditions facilitate intergovernmental working relationships that "pull together"? Given that the nature of these relationships is important, is it possible to predict when they are more likely to be positive among the individuals responsible for a program? This section presents one way of looking at such relationships.

At the risk of oversimplifying the complexity of federal–state interactions, two characteristics of working relationships seem most critical to predicting whether federal and state officials will respond positively to each other. The first essential characteristic is mutual trust. Individuals within a working relationship may vary in their belief that other participants are dedicated to effectively implementing the policy. High levels of trust are evident within a relationship when actors share goals, respect the actions of others, allow flexibility, and support individuals within the program. Accordingly, the typology creates two dimensions of trust: individuals have either low or high levels of trust for implementation colleagues outside their organization.

The second essential characteristic of positive working relationships is the extent of involvement by oversight personnel. The typology suggests that participants in different organizations (in this case, federal and state agencies) may have low or high levels of involvement in the program. Involvement may include formal or informal communication between federal and state staffs, the frequency and nature of oversight activities, provision of funding, sharing of resources, giving of advice, and personal and other contacts among actors.

Involvement, then, incorporates a wide range of possible interactions between federal and state officials. However, though trust is normative (more of it is better), involvement does not carry that connotation. In other words, high involvement among participants may not necessarily lead to positive working relationships. Federal staff involvement that is perceived by state officials to be nitpicking state programs or micromanaging state activities, for example, may be counterproductive to establishing the kind of working relationship that will facilitate implementation.

With the two characteristics of positive working relationships—trust and involvement—as the dimensions of the typology, four kinds of relationships are possible. The next paragraphs describe what life is like for the actors in each cell of the typology and the kind of relationships that result when these two characteristics are considered.

Pulling Together: High Trust and High Involvement

When high levels of trust are coupled with high levels of involvement, as shown in the upper right corner of figure 1.1, the strongest kind of working relationship results. The participants in the relationship are pulling together, and the result is synergistic: The accomplishments of pulling together are greater than the sum of what each participant could do alone. Clearly, this is the cell of choice for both participants in the program and for observers of federal–state relationships.

Federal overseers recognize the abilities, expertise, and dedication of state agency staff. In turn, state staff accord the same level of respect to their federal counterparts. Moreover, federal agency officials exhibit concern about the success of the state implementation efforts—not because that is their job, but because they have a genuine desire to see state staff accomplish good things. The nature of the involvement, then, becomes one of assistance, with ample doses of technical assistance, consultation, and even logistical support, if possible, for on-the-ground implementation.

High
trust

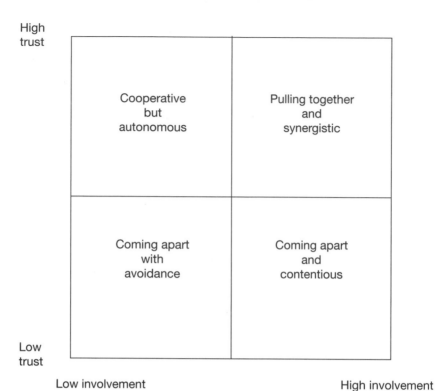

Cooperative but autonomous	Pulling together and synergistic
Coming apart with avoidance	Coming apart and contentious

Low
trust

Low involvement   High involvement

Figure 1.1.   A Typology of Federal and State Working Relationships

Skeptics may argue that high-trust, high-involvement relationships are nearly impossible to achieve and that federal and state officials seldom pull together. Indeed, the federal oversight role mitigates against establishing high levels of trust, whereas the desire of state officials to act autonomously mitigates against high levels of federal involvement. What is important is involvement based on a shared commitment to the policy objectives and a common recognition of the nature of the public problem to be solved. If interactions entail sharing knowledge, seeking advice and input, avoiding knee-jerk reactions to participant behaviors, and acknowledging positive activities, federal and state participants move toward the right kind of involvement and increased levels of trust.

Conversely, some people may argue that, after all, cooperative federalism suggests that federal–state relationships are usually harmonious. Functional expertise among the participants suggests that federal, state, and local personnel within programs work very cooperatively together because maintaining bureaucratic control over public programs is the paramount value. When political actors threaten programs, state and federal actors quickly circle the wagons to protect their programmatic turf.

Assuming that state and federal bureaucrats naturally work together in harmony because of their shared interest in the program is to ignore the stronger elements of federal–state relationships and the distinct roles that federal staff and state staffs play in policy implementation. For example, federal agency staff oversee the actions of state officials and promulgate national regulations, grant guidance documents, and state performance agreements; state officials run the inspection and enforcement programs, respond to public concerns and complaints, and promulgate state regulations and program requirements. Meanwhile, each actor must please a different set of constituents and stakeholders. Bliss within federal–state relationships is unlikely, given these constraints and the different federal and state perspectives of the program. As Miles's Law suggests, "Where you stand depends on where you sit."[68]

In short, expect relationships that pull together to be few and far between. Pulling together happens not by chance, or even by design. Pulling together is accomplished by the concerted efforts of both state and federal participants to achieve programmatic success.

Cooperative but Autonomous: High Trust with Low Involvement

When high levels of trust are combined with low levels of involvement, the result is a relationship that is cooperative but lonely, as is shown in the upper left corner of figure 1.1. Here, participants respect each other's roles but lack sufficient interaction to create synergy in the relationship and fully pull together. Participants have room to make their own decisions, but they may be unaware of what other participants in the same program are doing. Programs operate in quasi-isolation and state agency officials must go it alone—without the ability to learn from their federal counterparts. In turn, federal officials lack sufficient knowledge of what is happening in the states and are unable to provide adequate support for state efforts.

Similarly, the federal oversight agency is likely to act without fully seeking the counsel and opinions of state officials. The result may be less effective program implementation because neither actor has the opportunity to understand the activities of the other one. Information that is infrequently disseminated slows down a program and impedes organizational learning. Programs operate sporadically and become very dependent on state-level inducements and constraints, including the expertise of state staff. However, it is important to note that while federal–state contacts are infrequent and information channels are insufficiently used, communication when it does occur is aboveboard and open because both sets of actors trust each other. Sometimes, federal–state relationships gravitate to this cell because of the fiscal and resource constraints placed on the federal oversight agency. It is tough to have involvement when resources are lacking.

Coming Apart with Avoidance: Low Trust and Low Involvement

Low levels of trust result in suboptimal working relationships, as is illustrated in the bottom half of figure 1.1. Relationships that are coming apart can further be characterized as "coming apart with avoidance" or "coming apart and contentious," depending upon levels of involvement. As shown in the bottom-left quadrant, low involvement combined with low levels of trust characterizes working relationships that are coming apart with avoidance. Indeed, under these conditions, few reasons remain for federal and state program officials to work together, except for extrinsic statutory or legal obligations. These relationships are token, mandatory ones—with little expectations among the participants for positive outcomes or strong implementation performance. Neither side trusts the actions of the other, so communication among participants will likely be incomplete, confusing, and even dishonest.

Life for participants in this cell is like constructing a facade on a deteriorated building. From the outside, the building looks solid. But on the inside, the structure is crumbling. Residents of the building may be the only ones who know its true condition. Similarly, state and federal officials implementing a public program characterized by little involvement and low levels of mutual trust tend to avoid the obvious. That is, they seldom interact, and when they do, it is often to meet only the statutory requirements for contact. Thus, the facade is erected for the public to see, but little of substance is accomplished among the policy actors, and the relationship, like the facade, is only skin deep.

The implications for an intergovernmental program are serious. Individual actors may feel so detached that they engage in a "bare bones" operation of the program. Little reason exists to take risks and become a policy champion. Indeed, state officials who strongly embrace programmatic goals will find rapid, sure-fire implementation difficult at best, and probably impossible, without large infusions of support from citizens, state administrators, and legislators. By the same token, programs with this kind of working relationship are vulnerable during times of fiscal austerity at either state or federal levels, because policy professionals lack the necessary cohesion to present the need for continued political support. Thus, they are often unable to prevent the erosion of their program.

Coming Apart and Contentious: Low Trust and High Involvement

Little mutual trust combined with high levels of involvement characterizes working relationships that are also coming apart, as is shown in the bottom right corner of figure 1.1. Here, however, relationships are contentious. Participants are highly frustrated with what they view as unnecessary attention on the part of the other participants to administrative detail, program review, or organizational outputs. True, the participants are involved—but involved in the wrong way. Federal overseers pay attention to the actions of their state counterparts. Communication flows freely but does not often produce satisfying results. Frequent expressions by participants that they are being "micromanaged" would be common in relationships in this cell.

Below-board agendas are likely from both state and federal participants. State participants may comply with program requirements on paper while running the program as they want on the ground. Federal and state actors in this kind of coming-apart relationship hoard information that may be useful in operating the program. For example, state officials may shelter information about the compliance rates of the target group under a regulatory program or the actions of state inspection staff. Federal overseers, in turn, may obscure discussions pertinent to program reviews, oversight inspections, or new program guidance documents.

"End-running" may also be an outgrowth of this kind of relationship. State officials may "go around" federal regional staff to complain to federal staff at headquarters. Or they may seek a hearing in the political or judicial arena—playing their case to national politicians who have authority over the federal implementing agency. The arguments presented will go something like this: "We in the state of X are trying to run an effective enforcement program. The problem is that the federal oversight agency staff keeps getting in the way, by overstepping their authority, bogging us down in paperwork requirements, or engaging in countless bean-counting exercises while refusing to look at our accomplishments." End-runs become increasingly commonplace as the frustration level among actors rises.

In turn, federal participants respond by adopting the "gotcha syndrome" and look for ways to catch officials of the state implementing agency violating the dictates of the federal–state cooperative agreement or statutory mandates. State officials resent what they view as an unfair, unhelpful, and misdirected critique of their performance in the program. Hidden agendas and miscommunication become the hallmarks of this kind of relationship, and virtue and collaboration go out the window. Breaking this vicious cycle of negative responses within a relationship that is "coming apart with contention" requires an almost Herculean effort on the part of federal and state participants. Establishing trust is difficult after prolonged periods of obfuscation and control. Without dramatic intervention, this kind of relationship has its own force of gravity, destined to continued erosion of trust, resentment by all participants, and hypervigilance on the part of the overseer.

It is equally vexing and symptomatic of this kind of working relationship that participants often have a consensus about policy goals. The programmatic ends are not debated (e.g., both state and federal staffs want to reduce risks to public health or the environment); however, the means to that end are fiercely challenged. Ironically, this kind of relationship is prone to make participants lose sight of the bigger picture—the end goal of environmental protection that most of them share.

In sum, four kinds of working relationships are possible, and relationships that have high levels of trust coupled with high levels of involvement are the most desirable. When this type of federal–state relationship is observed, it is also likely that the actors in the implementation story will feel positive about how their program is going. By the same token, state implementers who feel micromanaged by their federal counterparts will likely feel less comfortable with their intergovernmental program.

This typology of working relationships suggests that—contrary to notions of cooperative, collaborative federalism—it is easier to have federal–state working relationships that are coming apart than pulling together, at least by the definitions offered here. The implications for public policy and policy implementation studies are twofold. First, actors must work harder to get the kind of relationship they want. Positive working relationships are not a given and must be sought. Second, without sensitivity to fostering positive working relationships, federal–state joint efforts may actually work against implementing a program effectively or efficiently.

Conclusions

The 1990s brought renewed attention to federal–state working relationships. States asserted that they were willing and capable of running environmental programs. At the same time, federal mandates were increasingly costly to state and local governments. Pressure from intergovernmental groups resulted in the Unfunded Mandates Reform Act, which was designed to curtail the number of unfunded mandates on subnational governments.

The ongoing devolution of environmental programs and the reinventing-government agenda of the NPR also produced a concerted effort by national politicians and top-level agency administrators to change the way they related to stakeholders and to partner with their state counterparts. As one EPA official wryly observed, "We're doing so much partnering these days, I don't know if I'm running an environmental program or going to a dance." Attempts by federal oversight agencies to redirect their approach to state environmental agencies so as to give state-level implementers more latitude in running their programs resulted in NEPPS and the REG 8 Directive. Both are major efforts at changing the nature of working relationships.

It would be nice if officials could simply say "abracadabra" and positive working relationships would jump out of a hat like the magician's bunny. However, a review of these innovations suggests it is not that easy. Getting to more synergistic relationships involves a lot of work, a commitment by all parties to fully implement the law, and the goal of consensus among regional and headquarters staff.

Working relationships do not exist in a vacuum. Rather, they are an integral part of the context of policy implementation. In turn, the rate and nature of policy implementation creates the environment in which federal–state working relationships are established. Implementation sets the parameters of the legal relationship, provides human and fiscal resources for working together, and creates a political, social, and economic arena for the program. Chapter 2 therefore looks at the larger picture of policy implementation, where the interactions of intergovernmental actors are part, but not all, of the reason for successful public programs.

Notes

1. James M. McElfish Jr., "Minimal Stringency: Abdication of State Innovation," Environmental *Law Reporter* 25 ELR 10003 (1995), www.elr.info/articles/vol25/25 .10003.htm (October 24, 2002).

2. Quoted in DeWitt John, *Civic Environmentalism: Alternatives to Regulations in States and Communities* (Washington, D.C.: Congressional Quarterly Press, 1994), 5.

3. U.S. Environmental Protection Agency, State/EPA Capacity Steering Committee, Joint Commitment to Reform Oversight and Create a National Environmental Performance Partnership System (Agreement signed May 17, 1995).

4. U.S. Environmental Protection Agency, Office of Water, *National Drinking Water Program Redirection Strategy*, EPA-810-R-96-003 (Washington, D.C.: U.S. Environmental Protection Agency, 1996).

5. Jonathan H. Adler, "A New Environmental Federalism," *Forum for Applied Research and Public Policy* 13, no. 4 (winter 1998): 55–61, at 55.

6. U.S. General Accounting Office, *EPA and the States: Environmental Challenges Require a Better Working Relationship*, GAO/RCED-95-64 (Washington, D.C.: U.S. General Accounting Office, 1995).

7. U.S. General Accounting Office, *EPA and the States*, 3.

8. National Academy of Public Administration, *Setting Priorities, Getting Results: A New Direction for the Environmental Protection Agency*, Report to Congress (Washington, D.C.: National Academy of Public Administration, 1995), 2.

9. National Performance Review, *From Red Tape to Results: Creating a Government that Works Better and Costs Less* (Washington, D.C.: U.S. Government Printing Office, 1993).

10. Bill Clinton and Al Gore, *Reinventing Environmental Regulation*, report issued by the White House, March 16, 1995.

11. Clinton and Gore, *Reinventing Environmental Regulation*, 10–11.

12. U.S. Environmental Protection Agency, Science Advisory Board, *Beyond the Horizon: Using Foresight to Protect the Environmental Future*, EPA-SAB-EC-95-007 (Washington D.C.: U.S. Environmental Protection Agency, 1995), 18.

13. Science Advisory Board, *Beyond the Horizon*, 18.

14. Testimony of Robert J. Uram, director of the Office of Surface Mining Reclamation and Enforcement, U.S. Department of the Interior, before the Subcommittee on Energy and Mineral Resources, Committee on Resources, U.S. House of Representatives, June 27, 1995.

15. Jóhn Kincaid, "From Cooperative to Coercive Federalism," *Annals of the American Academy of Political and Social Science* 509 (May 1990): 139–52, at 148.

16. International City/County Management Association, *Environmental Mandates Task Force: Policy and Legislative Strategy Meeting*, proceedings from the first meeting, December 8–9, 1992 (Washington, D.C.: International City/County Management Association, 1992).

17. See National Association of Counties, *The Burden of Unfunded Mandates: A Survey of the Impact of Unfunded Mandates on America's Counties* (Washington, D.C.: National Association of Counties, 1993); United States Conference of Mayors, *Impact of Unfunded Federal Mandates on U.S. Cities: A 314-City Survey* (Washington, D.C.: U.S. Conference of Mayors, 1993); Angela Antonelli, "Promises Unfulfilled: The Unfunded Mandates Reform Act of 1995," *Regulation* 19, no. 2 (1996), www.cato.org/pubs/regulation/reg19n2c.html (March 18, 2003).

18. For a rich scholarly discussion of unfunded mandates, see Paul L. Posner, *The Politics of Unfunded Mandates: Whither Federalism?* (Washington, D.C.: Georgetown University Press, 1998); also see Congressional Research Service, "Environmental Protection and the Unfunded Mandates Debate," CRS Report 94-739 ENR (Washington, D.C., Congressional Research Service, September 22, 1994), www.ncseonline.org/NLE/CRSreports/legislative/leg-4.cfm?&CFID=9395744&CFTOKEN=79637818 (August 5, 2003).

19. Public Law 104-4.

20. David Hosansky, "Federalism," *Congressional Quarterly Weekly Report* 54, no. 40 (October 5, 1996): 2824–25, at 2825.

21. See John Novinson, "Unfunded Mandates: A Closed Chapter?" *Public Management* 77, no. 7 (July 1995): 16–20.

22. Dan L. Crippen, director, Congressional Budget Office, CBO's Activities under the Unfunded Mandates Reform Act, Testimony before the Regulatory Affairs Committee on Government Reform, U.S. House of Representatives, May 24, 2001, www.cbo.gov/showdoc.cfm?index=2842&sequence=0 (March 18, 2003).

23. For an early treatment of state capacity, see James P. Lester, "A New Federalism? Environmental Policy in the States," in *Environmental Policy in the 1990s: Toward a New Agenda*, ed. Norman J. Vig and Michael E. Kraft (Washington, D.C.: Congressional Quarterly Press, 1990), 59–79. For a more recent discussion, see Adler, "New Environmental Federalism"; Michael E. Kraft and Denise Scheberle, "Environmental Federalism at

Decade's End: New Approaches and Strategies," *Publius: The Journal of Federalism* 28, no. 1 (1998): 131–46; and Barry G. Rabe, "Permitting, Prevention and Integration: Lessons from the States, in *Environmental Governance: A Report on the Next Generation of Environmental Policy*, ed. Donald F. Kettl (Washington, D.C.: Brookings Institution Press, 2002), 14–57.

24. John, *Civic Environmentalism*.

25. John, *Civic Environmentalism*, 7.

26. President's Council on Sustainable Development, *Sustainable America: A New Consensus for Prosperity, Opportunity and a Healthy Environment for the Future* (Washington, D.C.: U.S. Government Printing Office, 1996).

27. Thomas Anton, *American Federalism and Public Policy: How the System Works* (Philadelphia: Temple University Press, 1988), 3.

28. John Donahue, "The Disunited States," *Atlantic Monthly*, May 1997, 18–21, at 18; Richard Hofstadter, *The American Political Tradition* (New York: Alfred A. Knopf, 1948), 9.

29. Morton Grodzins, *The American System* (Chicago: Rand McNally, 1966), 80; quoted in David H. Rosenbloom, *Public Administration: Understanding Management, Politics and Law in the Public Sector*, 3d ed. (New York: McGraw-Hill, 1993), 123.

30. Daniel J. Elazar, "Cooperative Federalism," in *Competition among States and Local Governments: Efficiency and Equity in American Federalism*, ed. Daphne A. Kenyon and John Kincaid (Washington, D.C.: Urban Institute Press, 1992).

31. Terry Sanford, *Storm over the States* (New York: McGraw-Hill, 1967); quoted in *The Politics of Intergovernmental Relations*, ed. David C. Nice and Patricia Fredericksen, (Chicago: Nelson-Hall, 1995), 10.

32. Patricia Crotty, "The New Federalism Game: Primacy Implementation of Environmental Policy," *Publius: The Journal of Federalism* 17, no. 1 (1987): 53–67.

33. Joseph F. Zimmerman, "National–State Relations: Cooperative Federalism in the Twentieth Century," *Publius: The Journal of Federalism* 31, no. 2 (2001): 15–30.

34. Environmental Council of the States, "States Protect the Environment" (Washington, D.C.: Environmental Council of the States, 2000).

35. U.S. Environmental Protection Agency, Office of Wetlands, Oceans, and Watersheds, "State or Tribal Assumption of the Section 404 Permit Program," www.epa.gov/owow/wetlands/facts/fact23.html (July 20, 2002); Office of Wastewater Management, "National Pollutant Discharge Elimination System," http://cfpub.epa.gov/npdes/statestribes/astatus.cfm (July 20, 2002).

36. In its 2001 decision, *Solid Waste Agency of Northern Cook County v. U.S. Army Corps of Engineers*, the Supreme Court limited the use of the Commerce Clause to regulate environmental protection. In this case, brought by a coalition of twenty-three local governments, the Court found that the corps had gone too far in regulating isolated intrastate wetlands that were not contiguous to waters of the United States. See William Funk, "The Court, the Clean Water Act and the Constitution: SWANNC and Beyond," *Environmental Law Reporter* 31 (July 2001): 10741–72.

37. U.S. Environmental Protection Agency, *Joint Commitment to Reform Oversight and Create a National Environmental Performance Partnership System*, www.epa.gov/ocir/nepps/ovrsight.htm (July 30, 2003).

38. U.S. Environmental Protection Agency, Office of the Inspector General, "EPA Needs Better Integration of the National Environmental Performance Partnership System," Memorandum 2000-M-00828-000011, March 2000, 1.

39. Environmental Law Institute, *An Independent Review of the State-Federal Environmental Partnership Agreements for 1996*, ELI Project 941717 (Environmental Law Institute, 1996), 11.

40. U.S. Environmental Protection Agency, *Joint Commitment to Reform Oversight and Create a National Environmental Performance Partnership System*, www.epa.gov/ocir/nepps/ovrsight.htm (July 30, 2003).

41. U.S. Environmental Protection Agency, Office of Regional Operations and State/Local Relations, "Performance Partnership System: Frequently Asked Questions," November 21, 1996, www.epa.gov/regional/pps/faq.htm (December 20, 1997).

42. Donald Sutherland, "States Wary of Upcoming Environmental Performance Vote," *Environmental News Service*, February 9, 1999, www.ens.lycos.com/ens/feb99/1999L-02-09-01.html (February 26, 1999).

43. Donald Sutherland, "States Wary of Upcoming Environmental Performance Vote."

44. Environmental Council of the States, *Addendum to 1997 Joint Statement on Measuring Progress under NEPPS: Clarifying the Use and Applicability of Core Performance Measures*, signed April 22, 1999, www.sso.org/ecos/projects/cpms/JSA.htm (October 24, 2002).

45. Environmental Council of States, "Resolution Number 99-2: Approving FY 2000 CPMS and Joint Statement Addendum," April 1, 1999, www.sso.org/ecos/policy/resolution/REs%20Word%20Docs (October 24, 2002).

46. U.S. Environmental Protection Agency, "Trends in Performance Partnerships Environmental and Public Health Agencies, 1997–2000," June 23, 2003, www.epa.gov/ocir/nepps/pdf/neppstrends.pdf (July 31, 2003).

47. U.S. Environmental Protection Agency, "Grants Included in PPGs National Trend Summary," June 23, 2003, www.epa.gov/ocir/nepps/pdf/neppssummary.pdf (July 31, 2003).

48. U.S. General Accounting Office, *Environmental Protection: Collaborative EPA-State Effort Needed to Improve New Performance Partnership System*, GAO/RCED-99-171 (Washington, D.C.: U.S. General Accounting Office, 1999).

49. U.S. Environmental Protection Agency, "Performance Partnerships: Summary of Participating States and Territories," June 23, 2003, www.epa.ocir/nepps/pdf/trend_ 01.pdf (July 31, 2003).

50. U.S. Environmental Protection Agency, "Performance Partnership Agreements and Performance Partnership Grants: Environmental and Public Health Agencies Status and Trends," June 23, 2003, www.epa.gov/ocir/nepps/trends_status.htm (July 31, 2003).

51. U.S. Environmental Protection Agency, "Performance Partnerships: Summary of Participating States and Territories."

52. U.S. General Accounting Office, *Environmental Protection: EPA's and States' Efforts to "Reinvent" Environmental Regulation*, GAO/T-RCED-98-33 (Washington, D.C.: U.S. General Accounting Office, 1997).

53. U.S. General Accounting Office, *Environmental Protection: Collaborative EPA–State Effort Needed*, 3.

54. Jeanne Herb, Jennifer Sullivan, Mark Stoughton, and Allen White, *The National Environmental Performance Partnership System: Making Good on Its Promise?* Learning from

Innovations in Environmental Protection, Research Paper 12 (Washington, D.C.: National Academy of Public Administration, 2000); Leroy Paddock and Suellen Keiner, *Mixing Management Metaphors: The Complexities of Introducing a Performance-Based Partnership State/EPA Partnership System into an Activity-Based Management Culture*, Learning from Innovations in Environmental Protection, Research Paper 11 (Washington, D.C.: National Academy of Public Administration, 2000).

55. Herb et al., *National Environmental Performance Partnership System*, 14.

56. U.S. Environmental Protection Agency, "EPA Strategic Plan: New Ways of Achieving Our Overall Mission: Key Cross-Agency Programs (2001)," 82–83, at 82.

57. National Academy of Public Administration, *Environment.gov: Transforming Environmental Protection for the 21st Century* (Washington, D.C.: National Academy of Public Administration, 2000), 227.

58. William T. Gormley Jr., *Environmental Performance Measures in a Federal System* (Washington, D.C.: National Academy of Public Administration, 2000), www.napawash.org/pc_economy_environment/epafile13.pdf (July 31, 2003), 4.

59. U.S. Department of Interior, Office of Surface Mining, "REG 8 Directive: Oversight of State Regulatory Programs," June 20, 1996, www.osmre.gov/directives/directive844.pdf (March 23, 2003), 1.

60. Office of Surface Mining, "REG 8 Directive," I-2.

61. U.S. Department of Interior, Office of Surface Mining, "REG 8 Directive: Oversight of State Regulatory Programs: Annual Reports," October 9, 1987, www.osmre.gov/directives/directive384.pdf (March 23, 2003), ii.

62. Office of Surface Mining, "Annual Performance Agreement for Illinois Department of Natural Resources, Evaluation Year 1998," January 23, 2002, www.osmre.gov/paillino.htm (August 5, 2003), appendix A.

63. Office of Surface Mining, "Annual Performance Agreement for Illinois Department of Natural Resources," Introduction.

64. Office of Surface Mining, "OSM Oversight Team Wins Vice President's Hammer Award," press release on July 22, 1997, www.osmre.gov/news/072297.txt (August 1, 2003).

65. Office of Surface Mining, "Phase II Review of Oversight: Final Report of the OSM Oversight Outreach Team," October 1998, unpublished document.

66. Personal correspondence from the National Citizens' Coal Law Project, Kentucky Resources Council, Inc., to William J. Kovacic, director, OSM Lexington Field Office, August 28, 1996.

67. Robert Agranoff, "Managing within the Matrix: Do Collaborative Intergovernmental Relations Exist?" *Publius: The Journal of Federalism* 31, no. 2 (2001): 31–56; William Gormley, "Food Fights: Regulatory Enforcement in a Federal System," *Public Administration Review* 52, no. 3 (1992): 271–80; and Eugene Bardach, *Getting Agencies to Work Together: The Practice and Theory of Managerial Craftsmanship* (Washington, D.C.: Brookings Institution Press, 1998).

68. Quoted in Deil S. Wright, *Understanding Intergovernmental Relations, 2d ed.* (Monterey, Calif.: Brooks/Cole, 1982), 77.

· 2 ·

Implementing Environmental Laws

Suppose someone told you to go from Maine to California in seven days and offered a road atlas and a credit card. Suppose further that three other people would accompany you on the trip and share responsibility for a safe arrival. If fifty people were given this scenario, some would choose to rent a car, some would go by bus, others would go by train, and still others would fly. Even if the choices were further restricted—to require travel by car, for example—it is likely that not all fifty people would choose the same route, stay at the same motels, rent the same type of car, or arrive in California at the same time. With this scenario, it is easy to see how each new decision (mode of travel, route of travel, places to stay, etc.) results in a different experience. (Did you stop at Yellowstone? The Grand Canyon? Mom's place?) These collective experiences define the trip. Every time someone makes a choice, the story of the trip changes; and each trip, therefore, is unique.

Now imagine that you have rented a car and the four of you have begun your journey. How do you decide who drives? How long do you travel each day? How many road stops do you make? What would you do if you like listening to country music and the wind in your face, but other travelers like classical music and air conditioning? How you handle the decisions inside the car will certainly affect your perception and enjoyment of the trip. In short, the interaction of the travelers affects the quality of the trip as much as the choice of the vehicle, route, or places to stay.

The trip to California is like the implementation of an environmental law. Congress decides through legislative fiat that a trip must be made (or that a policy must be put into action). Then Congress defines the parameters of the trip narrowly (in this case, requiring that a car be used) or more broadly (just get to California). Similarly, Congress may impose additional constraints, including the amount of fiscal resources, extra staff, or time allotted to achieve implementation results. Extrinsic factors and events also affect implementation. A snowstorm may impede travel in January, but a tornado in March may really derail the trip. Envisioning what occurs inside a car during an extended road trip is one way of picturing how federal–state working relationships influence implementation. Certainly, the experience is prone to contention and conflict as the days get longer and the temperature (and tempers) inside the car get hotter. However, there is also the possibility that the trip will be pleasant and that by sharing driving responsibilities, you will arrive at your destination safely and in record time. The point is that both the nature of the trip itself (choice of car, route, lodging, etc.), which represents implementation, and the interaction of the travelers inside the car (cooperative, contentious, or somewhere in between), which represents working relationships, bring important insights to bear on the overall understanding of the implementation of any public policy.

The analogy also helps to explain why it is hard to fully understand intergovernmental policy implementation. Congress cannot control every decision made in implementing a public program anymore than someone might predict all the ways in which this trip could be taken or all the circumstances one might encounter along the way. As policy unfolds, no one can accurately predict every eventuality. Moreover, every policy contains the ability of implementers to make choices. Different people in any number of federal or state agencies, Congress, the judiciary, or the executive branch make decisions about how fast to go or whether it is wise to go to California at all. This simple metaphor also reinforces the importance of understanding what is happening to people who must undertake implementation responsibilities—because their willingness and ability to take on new activities affects the likelihood of implementation success.

This chapter presents the second premise of the book: that implementation of environmental policy is a story rich with contextual factors and high-stakes politics. Political factors are as inextricably wedded to the implementation process as they were at the time the policy was formulated. To return to the trip metaphor, the same array of political actors that argued for or against the trip to California are just as interested in how the trip unfolds. Thus, the best understanding of implementation of any environmental law comes from looking at national- and state-level political forces and the history of policy development and implementation. It also comes from examining statutory and regulatory language and court decisions, the nature of the group targeted for behavioral change, and state and federal officials and staff. And sometimes there are "implementation energizers," who—often despite political or bureaucratic forces to the contrary—continue to fight for effective implementation. Finally, as the asbestos and drinking water cases illustrate, implementation may change due to "refocusing" events, such as the discovery of a community at great risk of exposure to asbestos.

Defining Implementation and Measuring Performance

Legislators pass laws because they believe that the current state of affairs needs changing. However, the mere act of passing legislation is no guarantee that real changes will occur. One should think of law as a first, rather than a last, step in the process of producing desired policy results. What occurs after a law passes is implementation, and it is in this phase that policy goals may—or may not—be achieved.

In defining implementation in 1979, Carl Van Horn suggested that it "encompasses actions by public and private individuals or groups that affect the achievement of objectives set forth in prior policy decisions."[1] Malcolm Goggin and his colleagues defined the implementation of national policy by state governments as a "series of state decisions and actions directed toward putting an already-decided federal mandate into effect."[2] Both definitions contain the word "actions." Without action, there is no movement and no progress. However, these actions are a reflection of the interplay of multiple government institutions and the people inside them. Implementing officials respond to changes in their organizational, technical, and political environments. They make decisions about how much and what kind of activity to undertake and whether implementation efforts are meaningful from their frame of reference.

Implementing agencies are accountable for how much or how little action they undertake and for whether that action moves policy toward meeting its objective. Implementing policy is what agencies do. Measuring implementation progress is a matter of asking what has happened since the policy was adopted and how the implementing agency has contributed to achieving policy goals. Measuring performance is often expressed as outputs or outcomes. Outputs are typically activities undertaken by the implementing agency. Progress, then, depends upon the generation of appropriate responses by agency officials, as measured by activities such as the number of enforcement actions taken against a target group, regulations promulgated, inspections made, permits processed, and so on.

However, measuring implementation "success" on the basis of agency activity does not always correspond to the attainment of legislative objectives. In other words, outputs are indirect measures of results. For example, a state agency may meet its inspection quota, but numerous inspections may not lead to a cleaner environment because the inspector may not issue a notice of violation, or the regulated industry may prefer to pay a fine rather than to take corrective action. Moreover, even if the industry controls its effluent according to law (a fact verified in multiple inspections), it still is no guarantee that the beaches are safe to swim from or the water is safe to drink.

Conversely, fewer inspections coupled with a consultative approach may lead an industry to undertake corrective action. These actions, though fewer in number, are more likely to lead to a cleaner environment. However, they will not appear to be as successful, if success is measured by output alone. Moreover, as before, industrial compliance does not guarantee that the beaches are swimmable or the fish are edible, because industrial effluent is only one cause of water pollution. Thus, measures of agency output are only partially satisfying as surrogates for implementation performance.

The second method of measuring implementation "action" is through outcomes. Outcomes compare the results of programs and activities with their intended purpose or policy goal. Implementation is complete when policy objectives are met; for example, when drinking water is safe from harmful levels of contaminants. Outcomes, though more desirable, are more demanding to achieve than outputs. For one thing, outcomes in most public programs occur far in the future. For example, the "zero discharge" of pollutants into the water, the legislative goal of the Clean Water Act of 1972, has not been met—and by most accounts will probably never be achieved. Reclaiming mined lands, as required by the Surface Mining Control and Reclamation Act (SMCRA), may take ten or twenty years. Because fully realized outcomes of policy may not be known for decades, interim or intermediate measures of statutory goals may be useful. In the case of the Clean Water Act, policy analysts may look to the number of water bodies that meet water quality standards or to other indicators of improving water quality.

Another element complicating the ability to measure outcomes is the lack of data. Ample data exist in many environmental laws that are suggestive of implementation success, such as compliance data from a regulated industry. However, these data, though useful for monitoring a target group, are not easily translated into measures of policy outcomes. Take radon, for example. The number of radon awareness activities conducted by a state agency (an output measure) is much easier to quantify, and therefore to use to measure progress, than is knowing the extent to which radon levels have been reduced in homes (an outcome measure). Although all would agree that the latter measure of progress is more desirable, calculating risk reduction requires collecting information about the number of homes fixed for radon, as well as levels of radon present in the home before and after mitigation. Measuring improvements in water quality assumes that a state has sufficient data from which to make a judgment, and then that the federal oversight agency has commensurable data from all states. Data quality, continuity, and availability represent enormous challenges to developing indicators of performance. They also complicate the agency's ability to establish a baseline measure.[3]

Another problem that is often equally vexing is getting key stakeholders to agree on the "right" indicators or outcome measures. All stakeholders have different ideas about what constitutes the appropriate suite of indicators to measure progress toward policy outcomes. For instance, states and the U.S. Environmental Protection Agency (EPA) wrestled over the core performance measures under Performance Partnership Agreements (PPAs)—as described in chapter 1—just as EPA regional offices debated their colleagues at headquarters. As one EPA regional branch chief suggested, "I think everyone [in the agency] went overboard in developing indicators. Since we couldn't agree on a few good ones, we listed more indicators just to be impressed by the volume."[4]

Undeterred, Congress decided it would force agencies to demonstrate on-the-ground progress. Like the call for improving working relationships described in chapter 1, the mantra of governmental performance began in earnest in the 1990s and culminated when Congress passed the Government Performance and Results Act (GPRA) in 1993. Congress designed GPRA to "improve the confidence of the people in government by holding agencies accountable for achieving program results."[5] The law requires agencies to develop a strategic plan and annual program performance reports. In particular, GPRA requires federal agencies to establish annual performance plans that include performance goals and to specify those goals in "objective, quantifiable, and measurable form."[6] Congressional oversight committees, in turn, will use these performance goals and accompanying measures to assess the implementing agency's progress toward results-based management.

Herein is the rub. Federal agencies such as EPA or the Office of Surface Mining must now balance the demands of quantifiable goals under GPRA while simultaneously providing states with flexibility under state performance agreements. As was noted in chapter 1, this frequently complicates working relationships in the National Environmental Performance Partnership System, because states and EPA regional offices are held accountable for various output and outcome measures. At the same time, core performance measures under PPAs must be reconciled with requirements under GPRA and the statute itself. Preparing multiple progress reports—especially when each report must respond to a different set of output and/or outcome measures—creates implementation dysfunction, not to mention inter- and intra-agency discord.

Seven years after the passage of GPRA, EPA was relying primarily on the much easier, but far less satisfying, output measures to gage performance. Of the 364 performance measures set by the EPA for 2000, only 12 percent focused on final outcomes.[7] When the U.S. General Accounting Office investigated, it noted that the limited availability of data on environmental conditions was the major challenge to developing outcome-based measures. Still, outcome measures are likely to continue to make inroads as the tools of choice for measuring successful policy implementation.

Some scholars have argued that evaluating implementation patterns is a function of the kind of program, and therefore, not very amenable to direct or indirect measures of performance. Helen Ingram notes: "The challenge presented to implementers depends very much on the problems passed along to them by policy formulators. Success in implementation must be evaluated within the context of particular problems, and critical factors affecting implementation will vary with what is being attempted."[8] She suggests that many environmental laws contain clear goals and highly prescriptive procedures for the implementing agency. Given that environmental policies also embrace scientific uncertainties about the extent of risk, the best technologies, or necessary regulatory structures, the implementation of most environmental programs should be judged by the extent of policy learning that is acquired by key stakeholders.[9]

This is a very challenging organizational environment in which to implement laws. Whether one examines agency outputs, attempts to measure interim or final policy outcomes, or the amount of policy learning that has taken place, determining whether implementation has occurred is more difficult than one might think at a first glance. Seldom, if ever, does a policy analyst exclaim, "Eureka! Implementation is achieved." Nor is she likely to add, "I know how implementation works." If one general statement is common to studies of policy implementation, it is that the process seldom works as expected—on time and with satisfactory results.

Implementation as a Game of Strategy

The study of policy implementation is a study of strategies—"strategies" because for every program, different sets of actors adopt various strategic approaches to the program based upon their role orientations, available resources, the extent of behavioral change required, and the prevailing political winds, among other reasons. Implementing officials employ strategies to win—where winning is often implicitly defined as conserving agency resources, deflecting criticism and legal attacks, and maintaining stature in the pertinent political community.

Eugene Bardach used the metaphor of a game to describe implementation. He argued that these games are "also part of the larger game of politics and governance. Just as they draw their characteristic strategies and tactics from the game of politics, so too do they deliver their outcomes back to the larger game."[10] Players in the implementation game carefully calculate how they can best win, based upon what they regard as the stakes of the game, the strategies of the other players, the rules of playing, and the degree of uncertainty surrounding the possible outcomes. In an intergovernmental context, who holds the winning hand has been a subject of much debate. Just because federal agency staff may come to the table with more resources and control the rules of the game, they still have to play the cards they have, and those cards do not always provide a winning hand.

Martha Derthick was among the first scholars to identify the difficulties associated with getting new policies that relied on many levels of government off the ground. Noting the "great difficulty of organizing cooperative activity on a large scale," she suggested that national implementation hopes were pinned to limited federal incentives offered to local implementers.[11] The federal government could not easily compel subnational governments to perform. In turn, local officials tried to manipulate federal incentives in their best interests. Thus, bargaining among intergovernmental actors is an inevitable part of the implementation process.

Jeffrey Pressman and Aaron Wildavsky also described the "complexity of joint action" in intergovernmental implementation. They identify multiple clearance points and interdependencies among implementation actors as potential obstacles to policy success. Like Derthick, they suggest that state actors do not march in lockstep to the tune of the national government. Rather, national programs are reshaped or even undermined by strategies employed by state or local officials.[12] Daniel Elazar agreed: "Only in rare situations have federal grant programs served to alter state administrative patterns in ways that did not coincide with already established state policies."[13]

One commonly identified place in the implementation process for strategies to emerge is where administrative actions of street-level bureaucrats intersect with private choices. Richard Elmore, among other scholars, contends that this is the point at which implementation results are most affected. He examines the behaviors of the actors closest to the target group of the policy. Beginning with the last interaction (that between the street-level implementer and a receiver of the policy, e.g., a member of the regulated community), his "backward mapping" model moves up the chain of organizational command. This movement defines two characteristics for each subsequent set of actors: the ability of each level to affect the behavior of the target group and the lower-level bureaucratic agents; and the presence of resources sufficient to produce change in the target group. In this case, implementation depends upon the ability of actors at one level to influence actors at another, ultimately influencing the behavior of private groups or individuals.[14]

Michael Lipsky writes that the decisions of "street-level bureaucrats, the routines that they establish, and the devices they invent to cope with uncertainties and work pressures effectively become the public policies they carry out."[15] Frontline implementers, for example, make choices regarding policy depending upon their attitudes, values, or local theories about the substantive issue at hand. A state inspector may choose to comply with the dictates of the new policy and work toward substantive policy goals. Or the inspector may elect to maintain existing behavioral patterns and ignore the new policy. The street-level bureaucrat may try to change the policy by voicing distaste for implementation procedures to agency managers.[16] Really savvy street-level bureaucrats may simply go through the motions of what is required while not really changing anything.

Political pressures on street-level implementers increase once a state receives primacy and intergovernmental relations come into play. At least two kinds of situations may cause state enforcement personnel discomfort. First, they must now practice a "hands-on" enforcement strategy based upon federal, not state, prescriptions. State inspectors frequently find themselves in uncomfortable adversarial relationships with members of the regulated industry. Assuming an accommodating regulatory posture may alleviate this discomfort. Conversely, discomfort may increase with the presence of citizen or environmental groups pushing for rapid and strict implementation.

Second, regulatory policy such as SMCRA requires that a target group (i.e., coal miners) act according to a set of nationally derived instructions, despite the costs or behavioral change required. Substantial compliance costs may squeeze the profit margins of regulated companies, prompting their active interest in state enforcement activity. They express this interest through interactions with agency personnel and administrators, political appointees, or state politicians. In turn, state legislators and executive sovereigns may be inclined to listen to economically important industries within state boundaries. In the face of pressure from these regional or state economic powerhouses, it is no surprise that state officials are likely to be more sensitive to the costs associated with regulatory compliance than are their federal colleagues.

Thus, the nature of regulatory policy under primacy creates an environment with mixed local pressures on state officials charged with implementation responsibilities. Two extreme strategies are possible, with a wide range of behaviors in the middle. On the one hand, street-level implementers may exhibit what Bardach describes as "massive resistance" in the implementation game—using discretionary powers to ignore procedural requirements and forgive target-group performance.[17] On the other hand, these front-line implementers may also be the ones to rigorously pursue policy implementation, even in the face of political or administrative pressure to "back off" or "go easy" on the target group. In either case, the actions of persons charged with on-the-ground performance are an important element in understanding implementation and may influence the nature of federal–state working relationships as well.

The emphasis on the strategic activities of the bureaucratic staff reveals two important assumptions about implementation. First, real implementation power rests in equal or greater measure with the street-level bureaucrats as with legislative or administrative leaders.[18] Policymakers, therefore, do not wield the only determining influence over what happens in the implementation process. If this is the case, then a second assumption is apparent. Explicit commands are not an effective way of ensuring successful implementation. Other factors are also key variables—such as informal relationships between actors, symmetry in the dispositions of the staff and agency leaders toward policy goals, and the existence of countervailing external pressures from outside groups on the street-level bureaucrats.

In sum, three issues for implementation strategies are apparent. First, to minimize goal displacement, the disposition of the bureaucratic and the agency culture should be compatible with the policy goals of the new legislation. Second, the extent of behavioral change required of the target group is often inversely related to achieving implementation, because it is likely to engender conflict among the frontline implementers, the agency, and the regulated industry.[19] Third, the role orientations of enforcement personnel may influence the rate and nature of the implementation process, depending on whether a hard-line or negotiated regulatory posture is taken.

Implementation as a Story

A second element important for understanding implementation is to look for the legislative, administrative, and political elements of the implementation story. The story begins with the agenda-setting and formulation of the policy and profoundly influences the implementation process. Why use the metaphor of a story? As Peter Schwartz suggests, "Stories are about meaning; they help explain why things could happen in a certain way. They give order and meaning to events—a crucial aspect of understanding future possibilities."[20] Moreover, stories provide an opportunity to describe how different characters see events (in this case, implementation events), and cope with complexity. And there are "stories" rather than just one story, because each policy has its own legislative, administrative, and political legacy and current plot lines that determine, in large and small ways, the rate and progress of implementation. Central to the concept of stories is the notion that explaining implementation results is at least partially a function of policy-formulation dynamics.

Implementation stories are at least as interesting as the stories that prompted the legislation in the first place. Deborah Stone developed the notion of causal stories to explain the shape of political decisions about policies. She suggests that "the essence of policy making in political communities is the struggle over ideas."[21] During implementation, the struggle over ideas continues, involves more characters, and offers more entry points for individuals to add suspense to the story. Moreover, though policy formulation may be compared to a short story, policy implementation is more like a long novel, or whodunit, in which characters are developed over many pages and the plot is rich in detail.

Implementation stories have their origins in the legislative and political history of the law. To understand the beginning of the story, one has to ask the right questions. For instance, what interest groups testified before the congressional committee? What was the level and scope of the presidential administration's interest in the law? What event (if any) propelled this policy onto the agenda of Congress? Understanding the political discussions that shaped the law helps to explain why the process of putting the law into practice is so difficult. Take, for example, asbestos, described in the next chapter. Knowing that America's affection for this miracle fiber began at the turn of the twentieth century and continued for more than seventy years says a lot about why Congress passed the asbestos law it did when it did, and also why the law during the early years of its implementation resulted in hundreds of schools removing asbestos.

Parts of the story also include the availability of solutions to the policy problem, and the capacity of implementing agencies to respond. Discovering these parts of the story means asking such questions as these: How willing were the legislative architects to fund the program? What is the technical expertise of the agency? What is the scope and breadth of the problem? The answers to such questions begin to tell the story of implementation.

The work of implementation scholars helps identify important implementation variables or elements of the story. The approach of teams of scholars such as Donald Van Meter and Carl Van Horn and Paul Sabatier and Daniel Mazmanian is to describe the implementation success as hinging on variables that can best be manipulated from the top of the process.[22] Their "top-down" approach to understanding implementation contributes a comprehensive list of story elements. Sabatier and Mazmanian develop a model of implementation that places variables into three categories: statutory, nonstatutory, and technical (or problem tractability) variables. Being reluctant to accept the inevitability of street-level bureaucrats and target groups dictating implementation performance, Sabatier and Mazmanian provide a model that identifies legal and political mechanisms that constrain individual behavior.

A second element of Sabatier and Mazmanian's model looks at the nature of the problem. If the policy addresses a problem for which there are few technical solutions, poor causal theories, or a highly populated or hard-to-identify target group, or that requires substantial behavioral change, implementation will be impeded. A final model component addresses the influence of nonstatutory variables on implementation, such as public support, prevalence of interest groups, and the commitment of key legislators or executives. Thus, the structure of the statute, the nature of the problem, fiscal and staffing resources, and the ability of external actors to influence the process all change the character of implementation.

This and other top-down models that describe the elements of implementation are based on straightforward assumptions. First, they emphasis story elements over individual strategies. They assume that policymakers can usually control the organizational, political, and technical components of the implementation process through formal means. Thus, the intentions and carefully reasoned actions of policymakers at the top are more important than the dispositions of the bureaucrats at the bottom. A second assumption is that statutes or regulations, appropriated resources, and institutional relationships among agencies are the elements that should be manipulated to bring about successful policy implementation.

Several scholars have looked specifically at environmental programs using a top-down approach. William Lowry concluded that interstate competition for industry serves to dampen a state's enthusiasm for strong regulatory enforcement, whereas Evan Ringquist reviewed state air regulatory programs and found that strong federal regulatory requirements for states, coupled with adequate resources and enforcement, result in air quality improvements.[23] David Hedge and his colleagues found that the state political and economic milieu, as well as the orientation of state officials toward policy goals, play important roles in explaining implementation patterns and working relationships.[24] James Lester and his colleagues argued that federal funding is essential to creating and maintaining effective state programs. [25] A central thesis of these studies of comparative state environmental programs is the continued need for strong federal oversight and funding. Without the presence of the federal government, states' willingness to operate environmental programs varies dramatically.

Implementation and Refocusing Events

One area often missed by scholars looking at implementation is the power of events to change implementation direction and/or pace. John Kingdon and Roger Cobb and Charles Elder remind us that focusing events can push a public problem onto formal agendas for consideration.[26] Radon, which is discussed in chapter 4, is an excellent example of the ability of a dramatic event to propel an item onto the governmental agenda. A better known example is the Exxon Valdez oil spill of 1989, which spurred Congress to pass the Oil Pollution Act.

Events that capture the public eye can do more, however, than prompt the passage of a new law. Events may force implementing agencies to reconsider the effectiveness of programs designed to implement that law. In a typical implementation story, implementation moves along slowly, often taking years to develop. Implementers may recognize issues with their work but, due to the press of time or bureaucratic forces to stay the course, choose not to deal with it. When the popular media direct their attention to the issue, implementing agencies respond, often in the absence of a new congressional directive. On September 11, 2001, the media showed the tragic collapse of the twin towers of the World Trade Center. The dramatic pictures of clouds of dust—dust that contained asbestos fibers—would ultimately result in new energies directed toward asbestos by EPA, as is described in chapter 3.

Implementation Energizers

Good stories often contain heroes—characters who defy all odds to save the day. So, too, do implementation stories. Bureaucracies, where most of the story takes place, are replete with forces that hamper innovation. The unwritten rule of many organizations is to stay the course, to put in your time and go home. In the case of public bureaucracies, entrepreneurial spirit is often met with skepticism. Implementers in public agencies also face multiple, often conflicting, stakeholders, all of whom want to be satisfied. Nevertheless, just as policy entrepreneurs exist when policy is formulated, they exist when policy is implemented. These unsung heroes are not as rare as one might expect, given an environment of scarce resources, angry or demanding publics, and changing political whims. I call these heroes energizers because, like the little rabbit in the battery commercial, they keep going and going. During interviews, they exhibit extraordinary dedication to achieving on-the-ground results. Although most of the energizers I have encountered are in federal or state agencies, they may also exist outside public organizations.

An Implementation Framework

Figure 2.1 depicts a model of policy implementation that reflects the work of implementation scholars, integrates intergovernmental working relationships as a key factor in implementation, and employs strategies and stories as a way

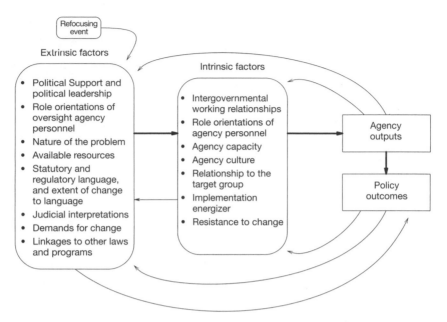

Figure 2.1. Model Framework of Extrinsic and Intrinsic Factors That Influence Policy Implementation

of explaining implementation variables. It also incorporates three new variables not found in the framework in the first edition of this book: refocusing events, linkages to other laws or programs, and implementation energizers. The framework approaches implementation from the perspective of the agency given the ultimate implementation responsibility, which is usually the state agency. It articulates factors both inside and outside the agency that influence the implementation process.

This model framework offers one conceptual approach to examining how and why public programs develop the way they do. The model takes as its starting point the concept of implementation stories and strategies described above. Extrinsic factors constitute most of the context for the implementation story. These components are extrinsic factors, or those variables that are outside the implementing agency's control. Strategic components, conversely, are intrinsic factors—those factors that are either within the agency's control or within part of the constellation of forces unique to a particular implementing agency. By attempting to be parsimonious, the framework may exclude certain implementation variables. However, the overall framework should offer an opportunity for examining the major implementation factors associated with environmental programs.

Extrinsic Factors: Parts of the "Story"

As was discussed above, implementation is influenced by the context of policy formulation as well as the current political and institutional environment in which implementation proceeds. These elements include political arrangements, role orientations of the federal oversight agency personnel, the nature of the problem, fiscal and human resource allocation, statutory language, judicial interpretations, and the legislative and policy history. Each will be described briefly in turn.

Political support and leadership, the first extrinsic variable, includes elements such as the support of national sovereigns, including the presidential administration and Congress. Much has been written about the ability of the administration to change the course of policy implementation. (See, e.g., the discussion of changes to environmental programs wrought by Ronald Reagan's administration and now by George W. Bush's administration.) Similarly, Congress, through its oversight activities and its ability to reauthorize or amend laws, may significantly alter environmental efforts.

Also important is the presence and intensity of interest-group involvement. Environmental groups closely monitor the implementation of environmental programs. Using citizen suits has frequently been effective at producing implementation performance on the part of EPA and other federal and state agencies. Similarly, interest groups affect the way regulations are written as well as the shape of the legislative amendments to current environmental laws. When the implementation of ambitious public programs stalls, these interest groups are forces that press implementing agency to recommit to policy objectives. Public support for the program may provide incentives to the agency to proceed with implementation, even in the face of resistance by the target group. The economic significance of the target group as well as the costs of compliance constitute potentially important elements of the political environment.

Other political factors include the extent to which the public perceives an environmental problem as serious and the presence of a "fixer" to encourage implementation. As Bardach suggests, "The character and degree of many implementation problems are inherently unpredictable. Even the most robust policy—one that is designed to survive the implementation process—will tend to go awry. . . . Someone or some group must be willing and able to set the policy back on course." Thus, he looks to external monitoring of the process by a fixer, a legislator or executive official who controls resources and may intervene when implementation falters.[27]

Also important as extrinsic factors in implementation are the role orientations of federal oversight personnel. As was discussed in chapter 1, the oversight posture taken by the federal agency profoundly affects the quality of the working relationship between state and federal staffs and may in turn change the way the state program is implemented. Also affecting implementation is the extent to which all players in the game agree on the goals of the policy, as well on the tactics for achieving these goals.

The third extrinsic factor shaping implementation is the nature of the problem. Here, elements include the seriousness and pervasiveness of the public policy problem and the size and heterogeneity of the group targeted for behavioral change. Many environmental problems are difficult to solve. Various factors may constrain program development—such as scientific uncertainty about causal relationships, difficulties in determining the extent of risk to ecological and human health from exposure to a contaminant, and the utility and availability of solutions to the problem.[28]

The nature of the problem may be also be defined by looking at the size and the characteristics of the members of the group targeted by the policy, as well as the extent of behavioral change required. For example, if the group is homogeneous and about equally affected by compliance costs and the extent of behavioral change is large, one could expect a unified, but more moderate, resistance to implementation because the consequences of implementing the new environmental standards will affect individual members equally. But if compliance costs will disproportionately burden some members of the target group, one could expect those members to fiercely resist rapid implementation.

A case in point is the U.S. coal mining industry. Before SMCRA, the Appalachian coal region contained many small "pick and shovel" coal-mining operations. After SMCRA, these small coal mines, already facing competition from large operations, could not meet new environmental requirements. Inspectors in those states found it hard to cite small operators that provided a living to many coal town residents.[29] Programs such as radon depend upon the voluntary compliance of the target group. Here, implementation success rests with the willingness of all American homeowners to voluntarily test their home for radon.

Closely related to political support for the environmental program is the provision of adequate fiscal and human resources. Virtually every implementation scholar includes resource allocation as an integral part of explaining the implementation of any program. Congress passed many environmental laws with inadequate or barely adequate federal resources to implement them. Limited budgets hamper the ability of agencies to run programs. Perhaps nowhere is this more the case than with the implementation of the Safe Drinking Water Act.

Another essential external factor in understanding the implementation of environmental programs is the language of the national law. A law that has clear and unambiguous goals, realistic timetables for implementation, adequate appropriations of fiscal resources, and appropriate delegation of authority often facilitates the implementation of environmental policy. In turn, a law that provides little guidance for policy implementers, or is too prescriptive in how it allows implementers to proceed, introduces obstacles to how a program evolves. In addition, environmental laws, the result of bargaining and compromise, reflect the prevailing political allegiances that were in power at the time. Thus, environmental laws, like other laws, contain exemptions and exclusions for the target group that affect policy outcomes. Also important is the congruence of the national law with related state laws.

A fifth external factor in environmental policy implementation is the role of judicial interpretation. The courts interpret statutory language as well as any promulgated regulations under the law. Court decisions may substantially affect the rate and nature of implementation. Environmental laws depend upon citizens suits for enforcement. Citizens can sue to compel federal or state agencies to perform nondiscretionary duties; they can also enforce the law by bringing violators into compliance. Environmental programs that mandate performance by a target group frequently involve the courts through challenges to regulatory language. Nearly 80 percent of all EPA regulations are challenged; the Office of Surface Mining was a party in six cases challenging its decisions in 1995 alone.[30]

Demand for change is an important external force. Often, when a law is passed, people assume that the problem is solved. If attention wanes, then it becomes even easier for the pace of implementation to slow. However, intense and continuing interest will speed up the pace of implementation.

Interconnectedness among environmental laws influences implementation of individual environmental programs. Sometimes, environmental laws connect in ways that benefit the implementation of both laws. For example, to the extent that states protect the source water of drinking water supplies (under the Safe Drinking Water Act), they also may protect lakes and other water bodies (under the Clean Water Act). Similarly, controlling for atmospheric emissions of mercury may ultimately reduce the levels of mercury found in the Great Lakes. However, this variable may not always work to facilitate implementation. Resources siphoned from one program to another reduce the probability that the first program will meet its goals.

Intrinsic Factors: Strategies

The second group of factors are intrinsic ones, which were defined above as those factors under the auspices of the implementing agency. Here, the major elements include working relationships, the role orientations of street-level implementers, agency capacity, agency culture, relationship to the target group, state-level political support, and resistance to change. Each factor is described briefly here.

The first intrinsic factor, working relationships, isolates the role between federal and state agencies charged with implementation responsibilities. Closely linked to the role orientations of federal oversight staff, positive working relationships develop because of mutual trust and the beneficial involvement of federal staff in state-level implementation. Facilitating trust is effective communication between levels of government, shared goals among federal and state officials, and the flexibility and effectiveness of methods chosen by federal staff to evaluate state performance. Federal-level involvement desired by states includes technical and financial assistance, as well as clear and timely guidance on changing federal policies and guidance. As was noted in describing the working relationship typology in chapter 1, working relationships with high levels of trust and helpful interactions among players pull together and produce synergistic implementation. Conversely, working relationships with low levels of trust and federal oversight perceived as micromanagement by state personnel often come apart, thereby slowing implementation progress.

In the 1990s, Congress, the Clinton administration, and students of environmental federalism recognized that positive federal–state working relationships were essential ingredients to achieving effective program implementation. As was explained in chapter 1, new federal oversight policies found in the National Environmental Performance Partnership System and the REG 8 Directive are a reflection of this high-level attention.

A second intrinsic element is the role orientation of agency personnel. As was discussed above, individuals given front-line implementation duties may have different perceptions about their enforcement roles than do state agency officials, federal agency officials, or other policy stakeholders. The strategies they employ—from resisting implementation through token enforcement to enthusiastically receiving their new responsibilities and zealously enforcing the law—affect the way implementation ultimately unfolds.

Agency capacity identifies elements within a state agency that affect how well an environmental program operates. Some agency capacity variables include adequate human and fiscal resources and the level of expertise among the agency staff. Capacity also involves the amount of jurisdictional control and statutory authority given to the implementing agency, and the extent to which programs are fragmented between departments.[31]

An agency's capacity to respond to a new program is also a function of the staff's willingness to take on this new task. This speaks to agency culture, or the collected set of organizational values and attitudes. To the degree that members of the implementing team share the values expressed in the new policy, implementation is facilitated. However, as Herbert Kaufman noted in his classic study of the U.S. Forest Service, agency culture can serve as a potent tool for maintaining the status quo and a level of homogeneity in staff perspective.[32] If attitudes within the implementing agency are strongly against the new policy, implementation will stall. Thus, the degree to which administrators and staff within the implementing state agency support the goals of the program, coupled with the congruence of legislative goals with existing agency culture, also may affect implementation.

In addition to agency capacity, agency culture—the individual role orientations of frontline implementers, and the existence of an individual or individuals to champion the program—can encourage implementation.[33] Much as the policy entrepreneur helps to propel a potential policy onto the legislative agenda, dedicated staff members or even a single individual can make a significant difference in whether or not the program succeeds. These are implementation energizers.

The relationship of the implementing agency to its immediate target group is often very important, for the same reasons mentioned above. The target group within a state may be diffuse, numerous, heterogeneous, or politically powerful. To the extent that it is a powerful political player in the state, the target group may influence the way that the agency perceives its implementation roles. Moreover, the ability of the target group to respond varies among states because the target groups may be different. For example, small coal mining companies operating in the Appalachian coal region look very different from the large, financially well-heeled coal operations in the West.

Political support for the program at the state level is a significant factor in understanding how implementation proceeds. Although a national law may compel states to undertake environmental activities, the mere presence of a law is no guarantee that state administrators, top agency officials, state legislators, and the governor can be persuaded to implement it. Nor is it a guarantee that states will pass their own strong regulatory programs. Important to levels of political support are the extent of public concern, interest-group and target-group involvement, and the willingness of a state to use its internal revenues if necessary to operate the program.[34]

Finally, the human tendency to resist change plays into the implementation of policy within a state. Just as there must be a certain amount of momentum to push implementation forward at the national level, implementers may vary in their willingness to change existing practices. This is especially true when organizations are being asked to take on additional tasks or to go against standard operating procedures.

Dynamics of the Model

The framework suggests that both extrinsic and intrinsic factors affect the ability of the implementing agency to implement environmental programs. Implementation produces both agency outputs (measures of agency activities, e.g., the number of inspections conducted or violations cited in the case of regulatory programs) and policy outcomes, or measurable improvements in the environment. Note that the model allows for the independent ability of extrinsic variables to influence policy outcomes. For example, individuals within a target group may change their behavior in response to a new law or federal regulation before the state implementing agency requests such changes. Similarly, advances in scientific understanding or improvements in technology may prompt policy outcomes without the direct intervention of the state implementing agency.

The model also recognizes that each factor intertwines and may influence other factors (thus, in figure 2.1, some factors are placed in the same box). For example, political arrangements may affect the resources available for federal oversight agencies or for states to use. The nature of the problem may affect the statutory language; internal variables such as agency culture and role orientations are often closely related. Or the political context of policy implementation (i.e., the support of sovereigns) may alter the state agency's capacity to implement the program.

Similarly, extrinsic factors influence intrinsic factors, as is indicated by the large arrow in figure 2.1. The kind of law passed, federal court decisions, the changing role orientations of federal oversight personnel, infusions of federal funding, and a new president or congressional oversight committee all will certainly affect working relationships, state political support, and agency capacity. To a lesser degree, intrinsic factors within an agency influence extrinsic factors, as is indicated by the smaller arrow between the boxes. For example, state agencies with little capacity to run the new environmental program may prompt Congress to allocate additional resources or pass amendments with agency-forcing provisions.

Finally, the model acknowledges that implementing environmental policy is an ongoing process. In figure 2.1, feedback loops emanating from both the "agency outputs" and "policy outcomes" boxes suggest that changes in the process may occur as decision makers become aware of performance and on-the-ground results. In short, the rate and/or intensity of implementation activities may vary over time, depending on changes in the external or internal factors, or in the repercussions from feedback into the process from agency output or policy outcome information.

Conclusions about Implementation

Implementation changes over time, not being stable, forward moving, or guaranteed. Furthermore, every point in the process is subject to a unique set of conditions and constellation of actors, employing various strategies to alter the course so as to maximize their position in the eventual outcome. And not only the course but also the rate of implementation may change depending on the strength of political forces at any given time as the policy evolves. This, in part, is what makes implementation stories so interesting.

Moreover, actors enter the process at the point that holds the most promise for shaping policy outcomes. Thus, environmental interest groups use the courts to force the agency with implementation responsibility to write regulations or enforce the law.[35] By the same token, target groups facing the legislative "promise" of regulation may choose to try to influence the regulatory process, to affect enforcement efforts after the regulations are promulgated, or to pursue legal remedies challenging the appropriateness of regulatory requirements.

Finally, federal–state working relationships form an important subset of policy implementation. As programs mature, the daily operations of federal and state agencies become paramount to policy success or failure. These regular interactions among personnel may greatly influence the eventual outcomes of a public program. Effective relationships, in turn, are based on mutual trust and adequate levels of appropriate involvement and vary among programs.

It is easy to see how each policy tells a unique implementation story. Though not unique in the same way as fingerprints, perhaps, each environmental program nonetheless involves distinct problems to solve, political arenas in which to solve them, and state and federal officials who may have very different opinions about their new roles as policy implementers.

Study Design and Rationale

It is now time to return traveling to California, paying attention to the elements of the trip and the atmosphere inside the car. (That is to say, looking at both implementation and federal–state relationships.) To that end, this book employs the typology of working relationships developed in chapter 1 and the implementation framework illustrated in figure 2.1 to examine the implementation of four environmental laws: the Asbestos Hazard and Emergency Response Act, the Indoor Radon Abatement Act, the Safe Drinking Water Act, and the Surface Mining Control and Reclamation Act.

A vital source of information for this study was the people working in state and federal agencies who are charged with implementing programs. Much of the data used in the book comes from responses to surveys and interviews of state program directors and federal regional staff. An extensive review of government documents and professional reports also helped to tell the implementation story. The perceptions of individuals involved in each program are central to explaining how the program works. The appendix to the book gives more information about the specifics of the research.

The book looks at federal–state relationships in two agencies, EPA and the U.S. Department of the Interior's Office of Surface Mining (OSM). This provides the opportunity to compare the organizational cultures and role orientations of two federal agencies with different perspectives. As was mentioned in chapter 1, EPA, which aims to control pollution and protect human health, is responsible for a wide array of environmental programs. OSM, as part of Interior, is a natural resource agency whose sole responsibility is to implement the surface mining law.

Each environmental program examined here differs from the others in several ways. First, not all the programs are regulatory. Three programs (asbestos, coal mining, and drinking water) are primarily regulatory, but radon is nonregulatory and relies on the voluntary participation of state and local officials. Second, working relationships vary by program. Radon has historically enjoyed positive federal–state interactions, whereas the drinking water and surface mining programs are more adversarial. Third, the programs vary in size. State drinking water programs and coal mining programs are generally larger than state radon or asbestos programs. Some programs have great resource needs and are in the public eye; others are not. The four programs thus have distinct political and legislative histories and, more essentially, each tells a wonderfully rich and varied implementation story.

Notes

1. Carl E. Van Horn, "Evaluating the New Federalism: National Goals and Local Implementors," *Public Administration Review* 39 (1979): 17–22, at 19.

2. Malcolm L. Goggin, Ann O'M. Bowman, James P. Lester, and Laurence J. O'Toole Jr., *Implementation Theory and Practice: Toward a Third Generation* (Glenview, Ill.: Scott, Foresman, 1990), 3.

3. For data quality issues, see U.S. Geological Survey, Intergovernmental Task Force on Monitoring Water Quality, "The Strategy for Improving Water-Quality Monitoring in the United States," Open-File Report 95-742, 1995, http://water.usgs.gov/wicp/Summary .html (March 23, 2003). For difficulties associated with performance measures, see Shelley H. Metzenbaum, "Measurement that Matters: Cleaning Up the Charles River Basin," in *Environmental Governance: A Report on the Next Generation of Environmental Policy*, ed.

Donald F. Kettl (Washington, D.C.: Brookings Institution Press, 2002), 58–117; International Joint Commission, Indicators Implementation Task Force, *Indicators Implementation Task Force, Final Report* (Windsor, Ontario: International Joint Commission, 2000); or Hallett J. Harris and Denise Scheberle, "Ode to the Miners' Canary: The Search for Environmental Indicators," in *Environmental Program Evaluation: A Primer*, ed. Gerrit J. Knaap and Tschangho John Kim (Urbana: University of Illinois Press, 1998), 176–200.

4. Telephone conversation with an EPA official, January 19, 2003.

5. Beryl A. Radin, "Searching for Government Performance: The Government Performance and Results Act," *PS: Political Science and Politics* 31, no. 3 (1998): 553–55, at 553.

6. Radin, "Searching for Government Performance," 553.

7. U.S. General Accounting Office, *Managing for Results: EPA Faces Challenges in Developing Results-Oriented Performance Goals and Measures*, GAO/RCED-00-77 (Washington, D.C.: U.S. General Accounting Office, 2000), 4.

8. Helen Ingram, "Implementation: A Review and Suggested Framework," in *Public Administration: The State of the Discipline*, ed. Naomi B. Lynn and Aaron Wildavsky (Chatham, N.J.: Chatam House Publishers, 1990), 462–80, at 470.

9. Ingram, "Implementation," 477.

10. Eugene Bardach, *The Implementation Game: What Happens after a Bill Becomes a Law* (Cambridge, Mass.: MIT Press, 1977), 278.

11. Martha Derthick, *New Towns In-Town* (Washington, D.C.: Urban Institute Press, 1972), 83.

12. Jeffrey L. Pressman and Aaron Wildavsky, *Implementation* (Berkeley: University of California Press, 1973), 93.

13. Quoted in Jeffrey R. Henig, *Public Policy and Federalism: Issues in State and Local Politics* (New York: Saint Martin's Press, 1985), 23.

14. Richard Elmore, "Backward Mapping: Implementation Research and Policy Decisions," *Political Science Quarterly* 84, no. 4 (1979): 601–11.

15. Michael Lipsky, *Street-Level Bureaucracy* (New York: Russell Sage, 1980), xii.

16. See Randall B. Ripley and Grace A. Franklin, *Bureaucracy and Policy Implementation*, (Homewood, Ill.: Dorsey Press, 1982); and Carl Van Horn and Donald S. Van Meter, "The Implementation of Intergovernmental Policy," in *Public Policy in the Federal System*, ed. Donald S. Van Meter and Carl E. Van Horn (Lexington, Mass.: Lexington Books, 1976).

17. Bardach, *Implementation Game*.

18. See Janice Love and Peter C. Sederberg, "Euphony and Cacophony in Policy Implementation: SCF and the Somali Refugee Problem," *Policy Studies Review* 7, no. 1 (1987): 155–73; and Goggin et al., *Implementation Theory and Practice*, 24.

19. See Eugene Bardach and Robert A. Kagan, *Going by the Book: The Problem of Regulatory Unreasonableness* (Philadelphia: Temple University Press, 1982).

20. Peter Schwartz, *The Art of the Long View: Planning for the Future in an Uncertain World* (New York: Bantam, 1991), 40.

21. Deborah A. Stone, *Policy Paradox and Political Reason* (New York: HarperCollins, 1988), 7.

22. Donald S. Van Meter and Carl E. Van Horn, "The Policy Implementation Process," *Administration and Society* 6, no. 4 (1975): 445–87; and Paul A. Sabatier and Daniel Maz-

manian, "Policy Implementation: A Framework for Analysis," *Policy Studies Journal* 8, no. 2 (1980): 538–60. For a fuller treatment of their framework, see Mazmanian and Sabatier, *Implementation and Public Policy* (Glenview, Ill.: Scott Foresman, 1983).

23. William R. Lowry, *The Dimensions of Federalism: State Governments and Pollution Control Policies* (Durham, N.C.: Duke University Press, 1992); and Evan J. Ringquist, "Does Regulation Matter? Evaluating the Effects of State Air Pollution Control Programs," *Journal of Politics* 55, no. 4 (1993): 1022–45.

24. David M. Hedge, Donald C. Menzel, and George Williams, "Regulatory Attitudes and Behavior: The Case of Surface Mining Regulation," *Western Political Quarterly* 41 (1988): 323–40; Denise Scheberle, "In the Eye of the Beholder: State and Federal Perceptions about the Surface Mining Control and Reclamation Act," in *Moving the Earth: Cooperative Federalism and the Implementation of the Surface Mining Act,* ed. Uday Desai (Westport, Conn.: Greenwood Press), 184–97.

25. James P. Lester, James L. Franke, Ann O'M. Bowman, and Kenneth W. Kramer, "Hazardous Wastes, Politics and Public Policy: A Comparative State Analysis," *Western Political Quarterly* 36 (1983): 257–81.

26. John W. Kingdon, *Agendas, Alternatives, and Public Policies* (Boston: Little, Brown, 1984); and Roger W. Cobb and Charles D. Elder, *Participation in American Politics: The Dynamics of Agenda-Building* (Boston: Allyn and Bacon, 1972).

27. Bardach, *Implementation Game,* 5.

28. See, e.g., Michael S. Hamilton, ed., *Regulatory Federalism, Natural Resources and Environmental Management* (Washington, D.C.: American Political Science Association, 1990); and James L. Regens, "State Policy Responses to the Energy Issue: An Analysis of Innovation," *Social Science Quarterly* 61 (1980): 44–59.

29. Denise Scheberle, "Scratching the Surface: State Implementation of the Surface Mining Reclamation and Control Act" (Ph.D. diss., Colorado State University, 1991).

30. U.S. Department of the Interior, Office of Surface Mining, *1995 Annual Report: Protecting the Natural Environmental, a Shared Commitment* (Washington, D.C.: U.S. Department of the Interior, 1996), 16.

31. For the effect of fragmentation on effective management of environmental programs, see Barry G. Rabe, *Fragmentation and Integration in State Environmental Management* (Washington, D.C.: Conservation Foundation, 1986).

32. Herbert Kaufman, *The Forest Ranger: A Study in Administrative Behavior* (Baltimore: Johns Hopkins University Press, 1960).

33. See Kingdon, *Agendas, Alternatives, and Public Policies,* for factors that put policies on the formal congressional agenda.

34. Evan J. Ringquist, "Is Effective Regulation always Oxymoronic? The States and Ambient Air Quality," *Social Science Quarterly* 76, no. 1 (1995): 69–87.

35. See, e.g., R. Shep Melnick, *Regulation and the Courts: The Case of the Clean Air Act* (Washington, D.C.: Brookings Institution Press, 1983).

· 3 ·

Unintended Consequences, Policy Retreat, and Refocusing Events in Asbestos Policy

Chapter 2 suggested that all laws tell unique implementation stories. Implementation stories may change when elements in political, intergovernmental, or policy landscapes shift, sometimes in dramatic and unpredictable ways. Asbestos policy presents just such an implementation story. America's initial high regard for asbestos-containing materials (ACMs) resulted in the deaths of thousands of people, the longest and most litigated toxic tort in the history of the country, and federal and state agencies that were whipsawed by political forces that first demanded protection from asbestos exposure and then seemingly just hoped the whole thing would go away. Indeed, this story's plot line weaves its way through virtually every extrinsic and intrinsic implementation factor presented in chapter 2's framework.

The primary focus of this chapter is the implementation of the only current national law dealing exclusively with asbestos, the Asbestos Hazard and Emergency Response Act of 1986 (AHERA), which was created as Title II of the Toxic Substances Control Act (TSCA). AHERA is designed to protect children from exposure to asbestos in schools. AHERA requires officials to inspect schools for ACMs and, if found, limit asbestos exposure through proper management. However, this law also intertwines with the government's changing attitudes toward asbestos and with asbestos regulation in other laws such as the Clean Air Act, the main provisions of TSCA, and the Occupational Safety and Health Act.

The chapter begins by telling a brief story of the use of asbestos in this country, the implementation of the AHERA program, including the U.S. Environmental Protection Agency's (EPA's) disinvestment in asbestos policy, and recent events that have kept asbestos on the national environmental policy radar screen. The story continues with the results of survey and interview research conducted in 1995 and 2002. The chapter concludes by discussing implementation patterns as well as the nature of federal–state working relationships.

History of Asbestos

Asbestos is a naturally occurring mineral whose name comes from a Greek word meaning inextinguishable or unquenchable. For centuries, people heralded asbestos for its unique properties. Its fibers can be spun into cloth (something done by the ancient Greeks), and it retains a remarkable ability to withstand heat. The fibers are incredibly small: Approximately 1 million individual fibrils of chrysotile asbestos (a type of asbestos accounting for 95 percent of the world's production) lie side by side in a linear inch.[1] However, even though small in size, asbestos fibers have high tensile strength and possess great powers to absorb and filter. When combined with its fire-resistant properties, this "magic mineral" promised to be the ideal insulation, fireproofing, and acoustical soundproofing material for the industrial age.

Expanding U.S. industry in the 1800s wanted to use asbestos. In 1858, H. W. Johns Manufacturing Company (later to become Johns-Manville) opened for business in New York to provide asbestos as a fire-resistant roofing material.[2] Twenty-eight years later, Manville Covering Company, the second company in the Johns-Manville Corporation, opened in Milwaukee to provide asbestos as a heat insulating material.[3] Asbestos eventually was used in an estimated 3,000 industrial applications in the United States.[4] Automobile manufacturers used it in brake pads and clutch plates. Pipe wrapping, roofing, wall and ceiling insulation, siding, flooring, and the insides of boilers all contained asbestos. During World War II, asbestos insulation was used extensively on U.S. Navy ships. In 1942 alone, the War Production Board used 40 percent of the estimated 36.8 million pounds of the asbestos-containing pipe insulation produced domestically in Navy shipyards.[5]

As is suggested in figures 3.1 and 3.2 by the Keasbey & Mattison advertisement in *Time* magazine and the photograph of "Cinema Asbestos," asbestos was widely accepted, and even embraced, by the U.S. government and many U.S. companies throughout much of the last century. Asbestos was easy to manipulate, yet strong and fire resistant. It seemed nearly perfect. The asbestos business was booming, and for decades the trajectory for asbestos use was only one way: up. Except for one deadly detail—those little asbestos fibers cause cancer and lung disease.

Health Risks Associated with Asbestos

Asbestos is classified as a human carcinogen. Asbestos poses a health risk when fibers are released into the air. The small size of asbestos fibers allows them to be inhaled more deeply into the lungs. Once inhaled, the fibers become trapped in the lungs, and the body cannot break down or eliminate them.[6]

Siding that resists fire and weather. Siding that *stops* rodents and termites. Siding that can't rust or rot. These are but a few of the practical advantages you get with "Century" Asbestos-Cement Shingles. And, as desirable as the wearing qualities, is the attractive, modern appearance these shingles give your home. What's more, you can count on the beauty to *last.* You can see and feel the texture of the authentic cypress grain. And the various colors offered are not pressed on the surface but are an integral part of the shingles, giving the best assurance of color permanence.

To make an old house look new— to build a new house that will keep its fresh "young" look throughout its lifetime, use K&M "Century" Asbestos-Cement Siding Shingles. Your local Keasbey & Mattison dealer will give you complete information on "Century" Shingles—we'll gladly send you information on *any* asbestos products.

Nature made Asbestos . . .
Keasbey & Mattison has made it serve mankind since 1873

KEASBEY & MATTISON

COMPANY • AMBLER • PENNSYLVANIA

Figure 3.1.   Keasbey & Mattison Advertise the Amazing Properties of Asbestos

Source: Time Magazine, March 5, 1951.

Figure 3.2.   Photograph of a Theater Using Asbestos Curtains

Source: Copyright Bill Ravanesi / Center for Visual Arts in the Public Interest, Inc.; used by permission.

The risk for asbestos-related disease depends upon the type of asbestos fiber, the level and duration of exposure, and whether the individual smokes. Each exposure increases the likelihood of developing asbestos-related disease.[7] Once exposed, the latency period between exposure and the onset of asbestos-related disease is ten to forty years.

Asbestos exposure is primarily associated with three diseases. Asbestosis is a serious scarring of the lung tissue that makes breathing difficult and is usually caused by occupational exposure to asbestos. No effective treatment exists. Lung cancer accounts for about half of all asbestos-related disease.[8] Asbestos workers are about five times more likely to develop lung cancer than are workers not exposed to asbestos in the workplace. Asbestos workers who smoke are fifty to ninety times more likely to develop lung cancer than nonsmokers. Mesothelioma, a cancer of the mesothelium or pleural linings of the lungs, is incurable and usually fatal within one year of diagnosis. Mesothelioma accounts for 10 to 20 percent of deaths due to asbestos exposure. More important from a risk point of view, mesothelioma rarely occurs without exposure to asbestos.[9]

Experts estimate that between 1940 and 1980, 27 million Americans had significant occupational exposure to asbestos.[10] The results were sometimes deadly; between 1980 and 1995, an estimated 149,350 people in the United States died of occupational asbestos disease. That number surpassed the combined total of 140,365 deaths from all other workplace injuries and illnesses during that period.[11] And more than 225,000 premature deaths due to asbestos-related cancers are estimated through 2009.[12] That number may be low, because it does not include deaths from complications due to asbestosis, or from asbestos exposure in nonoccupational settings, or exposure after 1979. Mesothelioma cases were predicted to peak at 3,000 or more in 2002.[13] Put simply, breathing asbestos fibers poses serious, even fatal, consequences—consequences Americans are still experiencing.

Though occupational exposures to asbestos have dramatically declined since the 1970s, the widespread use of ACMs in homes and buildings suggests that many Americans potentially have environmental exposure to asbestos. Insulation or ceiling tiles that have been in place for many years are degrading and potentially dangerous. Moreover, ACMs are still used, some of it imported from overseas. Data from the U.S. International Trade Commission indicate that import of some ACMs is actually increasing, potentially increasing asbestos exposure.[14]

The Government Responds to Asbestos

Given the serious health risks associated with asbestos, one might assume that the government would respond quickly to prevent more exposures. However, historically, that has not been the case. In fact, the government supported an industry that produced a wide range of products containing asbestos—even after World War II. Sadly, government officials were aware of the deadly results of asbestos exposure, even as they were promoting its use. The long history of policy avoidance, though not the major focus of this study, is still important to understanding the implementation of AHERA.

Health care professionals suspected that high levels of asbestos exposure posed significant health risks early in the twentieth century. Articles documenting the dangers of occupational exposure to asbestos appeared in medical journals as early as 1924. The government knew as well. In 1918, the U.S. Bureau of Labor Statistics published a report noting that American asbestos workers were experiencing early deaths and that some American and Canadian life insurance companies were refusing to issue policies to asbestos workers. By the 1930s, asbestos workers began to seek personal injury claims against Johns-Manville and Raybestos-Manhattan, the country's two largest asbestos manufacturers. Instead of choosing to limit occupational asbestos exposure, the companies chose to cover up the problem—a cover-up that lasted more than forty years.[15]

The U.S. Navy was not any better at protecting its shipyard workers. A Navy medical bulletin published in 1922 warned that working with asbestos was a hazardous occupation and suggested that respirators be used in the workplace. The Navy issued medical corpsmen handbooks advising them of the hazards asbestos workers faced. In a March 1941 letter to the Navy's surgeon general, Commander C. S. Stephenson, the Navy's chief officer for preventive medicine, wrote of asbestos workers in shipyards: "I am certain that we are not protecting the men as we should."[16] His warning would be deadly in its accuracy. As Bill Burke (2001) observed:

> Working in an American shipyard during World War II would prove to be almost as deadly as fighting in the war. The combat death rate was about 18 per thousand [armed] service members. For every thousand wartime shipyard employees, about 14 died of asbestos-related cancer, and an unknown number died of an asbestos disease called asbestosis, or complications from it.[17]

More troubling, the Navy did not protect its shipyard workers from asbestos until decades after World War II. Nor did the Navy ban the use of asbestos on new ships until 1973, and it then ignored its own ban until 1978.

With asbestos companies and the government choosing to look the other way, the medical community began to sound the alarm publicly. In 1962, Irving L. Selikoff, director of Environmental Health at Mount Sinai Medical Center in New York City, conducted a pioneering epidemiological study of 1,117 asbestos insulation workers. The study showed that developing asbestosis after long exposures to asbestos was almost unavoidable. Eighty-seven percent of men with twenty years of asbestos exposure developed asbestosis. Equally troubling, the incidence of lung cancer was seven times the expected rate.[18] In 1973, Selikoff testified before a congressional subcommittee and predicted that asbestos disease would kill 1 million American workers by 2000.[19]

By the 1970s, numerous professional medical journals featured articles on asbestos-related diseases. Researchers had plenty of data. The long latency period between asbestos exposure and cancer incidence had ended; thousands of shipyard workers exposed to high levels of asbestos during World War II provided ample case studies of asbestosis, mesothelioma, and lung cancer.[20] Though his work was generally focused on occupational exposure, Selikoff would later warn of the "third wave" of asbestos-related diseases. The first wave included asbestos miners and mill workers; the second wave included occupational exposures of insulation installers such as the shipyard workers; and the third wave would include school janitors, building maintenance workers, and members of the public, including children, who had suffered nonoccupational exposure to asbestos fibers.

Incredibly, the mass media, the public, and the federal government paid little attention to asbestos for decades.[21] State and federal health officials were reluctant to take any action to protect the public from asbestos exposure, even in the face of growing medical evidence of asbestos-related disease and mortality, and even as asbestos lawsuits were beginning to increase. Indeed, the chief industrial hygienist for the U.S. Public Health Service agreed to keep the dangers of asbestos exposure confidential when inspecting asbestos manufacturing facilities, and the Public Health Service did not make any recommendations to either asbestos workers or their unions about avoiding asbestos exposure.

Legal and Media Attention to Asbestos in the 1980s

With mounting epidemiological evidence, asbestos lawsuits proliferated. By 1982, roughly 30,000 lawsuits had been filed by asbestos victims or their heirs against asbestos manufacturers. Almost half of the lawsuits were brought by people exposed by direct action of government.[22] The leading supplier of asbestos insulation for ships and airplanes during World War II, Johns-Manville, filed for bankruptcy protection in 1982. Six years later, the company emerged from Chapter 11. On April 1, 1996, Johns-Manville became Schuller Corporation, after paying more than 94,000 asbestos-injury claims and more than $1.5 billion in settlements.[23] (Though the media declared that Johns-Manville was no more, the company always remained intact and readopted its historic name in 1997. Johns-Manville was acquired by Berkshire-Hathaway in 2001.)[24] Fifteen other companies with significant asbestos liability would file for bankruptcy in the 1980s.[25]

The feeding frenzy of asbestos lawsuits stirred the interest of the media. For example, in 1983 the Public Broadcast System aired a special titled, "Asbestos: The Lethal Legacy," which highlighted the government's failure to protect the public from occupational exposures to asbestos. Consumer advocates Ralph Nader and Paul Brodeur soon became involved in warning the public about asbestos. More than 100 articles on asbestos were published between 1982 and 1985 in major media outlets. More important from the perspective of the AHERA program, states became embroiled in local conflicts about asbestos in schools. As the next section explains, schools soon became a focal point (or lightning rod, depending upon one's perspective) for public asbestos concerns. In any event, by the mid-1980s many Americans understood asbestos dangers and that the government had failed to protect them. AHERA was crafted in this climate of public fear and mistrust of government.

Congress Develops an Asbestos Law

After decades of ignoring asbestos as a public health danger, Congress finally moved in the 1980s to protect one subset of the population—children—from asbestos exposure. In large part, Congress responded to political forces. During a series of congressional hearings in the late 1970s and early 1980s, educational lobbies pressed for national regulation of asbestos in schools. Local school officials were beginning to hear from angry parents demanding asbestos-free schools.[26] Congress passed two laws in rapid succession: the Asbestos School Hazard and Detection Act of 1980 and the Asbestos in Schools Act of 1982. The first law required the U.S. Department of Education to develop a grant and loan program for schools, but it was never funded. The Asbestos in Schools Act required schools to inspect for friable (meaning crumbles when touched) ACMs but provided no guidance or oversight. In 1984, Congress authorized a federal grant and loan program to assist schools in asbestos management under the Asbestos School Hazard Abatement Act. That act authorized expenditures of $50 million for the program in 1985 and $100 million per year for each of the next five years to assist schools with financing asbestos removal or control, mostly in the form of no-interest loans.[27]

AHERA was passed in 1986 as Title II of TSCA to strengthen the federal directive to control asbestos exposure in schools. In creating AHERA, Congress criticized EPA and explained that it was making up for inadequate EPA responses to asbestos in schools. "As a result of the lack of regulatory guidance from the EPA, some schools have not undertaken responsive action, while many others have undertaken expensive projects without knowing if their action is necessary, adequate, or safe. Thus, the danger of exposure to asbestos continues to exist in schools, and some exposure actually may have increased due to the lack of federal standards and improper response action."[28] That Congress chose to chastise EPA for its failure to regulate asbestos appropriately was a bit disingenuous. After all, the federal government had supported the asbestos industry for decades.

AHERA went beyond the grant and loan provisions to require that public and private schools be inspected for asbestos, that the public be notified if asbestos was found, and that schools initiate appropriate asbestos management plans. AHERA also called for certification of asbestos contractors that work in schools and required EPA to issue model accreditation plans for training and certification through state- or EPA-sponsored courses. It further required EPA to conduct a study of asbestos risk in public buildings, creating the potential for a program like AHERA to regulate asbestos management in buildings.

AHERA mandated action on the part of EPA by requiring the agency to write regulations for the management of asbestos, inspect schools for compliance, and conduct studies of asbestos exposures in public buildings. It also mandated significant performance from local education agencies (LEAs), which were required to establish asbestos management programs for school buildings. To manage asbestos properly, LEAs had to identify someone to run the program—in the parlance of the law, a "designated person." Then, the designated person had to locate and identify ACMs, determine the appropriate action to take, and periodically reinspect for friable and nonfriable asbestos. LEAs also had to identify a designated person to oversee the plan, ensure that only properly trained and certified persons performed asbestos removal and repair operations, and train operations and maintenance personnel who might work with ACMs.

AHERA was not a delegated program. LEAs (not states) were the regulatory target of the law. Few requirements were placed on states. LEAs had to submit their management plans to the state's governor (or his or her designee) for approval. After approving the plans, the state had no further mandated role. However, the law did not preclude states from establishing a more rigorous asbestos control program, and some states did.[29]

Without express statutory authority to implement AHERA, the role of states was determined through their participation in the enforcement of AHERA and their decision to participate in EPA's model accreditation plan for training and certifying asbestos contractors and inspectors. States that chose to do neither one of these activities had an implementation role limited to approving school management plans.[30] However, states with an approved enforcement program received a "waiver" from EPA, which allowed state officials to monitor LEAs for compliance with regulatory requirements under AHERA.[31]

In developing AHERA, Congress seemed ready to champion the protection of children at all costs. AHERA explicitly states that asbestos control must protect human health regardless of cost. Even the title of the law, which includes the words "emergency response," suggests that Congress viewed asbestos in schools as a serious problem in need of immediate attention. AHERA demanded rapid implementation. It required EPA regulations governing asbestos in schools to be in place by 1987, and school management plans were to be submitted to state agencies the following year. Only when Congress realized that the timetable was unworkable and that asbestos removal contractors were in short supply did it amend AHERA to extend the deadline for LEAs to comply to May 9, 1989.[32]

Now that the law was in place, congressional architects of AHERA were eager to get EPA to address asbestos in schools but also to make the agency a scapegoat for decades of government inattention to asbestos. During AHERA oversight hearings in 1987, Representative Mike Synar (Okla.) declared: "EPA has a responsibility to enforce the law of this country. I am hopeful that we have jogged them into recognizing that Congress is going to do the type of tough oversight until we get the type of response that we demand and that the American public demands."[33] When EPA released its 1988 report to Congress suggesting that asbestos in commercial buildings posed little risk to the public, several members of Congress, including Frank Lautenberg (N.J.) challenged EPA for its lack of concern for America's health.[34]

In a 1991 public hearing concerning asbestos, Senator Malcolm Wallop (Wyo.) summarized the collective congressional mindset regarding AHERA: "Five years ago the Congress reacted to the growing national phobia about asbestos by enacting AHERA, conveying all of the proper terminology, to alarm the public about the latest threat to their health while reassuring them that Congress would take care of the problem. The bill passed the Senate with little debate and no dissent. We were all anxious to ensure that our schools posed no threat to the health of our children."[35]

In short, the role of Congress was to move to protect children (without fully comprehending the extent of the health risks associated with removing ACMs) and to make certain that EPA responded quickly to the dictates of AHERA. It fell to EPA, the LEAs, and the states to make the asbestos control program under AHERA a reality.

EPA Develops Asbestos Regulations

EPA regulatory action to control asbestos preceded the passage of AHERA. EPA had responded to concerns about asbestos under different statutory authorities. In 1971, EPA first listed asbestos as a hazardous air pollutant as part of its new authority under Section 112, the National Emission Standards for Hazardous Air Pollutants (NESHAP) provisions of the Clean Air Act. The NESHAP standard required building owners and contractors to notify EPA and/or the state before removing asbestos.[36] No visible emissions of dust were allowed during the removal, transportation, and disposal of ACMs. EPA also prohibited the spray application for most uses of friable asbestos in 1978.[37] Subsequently, additions to EPA's Asbestos NESHAP regulations in 1974, 1975, and 1990 strengthened requirements for the removal of friable ACMs from commercial and certain other buildings, including schools, undertaking major renovation projects.[38]

The NESHAP rule, however, affected buildings where physical alterations were planned, through either outright demolition or renovation. It was silent about ACMs in existing buildings that were not undergoing major remodeling, which included most schools. How, then, did schools get involved in asbestos removal, both before AHERA and as part of responding to AHERA?

Clues to how the federal government may have promoted the idea that removal of asbestos was a prudent practice for schools can be found in EPA's earliest guidance documents. In 1979, EPA produced a guidance document for asbestos management in schools and buildings, referred to as the Orange Book. The Orange Book, and a subsequent guidance document published three years later, the Blue Book, did little to discourage the removal of asbestos. Indeed, the Blue Book suggested that removal was "always appropriate, never inappropriate."[39] In fact, EPA considered regulations that would have required schools to remove or cover exposed asbestos, but it abandoned those efforts in 1981.[40]

Then, in 1982, EPA promulgated the "Friable Asbestos-Containing Materials in Schools; Identification and Notification Rule" (40 CFR Part 763). Known simply as the Asbestos in Schools Rule, it required all primary and secondary schools, both public and private, to inspect, sample, and analyze all friable materials for asbestos. Under the rule, schools had to document their findings and inform school employees and parent–teacher organizations (or just parents and guardians) of the location of friable asbestos.[41] The deadline for compliance was 1984, and the decision to remove, contain, or simply manage asbestos was left entirely up to the schools.[42]

By the mid-1980s, EPA had modified its position on the appropriateness of asbestos removal. In 1985, EPA officially put management of asbestos in place ahead of removal when it issued a third guidance document, referred to as the Purple Book.[43] However, even that guidance suggested that while the choice of abatement method is determined by the condition of the ACM, "removal has the widest applicability" and "is the only truly permanent solution."[44] In 1987, EPA once again left the choice of removal or management in place of asbestos up to LEAs: "Nothing in this rule shall be construed to prohibit removal of asbestos containing building materials from a school building at any time, should removal be the preferred response action of the LEA."[45]

Only in later guidance did EPA strongly advocate managing asbestos in place.[46] In 1990, the agency went so far as to say that "removal is often not a school district's best course of action to reduce asbestos exposure" and that "improper removal can create a dangerous situation where none previously existed."[47] However, given the emerging mountain of asbestos litigation, EPA's initial inclination to require asbestos removal or encapsulation, and earlier EPA language found in the first guidance documents, it is easy to see how the message of asbestos removal was what was heard by school officials.

Yet another EPA action under different authority occurred in 1989, when EPA issued a rule under TSCA to ban all asbestos products. When issuing the rule, EPA stated, "It is well recognized that asbestos is a human carcinogen and is one of the most hazardous substances to which humans are exposed in both occupational and non-occupational settings."[48] The ban on all asbestos products was later overturned by the U.S. Court of Appeals for the Fifth Circuit in 1991 for being overly broad and creating an unreasonably expensive prohibition.[49] EPA did not challenge the decision, and only the threat of toxic tort or product liability litigation would slow the production of ACMs into the 1990s.

In sum, EPA regulatory actions regarding asbestos have occurred in several areas and generated a number of mixed signals for policy implementers. The NESHAP standards have been directed at asbestos removal in commercial buildings but do not regulate daily exposure to asbestos in schools absent a renovation or demolition activity. Early guidance for schools to manage asbestos suggested that asbestos removal was prudent, although later guidance suggested otherwise. In 1989, EPA sought to ban outright the production of this "most hazardous substance," but its rule was overturned by the court. Thus, it seems easy to understand how state officials, school officials, the public, and even EPA staff might be confused about the agency's posture regarding asbestos removal, though current agency guidance documents and the recent rhetoric of EPA administrators suggest a tempered response.

The Early Years of Implementing AHERA

The years immediately following the passage of AHERA were turbulent ones for asbestos policy, as scholars and medical professionals began to criticize what they saw as unnecessary asbestos removal in schools. From this point of view, the federal government had come full circle. For years, it had refused to develop a reasoned asbestos policy; now it had seemingly gone too far, and as a result, school officials were needlessly removing asbestos-containing ceiling tiles, floor tiles, and insulation.

In the 1980s, asbestos exposure may have increased because school officials often chose to remove asbestos.[50] They were caught in the cross fire between intense public reaction against asbestos, a stiff congressional posture to protect children "at all costs," and changing guidance on asbestos management from EPA. Thus, they responded in an understandable fashion: Why risk lawsuits or community backlash by just "managing" asbestos? Asbestos litigation made school officials wary, and states across the country became embroiled in local conflicts about asbestos in schools.

Alabama's attorney general filed suit in October 1982 against the governor when he learned that his child's school had asbestos ceiling tiles. Less than two months later, Governor Forrest James signed an out-of-court settlement releasing $75 million in bonds for schools to remove (not just control) asbestos.[51] School districts in other states closed schools temporarily because of concerns about unsafe asbestos levels. Senator Wallop—after relating a story of Kelly Walsh High School, a Wyoming school that closed for a year because ACMs were found—stated, "I have talked to school superintendents who feel that they have no choice, that if they allow it there [asbestos in schools], they will soon be on trial for irresponsibility and liability for not having removed it regardless of what the law says."[52]

In late 1989 and early 1990, two articles written by prominent U.S. and international health professionals published in the *New England Journal of Medicine* and *Science* proved to be watershed events in focusing attention on concerns about unwarranted asbestos abatements that actually increased airborne asbestos fibers.[53] EPA administrator William Reilly declared that removal of asbestos by schools was an unintended consequence of EPA asbestos regulations and that "a considerable gap has opened up between what EPA has been trying to say about asbestos and what the public has been hearing."[54] Since 1992, articles criticizing the frequent removal of asbestos in schools have appeared in such major news magazines as *Time* and *U.S. News & World Report*. Articles in medical journals and safety magazines have also pointed to the needless exposure of school custodians.[55]

In addition to possibly increasing exposure to asbestos fibers, removing and disposing of asbestos is expensive. A U.S. General Accounting Office report on the condition of American schools suggested that schools spent more money on asbestos management than on any other environmental pollutant: 57 percent of school districts studied had incurred asbestos-related expenses (compared with 25 percent that had incurred expenses for dealing with lead-based paint or lead in the water and only 18 percent that reported radon-related expenses).[56] Moreover, the General Accounting Office estimated that $11 billion was needed to remove or correct asbestos, lead in water or paint, and radon, and that most of the cost was attributable to asbestos.[57]

Although Congress passed the Asbestos School Hazard Abatement Act to provide federal funding to assist schools in asbestos management, the funding has never been sufficient to cover the number of requests. Between 1988 and 1991, EPA received 1,746 qualified applications from LEAs requesting financial assistance totaling nearly $600 million, but it awarded only $157 million to the 586 school districts with the "worst" asbestos problems.[58] LEAs, in turn, had to seek other sources of funding (most often from school operation and maintenance budgets) to manage ACMs in school buildings.

In sum, the legacy of governmental neglect of the health dangers associated with asbestos exposures for more than a half-century resulted in a number of unintended consequences, not the least of which was thousands of lives lost due to asbestos-related disease. In turn, class-action lawsuits by people with occupational exposures to asbestos continue today. Shifting EPA guidance placed school administrators in a difficult position: Remove asbestos now or deal with it forever, as part of an asbestos management program. This set the stage for political conflicts and resistance by LEAs.

Conversely, the early years of AHERA implementation signaled that exposing children to unsafe levels of asbestos would not be tolerated. Though some schools may have acted hastily in removing floor or ceiling tiles that posed minimal health risks, they nonetheless did comply with the initial regulatory and statutory requirements. An EPA-sponsored study in 1989 found that 92 percent of schools had at least conducted a general inventory of their buildings. AHERA in the early years was full of political maneuvering and initial misunderstanding of what was required to comply, but it was also a time that EPA, the states, and certainly local governments paid attention to the deadly traits of this "miracle fiber." With most schools having management plans in place, how would the rest of the AHERA implementation story unfold?

Implementing AHERA Today

How one views the story of AHERA implementation today depends in part upon one's perspective. The late 1990s and early 2000s tell a story of EPA's continued pullback from AHERA. To some, this seems a reasonable approach, if one believes that schools are well acquainted with asbestos problems. It certainly seems reasonable in an era of devolving authority down to state and local governments. To others, however, EPA's pullback from AHERA implementation is premature and troubling.

The declining interest in AHERA is evident in the availability of federal funding. For fiscal 1995, the administration's budget submitted to Congress included a disinvestment from TSCA state grant programs of more than $1.4 million.[60] Further cuts for asbestos cooperative agreements would be forthcoming as the agency made choices about how to spend its funds. EPA's Office of Enforcement and Compliance Assurance identified three areas for priority funding in fiscal 2001: lead-based paint, wetlands, and unpermitted releases under the Oil Pollution Act.[61] For the agency to invest in these priority programs, it meant that it would have to shift money from the other small compliance and enforcement programs, most notably AHERA. Disinvesting from AHERA at the EPA headquarters level meant that the ten EPA regional offices would have fewer resources to implement the asbestos program.

The practical effect was to limit inspection and enforcement efforts under AHERA. Most EPA regions allocate only one or two full-time equivalent employees for the AHERA program. Not surprisingly, several regional officials reported conducting only a handful of AHERA inspections in 2002, and one regional official observed that it was impossible to complete any inspections, given the pressing demands of other, higher-priority programs. Some regional offices have cut AHERA positions in half since 1990. For example, EPA Region 2, which serves the states of New York and New Jersey as well as Puerto Rico and the Virgin Islands, reduced the number of AHERA inspection staff from six to two in 1996.[62] Each inspector may budget for no more than one inspection per month, which would total twenty-four inspections per year for that region.

Also in response to EPA headquarters efforts to consolidate the enforcement of many regulatory programs, enforcement activities have been shifted into one division in many EPA regional offices. Asbestos program staff located in EPA regions may not run the inspection and enforcement program. Many regional offices have some support for AHERA inspections through the use of Senior Environmental Employment Program employees, but these are not permanent federal employees and they seldom exclusively work in the asbestos program.[63]

Critics of EPA's divestiture of AHERA include people inside the agency, both at the headquarters and regional levels. Seven of nine EPA asbestos officials interviewed in 2002 and 2003 would like to see more money dedicated to AHERA implementation. "We used to have an adequate program," lamented one EPA official. "Now we have misery." Another EPA staff member concluded that "we do what we can, given that we're very short on resources, but mostly we rely on tips and complaints [about schools] to set our inspection schedule." A third official agreed: "We don't have adequate funding to do compliance inspections, not to mention to do outreach efforts. There are a lot of new designated persons in school districts that were not around at the beginning [of AHERA implementation]. They don't have a clue what to do—they may not even be aware that they are the designated person handling asbestos surveillance and reinspections." Yet another EPA official commented, "We're always doing more with less. Often it's just me, and with not much of a budget. It's very difficult to understand the decisions that have been made."

When asked about how it would be possible for EPA to truly "divest" from statutorily required duties, an EPA official suggested "divesting is an unfortunate choice of words. We would have to repeal the regulation if we really divested. Instead, the [EPA] regions are in this 'nether world' expected to do something with nothing. We've taken people from the asbestos program and not replaced them as resources have steadily eroded."

As one EPA official put it, "AHERA started as a well-funded, very successful, very good program. Then, no sooner had it reached its pinnacle than AHERA succumbed to steady erosion in funding and resources. We have substantial noncompliance from schools now because we [EPA] have pulled back. Take, for example, charter schools. We are finding schools that have not heard about AHERA and have not managed asbestos risks. Many designated persons are not trained because the guard has changed."[64]

The EPA Office of the Inspector General (OIG) sharply criticized the AHERA enforcement activities of Region 3, observing that "the Region inspects only an infinitesimal number of schools because it can only respond to tips and complaints it receives about possible asbestos problems in schools."[65] The report concluded that the region should consider expanding rather than curtailing the AHERA program, especially in light of new charter schools, many of which have not heard of AHERA.

The OIG used the compliance problems of the Washington, D.C., public schools to illustrate its point. After students refused to attend a high school in the city that was undergoing asbestos abatement, Region 3 AHERA personnel inspected the building. Failing to find a management plan for the school, the EPA inspector expanded the inspection to include all schools in the city. The region subsequently determined that none of the 175 schools had any documentation required by AHERA (management plans, training records, reinspection, and periodic surveillance records).[66] Further inspections revealed that many of the city's schools had "major asbestos fiber releases" (the dislodging of more than 3 square or linear feet of friable asbestos). As a result, 55 of the 175 schools had to partially or fully close for asbestos abatement actions in 1999.[67]

Though most EPA officials interviewed would like to see restoration of funding to levels seen in the early 1990s, not everyone agrees. Some people inside the agency believe that most of the work of implementing AHERA has been done and that funding, therefore, is rightfully allocated to more pressing needs. As one EPA official suggested, "AHERA has been around for over fifteen years. Schools have responded. The last thing schools want is to be liable for asbestos exposure. Liability is a strong motivator." Two officials agreed that divesting made sense when faced with too much to do with too few dollars. One observed, "Personally, I think lead-based paint is a hotter issue." A second official commented, "Most states are inspecting schools even though they are not funded to do it under AHERA. They use the money available from NESHAPs [requirements]. It's not the same program, but it still gets inspectors into schools. Many AHERA violations are just paperwork violations, such as not having an up-to-date management plan. NESHAPs are more important to enforce."[68]

Refocusing Events: Libby, Montana, the World Trade Center, and Litigation

As was mentioned in chapter 2, unexpected or dramatic events can trigger changes in implementing a policy just as it does in creating a policy, even in the face of forces that otherwise would maintain the status quo. The implementation landscape shifts, sometimes exposing long-standing fault lines in government programs. The good news is that sometimes these events inject new energy into the implementation process, bringing positive programmatic change. Of course, this is not always the case. It may be that these events, like fireworks, capture a lot of attention but quickly fade. Two recent tragedies, one in Libby, Montana, and the other in New York City, have each directed much attention to asbestos exposure and its health risks, to the insufficiencies of EPA's regulatory approach toward asbestos, and to AHERA. Also complicating asbestos policy is the rapid increase in asbestos litigation.

The 2,700 residents of Libby, Montana, are perhaps more aware of asbestos than citizens of any other American community. The death rate from asbestos-related diseases in Libby is sixty times the national average.[69] The culprit is an inactive vermiculite mine that was operational from 1921 to 1990. The mine was owned by the Zonolite Company until W. R. Grace bought the mining operations in 1963. Vermiculite is widely used as insulation material for homes and buildings and as a soil conditioner. Unfortunately, the vermiculite from the Libby mine contained tremolite asbestos.[70]

In response to citizen complaints and newspaper articles (more than eighty of which have been published by the *Daily Inter Lake* newspaper in Kalispell, Montana, and in the *Seattle Post-Intelligencer*), EPA Region 8 acted under its Superfund authority to send an Emergency Response Team to Libby in November 1999.[71] What the team found was overwhelming. EPA tests revealed that dangerous levels of asbestos were present in Libby—not only at the mine but also in homes and buildings. W. R. Grace had given away residue from the mine to the residents of Libby, who used it for insulation, mulch, and even cat litter. Most troubling, Libby's children played in the powdery substance.[72]

In January 14, 2002, in a letter to EPA, Montana governor Judy Martz declared that Libby "presents the greatest danger to public health or welfare or the environment of known Superfund facilities in Montana." She designated the Libby site as the highest-priority release site in the state and requested that it be placed on the National Priorities List for Superfund remediation as soon as possible.[73] (Under the Superfund law, states are permitted only a one-time privilege of naming a site as the highest priority.) EPA subsequently added the Libby site to the National Priorities List on October 23, 2002, thus making it eligible for extensive, long-term cleanup.[74] EPA agreed to clean up more than 600 homes in Libby, at a cost of more than $20 million.[75]

As the Libby, Montana, story garnered the attention of the national media, EPA was becoming embroiled in a political brouhaha. The first turmoil was over EPA's oversight of vermiculite. EPA was sharply criticized for failing to alert the public to the dangers of vermiculite, even though agency officials knew as early as 1982 that asbestos-containing vermiculite causes "significant adverse health effects."[76] Agency officials ignored evidence in the 1982 EPA inspection report that found alarming levels of asbestos in vermiculite, opting instead to accept the much lower figures of W. R. Grace.[77]

As if that were not enough, the beleaguered agency was also engulfed in an internal firestorm. At issue was whether or not the agency should warn the public about the potential dangers of Zonolite insulation—insulation that was present in an estimated 10 to 35 million homes. The EPA Region 8 Libby response team, led by Paul Peronard, argued that tremolite asbestos was dangerous. "When it comes to Zonolite being deadly, there's no maybe involved here," said Aubrey Miller, a U.S. Public Health Service physician assigned to EPA's Libby team. "The hundreds of deaths and the very large numbers of people with early signs of asbestos-related disease from exposure to Zonolite should be more than adequate for the most skeptical person."[78]

Nevertheless, some officials at EPA headquarters were not convinced. At issue was whether homeowners would disturb insulation, not unlike the hasty removal of asbestos in schools. Also at issue was the $10 billion potential price tag associated with fixing homes with Zonolite insulation. After months of internal wrangling, EPA decided to issue a warning to the public that exposure to Zonolite insulation could be dangerous on April 5, 2002.[79] However, that warning never came. Just as EPA was on the verge of warning millions of Americans that their attics and walls might contain asbestos-contaminated insulation, the Office of Information and Regulatory Affairs in the White House's Office of Management and Budget derailed the declaration. EPA finally announced a national consumer awareness campaign for vermiculite attic insulation that may contain asbestos on May 21, 2003.[80] A date more than a decade after EPA discovered asbestos in Zonolite and other insulation, more than a year after EPA first wanted to issue a warning, and one day after EPA administrator Christine Whitman announced her resignation. The following day, Senator Patty Murray (Wash.) introduced a bill banning the manufacture or import of asbestos-containing materials.[81]

In short, the tragedy in Libby, Montana, is important to the asbestos policy implementation story because it brought national attention once again to the dangers of asbestos exposure. However, the Libby story also revealed the political nature of asbestos policy management, at both EPA and the White House.

When the twin towers of the World Trade Center collapsed on September 11, 2001, few people were thinking about asbestos exposure. All eyes were on efforts to find survivors, and all hearts went out to the more than 2,792 victims and their families. However, EPA, the state of New York, and New York City also had to be concerned about environmental risks, most notably asbestos. It seems odd that the cleanup of the World Trade Center site would involve AHERA, but it did. AHERA provided EPA with the standard for a "safe" level of exposure to airborne asbestos fibers. The agency chose the AHERA standard because it was the "most stringent and protective."[82] However, it also brought to light a painful reality: EPA did not have relevant environmental standards for asbestos dust, indoor air, or soil.

Two problems emerged with the AHERA standard. First, AHERA provided an indoor clearance standard to determine when children could safely reenter schools after an asbestos abatement had occurred. (The clearance standard is 70 or fewer structures, or fibers, per square millimeter.) The test counts the number of asbestos fibers on air filters collected from monitoring equipment and compares the results against the clearance threshold. The process requires that the inside air be disturbed during sampling to provide the "worst-case" scenario. One EPA official described the protocol as similar to standing next to a leaf blower, where all sorts of debris and dust enter the ambient air. However, the testing protocol was not feasible for many areas around the World Trade Center site.

A second issue was asbestos dust. According to EPA's definition, a substance must contain at least 1 percent asbestos to be considered an ACM. EPA employed the rule to classify the dust around the World Trade Center site as an ACM (figure 3.3). Dust that contained less than 1 percent asbestos was, therefore, not unreasonably hazardous. This prompted a negative reaction from officials inside the agency and from public health officials who argued that dust was easy to inhale—far easier than insulation or ceiling tiles—and, therefore, potentially hazardous below the 1 percent threshold. One EPA official commented, "Dust with 1 percent asbestos is really bad—you can make a blizzard of asbestos fibers from dust."

New York City also used the 1 percent threshold to determine whether the removal of indoor dust was subject to its asbestos control program. In the dust-laden aftermath of the towers' collapse, more than 25 percent of the bulk dust samples that EPA collected showed the presence of asbestos above the 1 percent threshold.[83] Although airborne levels of asbestos would decline as the dust settled, some EPA officials remained concerned about the arbitrary 1 percent standard. As an EPA Branch Chief noted, "1 percent asbestos in a material is not a safe level of asbestos . . . one-half percent ACM could be just as hazardous as 20 percent ACM, depending on the condition of the material and how it is handled."[84]

Cate Jenkins, a senior chemist with EPA's hazardous waste identification division, was perhaps the most strident critic of EPA's policy. Calling asbestos exposure in homes around Ground Zero comparable to exposures in Libby, Montana, she argued that Lower Manhattan should be declared a Superfund site.[85] In her January 11, 2002, memo to "all affected parties and responsible persons," she warned that proper asbestos abatement procedures were not being followed in cleaning up homes and buildings, because most dust did not qualify as ACM. EPA responded by offering free testing and cleaning of homes to residents of Lower Manhattan.

We Protect More Than the Environment...

Home is where we live our lives and feel safe with our loved ones. For some living in lower Manhattan, the possibility that dust from the collapse of the World Trade Center may linger in their homes has raised concerns.

That is why the EPA, along with FEMA, New York City, New York State and OSHA is offering residents of lower Manhattan — south of Canal, Allen and Pike Streets — the option of having their homes professionally cleaned and/or tested for airborne asbestos contamination free of charge.

While scientific data does not point to any significant long-term health risks, people should not have to live with uncertainty about the future.

Call **1-877-796-5471** or visit **www.epa.gov/wtc** to schedule an appointment to have your apartment cleaned and/or tested or for further information.

www.epa.gov/wtc
1-877-796-5471

Created by Fenn & King Communications • 202-337-6995

Figure 3.3.   The EPA Advertises Asbestos Testing for Residents around the World Trade Center Site

Note: EPA = U.S. Environmental Protection Agency.

While the EPA Office of Inspector General (OIG) stopped short of recommending that Lower Manhattan be listed as a hazardous site, it was nonetheless critical of the way in which EPA warned residents about the danger of airborne pollutants, including asbestos. In its report released in August 2003, the OIG found fault with EPA's failure to alert people to the dangers of even low levels of asbestos. In the days following the tragedy, the White House screened EPA press releases. As noted in the report, "We were unable to identify any EPA official who claimed ownership of EPA's World Trade Center press releases issued in September and early October 2001. When we asked the EPA chief of staff whether she could claim ownership of EPA's early press releases, she replied that she was not able to do so "because the ownership was joint ownership between EPA and the White House," and that 'final approval came from the White House.'"[86]

A September 13 press release illustrates how language shifted from the draft to the final release. According to the OIG, the draft press release stated in part: "Preliminary results of EPA's sampling activities indicate no or very low levels of asbestos. However, even at low levels, EPA considers asbestos hazardous in this situation." The final release was far more optimistic in tone: "EPA is greatly relieved to have learned that there appears to be no significant levels of asbestos dust in the air in New York City."[87]

If Libby and New York prompted public sympathies for government action to do more to protect people from asbestos, the rise of asbestos litigation brought to light the enormous economic expenses associated with previous asbestos exposure. By 2002, more than 600,000 claimants had filed lawsuits against 6,000 defendants, and projections are that the number of claimants could exceed 1 million.[88] In contrast, only 21,000 claimants had filed asbestos-related suits in 1982. Costs already totaled $54 billion, and estimated future costs range from $145 billion to $265 billion.[89] At the end of 2002, sixty-one companies had declared bankruptcy, one-third of those between 2000 and 2002.[90] Perhaps most troubling was that about 65 percent of the compensation awarded under these lawsuits has gone to nonmalignant claimants—that is, to people who have been exposed to asbestos but show no serious adverse health effects—and that percentage is rising.[91] This steady and unprecedented rise in asbestos lawsuits prompted the Senate to hold hearings in 2002 on possible changes to the tort system for trying asbestos-related claims. In 2003, Senator Orrin Hatch (Utah) introduced S. 1125, the Fairness in Asbestos Injury Resolution Act of 2003 (or the FAIR Act of 2003), which would create a privately funded, publicly administered asbestos trust fund to provide resources for an asbestos injury claims. Asbestos is, once again, front and center in Congress.

It is too soon to tell whether the asbestos concerns in Libby or Manhattan, or the rising number of class-action lawsuits, will change the intensity of AHERA implementation or EPA's inclination to keep asbestos low on its list of priorities. However, these events have triggered several political firestorms that have refocused public attention on asbestos. In addition, they did prompt EPA to take a hard look at its national asbestos program. In October 2002, the

Global Environmental and Technological Foundation, through a contract with EPA, sponsored a stakeholder forum titled "Asbestos Strategies: Lessons Learned about the Management and Use of Asbestos" in an effort to identify the most promising new directions for national asbestos policy.[92] Many of the people at the table implement AHERA.

A View from the States

In contrast to many environmental laws that permit EPA to delegate programmatic authority to states, AHERA provides only that EPA may grant a state a waiver. Once granted a waiver, the state may operate the full AHERA inspection program. However, where delegation (e.g., in the drinking water or coal mining programs discussed in other chapters) provides the "carrot" of federal funding, the granting of a waiver under AHERA comes with no direct federal support, though states do receive money through the TSCA cooperative agreements, as discussed above. Only nine states have sought and been granted waivers to run the AHERA program: Connecticut and Rhode Island in 1989; Colorado, Louisiana, and Utah in 1995; Maine in 1996; Massachusetts in 1998; and Texas and Oklahoma in 2000.[93] However, this does not mean that other states are not involved in the implementation of asbestos policy.

States deal with asbestos in at least three ways. First, most states operate the model accreditation plan, which certifies and trains asbestos inspectors and abatement contractors. Running the training and certification program is appealing to many states, in part because it generates fees. State and local governments are used to dealing with building inspectors and contractors. Moreover, training and certification programs are not the political lightning rods that inspecting schools for asbestos are. Second, nearly every state has delegated authority to run NESHAPs, and therefore to manage asbestos in building demolition or renovation. Many also oversee occupational exposures to asbestos and thus work closely with the federal Occupational Safety and Health Administration.

Third, states with or without waivers receive federal funding under TSCA to engage in enforcement activities under AHERA. With TSCA funding, states conduct a required number of inspections, providing EPA regional offices with inspection reports and copies of warning letters to schools not in compliance, develop and implement a Neutral Administrative Inspection Scheme, and detail staff and travel expenditures.[94] TSCA grant guidance requires that states provide at least 25 percent matching funds for the program.[95] The administration of these grants is conducted at the EPA regional level, and states with waivers or partial waivers often receive priority consideration for federal grants.

EPA regional offices receive TSCA funds for cooperative agreements for states from EPA headquarters, and decide how much states in their region receive, based upon state requests and other factors. As was mentioned above, the decision of EPA headquarters to focus on other priority TSCA programs reduced the amount of money available for asbestos agreements under TSCA. EPA regions also made internal decisions about how to allocate funding to states within their borders, in some cases reducing even further the amount of money available for AHERA in order to address higher regional priorities. This disinvestment from asbestos has implications for state programs.

As is shown in table 3.1, the total amount available for TSCA asbestos, lead, and polychlorinated biphenyls (PCBs) programs was $5.2 million in fiscal 2002. Less than half of that amount, or $2.1 million, was given to states to operate asbestos inspection programs. EPA Region 5 allocated all of its $571,700 TSCA enforcement cooperative agreement funding to the PCB control program, leaving nothing for AHERA. Regions 7 and 10 also made no distributions to states under the TSCA cooperative agreement allocations to run AHERA inspection programs. Indeed, only eighteen states received any allocation for AHERA under these TSCA cooperative agreements. Of those, only two states, New Jersey and Oklahoma, received more than $200,000 to operate inspection programs for asbestos. To put it another way, most states receive no funding to run AHERA inspection programs, and those that do receive very small amounts. Thus, both states and EPA regional offices are hard-pressed for funding.

The next section describes the perceptions that state asbestos program officials have about the implementation of asbestos policy. The perceptions reported here are from responses to mailed surveys and interviews with state asbestos program directors. In 1995, fifty surveys were sent to state officials responsible for state asbestos programs; thirty-seven were returned, for a response rate of 74 percent. Ten interviews were conducted with asbestos directors in 1995. In 2002, surveys were once again sent to state asbestos program officials. Twenty-five surveys were returned, for a response rate of 50 percent. Nine interviews were conducted with state officials and nine with EPA officials in late 2002 and early 2003. In some cases, follow-up e-mails continued the conversations.

Many state officials directing asbestos programs wear two or more hats; they enforce the NESHAP provision for asbestos under the Clean Air Act, they certify and license asbestos contractors, they provide or supervise training in asbestos management, and they may operate the AHERA inspection and compliance program. Sixty-eight percent of state officials responding to the 2002 survey manage regulatory requirements under NESHAPs and AHERA. They also oversee state asbestos programs that may include additional activities.

Table 3.1. TSCA Enforcement Cooperative Agreement Funding: Summary for States and Other Jurisdictions Receiving Funding for PCBs, Asbestos, and Lead in Fiscal 2002 (dollars)

State or Jurisdiction	PCBs	Asbestos	Lead
Alabama	$153,669	$0	$40,000
Arkansas	0	0	51,011
California	104,096	50,000	40,500
Colorado	0	154,267	41,650
Connecticut	200,000	100,000	100,000
District of Columbia	0	0	28,189
Georgia	0	0	24,500
Hawaii	0	198,058	0
Iowa	192,500	0	41,650
Illinois	100,000	0	148,691
Indiana	135,000	0	95,191
Kansas	0	0	41,650
Kentucky	54,000	60,000	0
Louisiana	0	150,000	0
Massachusetts	0	100,000	51,000
Maryland	0	103,737	46,216
Maine	0	100,000	0
Michigan	0	0	48,691
Minnesota	90,000	0	48,691
Missouri	105,466	0	41,650
Mississippi	0	80,518	35,373
North Carolina	0	88,817	30,000
North Dakota	21,000	0	0
New Hampshire	0	50,000	50,000
New Jersey	0	204,000	83,127
New York	0	146,189	0
Ohio	0	0	48,691
Oklahoma	0	221,876	100,000
Pennsylvania	0	0	46,216
Puerto Rico	115,970	0	0
Rhode Island	0	100,000	0
Tennessee	0	0	30,000
Texas	121,090	0	0
Utah	0	134,400	41,650
Virginia	0	0	48,648
Vermont	0	0	49,000
Wisconsin	0	0	148,691
West Virginia	0	144,000	38,918
Total	1,392,791	2,185,862	1,639,594

Note: Jurisdictions that did not receive any funding are omitted from the table. PCBs = polychlorinated biphenyls. TSCA = Toxic Substances Control Act.

Source: Data taken from two internal documents of the U.S. Environmental Protection Agency.

About half of the state officials responsible for running the asbestos program are located in state departments of environmental quality; the rest are located in state departments of public health, labor, or education. Some states, such as New York, divide asbestos duties between departments. New York assigns responsibility for oversight of licensing of asbestos abatement projects to the Department of Labor and for accrediting asbestos training programs to the Department of Health. Thus, for many state officials, administering an asbestos-in-schools program is only part of what they do.

As was mentioned in chapter 2, national environmental laws influence not only the shape of federal bureaucracies but state agencies as well. Although nineteen state asbestos programs predate the passage of AHERA, 49 percent of state officials identified the passage of AHERA as the reason for establishing their state programs. Forty-two percent believe that state laws governing asbestos were more fundamental to creating the program.

State asbestos programs tend to be small, with 56 percent of the respondents in 2002 reporting a staff of five or fewer full-time equivalent people—and they do not expect any increases to budgets or staff. Indeed, nearly all state officials report that state asbestos programs are either stable or decreasing in size.

Factors that Facilitate or Hinder Implementation

Table 3.2 lists the factors that asbestos officials identified most often as ones that constrain the implementation of an effective AHERA program. Table 3.3 reports state officials' perceptions about various elements in the asbestos program. Nearly every asbestos official is concerned about budgets and the lack of EPA involvement in AHERA, both financially and in offering technical and inspection support. As is shown in table 3.2, concerns about inadequate funding and personnel resources clearly top the list of implementation obstacles. In 2002, only 20 percent of state asbestos program directors believed that their asbestos programs were adequately funded (down from 54 percent in 1995), as is shown in table 3.3. As one state official commented, "Over the past years, the state's program has changed little. We routinely inspect 50 LEAs per year and that number has remained the same for 10 years. We are an EPA waiver state or likely we would have no AHERA component to our state asbestos program. If the money dried up, I don't know if we've do AHERA at all."

Another official suggested that the state was more confident about TSCA funding if it had a waiver to run the AHERA program. Therefore, the state sought and received a waiver. However, many state officials feel differently about running the AHERA inspection program through an EPA waiver. As one state official put it, "There was a concern on two fronts: (1) attempting to

Table 3.2. Factors That Hinder the Implementation of AHERA as Ranked by State
Officials, 2002

Factor	Percentage identifying as an issue (N = 34)
Insufficient resources	85
Lack of EPA involvement in AHERA	67
Schools not being aware of or ignoring AHERA requirements	56
Lack of support of state administrators or policymakers	53
Presence of fraud among asbestos abatement contractors	26
Problems with regulatory or statutory language	21

Note: AHERA = Asbestos Hazard and Emergency Response Act. EPA = U.S. Environmental Protection Agency.

change the existing state laws regarding asbestos to incorporate requirements of AHERA could put the existing program in jeopardy; (2) funding from EPA to develop and maintain an AHERA program was already dwindling and continuance of such funding was at best unreliable."

Precarious funding, together with the lack of a strong federal presence in asbestos, influence the perceptions that state officials have about the effectiveness of their program. Although most officials see their programs as effective (81 percent in 1995; 64 percent in 2002), only 36 percent of state officials believe that the program is stronger now than three years ago. Most written responses indicate that state officials feel that asbestos programs are in a kind of "holding pattern"—with few initiatives under way, but not much retrenchment either. (In contrast, 73 percent felt the program was improving in 1995.)

State officials who felt their programs were stronger often pointed to an initiative that they had undertaken—initiatives often undertaken without additional revenue. For example, one program official noted that his staff had made a concerted effort to review all three-year reinspection reports (nearly 4,000 of them) because they felt it was important to keep schools "on track." Another had leveraged the support of parent–teachers associations in the state to increase awareness of the AHERA program and to make sure that schools were conducting inspections. Yet another state official commented that his state had developed and disseminated a newsletter to schools, trained the entire staff to conduct AHERA inspections, and even trained EPA and other personnel on AHERA inspections and reports.

When asked what they would change about their state's asbestos programs, responses varied. Among the most frequent response was a desire for more state inspection and enforcement staff. As one state official put it, "To have an effective program, you must maintain a presence in the field. Currently, only one individual is responsible for field inspections for the entire state." One

Table 3.3. Perceptions of State Asbestos Officials about State Asbestos Programs (percentage indicating that they strongly agree or agree), 1995 and 2002

Perception	1995 (N = 37)	2002 (N = 25)
Program is effective	81	64
Program is stronger than three years ago	73	36
Program is adequately funded	54	20
Staff is adequately trained	89	80
Citizens are aware of asbestos dangers	51	48
Asbestos is a top environmental priority	60	36
School officials are very supportive	n.a.	16
A strong program depends upon state inspectors citing all violations	n.a.	40

Note: n.a. = not available.

state official suggested that too few inspections were conducted. "You must perform frequent inspections in order to have a viable asbestos program. If the state presence is not maintained, contractors become lax in following work practice requirements." Another official agreed: "We don't have adequate staffing resources. . . . We conducted a noncompliance study of NESHAPs and discovered that only 22 percent of our contractors or building owners complied with the requirement to notify the state before removing ACMs. That tells me that we need more inspectors in order to cover the state."

The recent reduction in EPA funding and availability of EPA inspection personnel jeopardizes AHERA implementation. "Most of our schools are in compliance now. They have approved management plans and conduct periodic inspections. It doesn't mean they're going to stay that way [in compliance], especially since they know that no EPA person or state inspector is going to come knocking at their door."

Other state officials felt that local jurisdictions should be more involved and interested in implementing AHERA. Only 16 percent of state asbestos officials perceive that local school districts are supportive of the AHERA program, as is shown in table 3.3. One official commented, "We [the state department staff] developed the management plans for 456 schools. We continue to do so, and look forward to the day when more local people get on the band wagon and develop their own plans." Another observed that wealthy school districts could comply with AHERA, but poorer districts were not equipped to monitor or update asbestos management plans. Still another observed that charter schools had not submitted any management plans at all.

A frequently mentioned factor complicating AHERA implementation are personnel changes in school districts, which mean that staff are not aware of or ignore the requirements (table 3.2). School operations and maintenance personnel have changed since the early days of AHERA. State officials (and EPA officials as well) are concerned that new people involved in school operations may not be trained in asbestos management and may not know how to conduct inspections or periodic surveillance. Indeed, new school personnel may not even know that they are the "designated persons" to fulfill the AHERA compliance requirements.

As was noted in earlier sections of the chapter, for some schools, involvement in the asbestos program is synonymous with spending significant resources for asbestos management in their buildings. In an era of tightening school budgets, spending money for asbestos management or removing asbestos may come at the expense of other school programs. As one state official put it, "Schools do not have any financial support for asbestos management from either the state or the federal government. Is it any surprise, then, that a lot of small schools have problems complying with AHERA?" Several state and EPA officials observed that this is particularly true for charter schools, many of which were created many years after the passage of AHERA.

The unintended consequence of LEAs interpreting AHERA to mean asbestos removal rather than management in place has negative consequences in some states, with state officials feeling that asbestos programs are political targets of state legislatures and executive administrations. More than half of the state

officials interviewed felt that their state legislatures were not strong supporters of AHERA. As one noted, "Believe me, there's some people in the state who would like to see the end of AHERA." Others noted the political backlash that asbestos abatement actions have received. "Our program is susceptible to continual changes in the political atmosphere, not only in Washington but in our state legislature." Another hoped that his state would "bring back the policymakers who recognize the potential hazards of asbestos and who will promote commonsense, level-headed approaches to preventing problems and controlling hazards." One state official observed, "Our legislature typically doesn't like environmental regulation. We have to continually make our case that asbestos poses risks to the public in order to maintain our program."

Despite this situation, most state officials believe that asbestos exposure in schools remains a serious problem that needs monitoring. They mention the refocusing events described above: "Recent events such as the World Trade Center and Libby, Montana, . . . point out that the asbestos issue is not behind us and that regulations put in place twenty to thirty years ago do not appropriately deal with [asbestos] hazards."

Yet another implementation challenge recognized by some state asbestos staff was the fragmented nature of asbestos activities. "We need better coordination among various state agencies; we also need to reduce overlapping

responsibilities." As another official commented, "In our state, controlling asbestos exposures is divided among three departments. We have close communications and working relationships, but this division sometimes makes
it difficult to coordinate activities." Others noted differences between EPA and
Occupational Safety and Health Administration regulations, and the lack of
consistency between federal and state agencies.

Several state officials voiced concern about the increase in fraud in asbestos
removal projects. In some cases, contractors have fraudulent accreditation
cards and training certificates. In other cases, contractors may actually be removing ACMs and replacing them with building materials that also contain
asbestos. Thus, schools that pay to have asbestos removed may be unwittingly
putting it back into schools.

Federal and State Working Relationships

Concerns that state officials have about their programs, however, seem small
when compared with the perceptions they have about federal efforts to oversee AHERA. State asbestos officials are less likely to believe that the EPA asbestos program is adequately funded (8 percent) than believe their own programs are adequately funded (20 percent), as is shown in tables 3.3 and 3.4.
This is down from 1995, when 25 percent felt EPA was adequately funded. To
put it another way, nearly every state official responding to the survey or interview questions believes that EPA regional offices lack sufficient resources to
implement AHERA.

These comments illustrate the concern of state officials about EPA: "Initially, EPA did provide some support in the state for the AHERA program
through workshops, site inspections, etcetera. Current activity has been spo-
radic, with occasional training course audits, infrequent site inspections (typically conducted in conjunction with other EPA inspection activity], and mail-
ings to targeted audiences. Charter schools are a recent example. However,
there is no plan [by EPA] for follow-up to determine if charter schools are in
compliance." "EPA is broke." "They need more funding so they could properly follow-up on complaints and referrals." "State and federal resources are
insufficient to carry out a proactive program." "They [EPA] need a bigger staff
and more funds." "We get very little assistance with running our asbestos program." "EPA should partner with the states, particularly financially. States ba-
sically do the work, but the money is drying up and the asbestos program will
cease to exist in many areas."

Many officials expressed concerns about EPA pulling out of the asbestos
program, as is evident in these comments: "Most states have functioning asbestos programs. However, EPA is taking on fewer asbestos activities, assum-

Table 3.4. Perceptions of State Asbestos Officials about Working Relationships with EPA (percentage indicating that they strongly agree or agree), 1995 and 2002

Perception	1995 (N = 37)	2002 (N = 25)
I have a positive relationship with EPA regional asbestos staff	86	80
I have a positive relationship with EPA Headquarters	39	52
EPA staff has a high degree of technical expertise	n.a.	24
EPA asbestos program is adequately funded	25	8
Oversight is flexible	69	64
Regional and Headquarters officials view program similarly	28	12
EPA clearly communicates goals and requirements	19	24
Without the EPA, the state would not be as serious about running an asbestos program	16	16

Note: n.a. = not available. EPA = U.S. Environmental Protection Agency.

ing that the states are handling everything. This isn't true. The states need continued funds and support from EPA." "The lack of EPA involvement [constrains] our program. EPA pulled back from its emphasis on asbestos as a public health issue." "EPA needs to reinvest itself in asbestos issues." "The deemphasis of the asbestos program within EPA only leaves the state programs more vulnerable. Our program is in jeopardy because our state legislators are all too willing to bow out of AHERA implementation. There's still a lot of asbestos to be dealt with, so I hope something changes." "[Asbestos] may not be as large a lion as it once was, but it does still continue. Without continued interest at the federal level, the concern at the local level will begin to disappear, as it has already."

One way states are dealing with the absence of federal leadership in asbestos is through the creation of five regionally based consortiums. For example, the Mid-West Regional Environmental Consortium created in 1999 serves as a forum for state and federal asbestos officials to address asbestos issues cooperatively.[96] These five consortia took over the preparation of annual conferences after EPA stopped holding annual asbestos meetings for state personnel.

In addition to more federal funding and increased federal commitment to the asbestos program, several state officials perceived opportunities to improve EPA's management of the program. Some officials pointed to inconsistent implementation among EPA regions. As one official noted, "EPA should coordinate more efficiently between the regions. Regional offices interpret the regulations and reporting requirements in different ways—our regional office is far more restrictive than other regions."

Still other state asbestos officials felt that the reporting burden under the cooperative grant program is too onerous. One state official said that they refuse EPA grants because the grants are small and do not justify the paperwork involved. Several officials pointed to what they perceived as a lack of knowledge at EPA headquarters of field conditions, or what implementation would be like for small, fiscally stressed school districts. For example, some state officials believed that EPA engaged in rule-making activities without bringing them into the process and without understanding what the effect of new policies would have in the states.

"Before implementing AHERA, EPA should check and see if there are enough expert inspectors and management planners in the workforce. Most of the asbestos management plans done by schools in our state were poorly done, because we did not have enough trained consultants and contractors to help school officials." Finally, several state officials noted a lack of agency trust of the state program to accomplish implementation. As one official suggested, "EPA should either respect the way our [state] program is run, or give us some money to help run it."

However, state officials still view working relationships between state agencies and EPA regional staff as positive, albeit with infrequent contact. Eight of out ten respondents agreed that positive working relationships exist between states and the regional office. As one state official commented, "Since I am the only one for our state when it comes to asbestos, EPA has been a great help to me for guidance and answering any questions that I have." Another agreed: "EPA always makes sure we have a program, even though the funding is reduced." However, just half of state asbestos directors responding to the survey perceive that they have a positive relationship with EPA headquarters.

Why do state officials perceive that they have the support of EPA regional staff but not of EPA headquarters staff? One reason stems from the feeling of some state officials that EPA has done a poor job of communicating its program requirements. Only about one-fourth of state asbestos officials agree that EPA has clearly communicated its program goals and requirements to states. One official pointed to the model accreditation plan provisions as being too inflexible; another simply stated that EPA should spend more time with state program managers before issuing policies and regulations; and yet another suggested that the reporting requirements for AHERA inspections were duplicative and a waste of time.

When referring to EPA headquarters, one state official commented, "They never really envisioned how the asbestos program would work from the ground up. They should partner with us both philosophically as well as financially." This comment identified the feeling of other state program coordinators that they were left out of the picture. "EPA should provide states with advance copies of pending legislation and EPA guidance documents. We should have more say in interpreting the guidance. Even better, the EPA should provide clarification materials and more written correspondence so we know what is going to happen."

Conclusions about the Asbestos Program

The story of AHERA implementation is like that of many programs that begin in earnest and then fade as policymakers perceive that they have solved the problem and new issues emerge that require their attention. However, asbestos is like a sleeping giant—a dangerous sleeping giant who, once awakened, poses significant risks to human health. Though ACMs are not produced in the United States at the same rate as thirty or forty years ago and few of us face the same level of exposure to asbestos fibers as the residents of Libby, Montana, asbestos is still lurking in homes, schools, and workplaces. Asbestos exposure in many U.S. schools is still a potential reality, and we still need AHERA. EPA's strategy of disinvesting from asbestos prompted the concern of EPA and state asbestos on-the-ground implementers.

This story reveals the poignancy of the policy history: Delay by the federal government in dealing with asbestos health risks in turn exposed more people to ACMs—a costly delay for victims and for corporate America. Almost weekly, reports of businesses hit by asbestos lawsuits are in the news. AHERA directed political and bureaucratic attention to schools, which were ill equipped to deal with the "asbestos scare." Making matters worse, EPA vacillated on its guidance to states and to school districts in the 1980s, prompting confusion on the part of the target group (schools) about how to comply. Compliance has been expensive when it has led school districts down the path of asbestos removal, which may not even be the optimal policy choice. In the midst of public controversy and misunderstanding, some national policymakers and state politicians wish that AHERA would just go away.

In the meantime, EPA officials have responded to other emerging issues, such as protecting children from exposure to lead-based paint. Within the context of limited funding, shifting priorities to new "hot" issues is an understandable EPA course of action—provided those new priorities pose a greater danger to the public. (This is something strongly challenged by most of the state and EPA officials interviewed.) Most Americans, meanwhile, believe that asbestos is a relic of history, so they exert very little pressure on politicians or agency officials to continue to press hard for AHERA implementation.

Intriguing, then, is the potential for two refocusing events, one in Libby, Montana, and the other in Lower Manhattan, to renew the attention of policymakers and EPA to asbestos. Congressional architects of asbestos tort reform may reshape public attitudes toward asbestos once again—but not in the direction of more funding for AHERA. Equally vexing is that our environmental laws do not prohibit the importation of ACMs. Stay tuned, because the story of asbestos policy is far from over.

According to the working relationship typology given in chapter 1, the interview and survey data suggest that intergovernmental relationships in asbestos are best categorized as falling somewhere between "cooperative but autonomous" and "coming apart with avoidance." Concern over agency disinvestment in asbestos has prompted two reactions among many (but not all) state officials. One reaction is for states to leap over the intergovernmental divide and try to rally for their EPA regional asbestos counterparts. State asbestos officials feel that the federal program is important to the extent that it provides leverage in their state for these officials to continue the asbestos programs.

Most states run the accreditation program to license asbestos inspectors and abatement personnel, and they have delegated authority to run NESHAPs. However, because forty-one states do not have waivers to run the AHERA inspection program, they look to EPA to complete AHERA implementation. The combination of separate and multiple state activities in asbestos coupled with a reliance on EPA inspections and enforcement of AHERA leads working relationships to be cooperative but autonomous, with relatively higher levels of mutual trust between state and federal program staff but very little involvement with states on the part of EPA.

A second reaction is for state officials to feel betrayed by EPA. Many state officials believe that EPA, when considered as a whole entity (as opposed to thinking about particular regional program officials) is not very concerned about public health risks associated with asbestos in schools, nor is the agency particularly effective at implementing AHERA. Most of this ineffectiveness is clearly linked to a lack of funding, but some ineffectiveness is associated with less than stellar program management, at least from the perspective of state officials. Inadequate funding and few, if any, EPA inspections lead to some perceptions that EPA is simply avoiding AHERA implementation. Thus, the relationship is like the "coming apart with avoidance" quadrant of the typology. An improved asbestos program in the minds of many state officials would include more federal–state interaction, more continuity among EPA regional offices, and a more consistent federal posture toward asbestos.

Notes

1. Paul Brodeur, "The Asbestos Tragedy," in *Breath Taken: The Landscape and Biography of Asbestos*, ed. Bill Ravanesi (Newtonville, Mass.: Center for the Visual Arts in the Public Interest, 1991), www.bumc.bu.edu/SPH/Gallery/monograp.html (March 26, 2003).

2. Johns-Manville Corporation, "Johns-Manville Corporate Chronology," www
.johnsmanville.com/corporate/history.shtml (March 28, 2003).

3. Johns-Manville Corporation, "Johns-Manville Corporate Chronology."

4. U.S. Environmental Protection Agency, Office of Public Affairs, *Asbestos Fact Book*, A-107/86-002 (Washington, D.C.: U.S. Environmental Protection Agency, 1986), 2.

5. Bill Burke, "Shipbuilding's Deadly Legacy: A Special Report," *Virginian Pilot* [Norfolk], May 6, 2001, www.pilotonline.com/special/asbestos/index.html (March 28, 2003).

6. Pascale Krumm, "The Health Effects of Asbestos," *Journal of Environmental Health* 65, no. 2 (2002): 46.

7. U.S. Environmental Protection Agency, *Asbestos Fact Book*, 3.

8. Krumm, "Health Effects of Asbestos," 46.

9. U.S. Environmental Protection Agency, *Asbestos Fact Book*, 3.

10. William Nicholson, "Occupational Exposure to Asbestos: Population at Risk and Projected Mortality 1980–2030," *American Journal of Industrial Medicine* 3 (1982): 259–311; cited in Stephen Carroll, Deborah Hensler, Allan Abrahamse, Jennifer Gross, Michelle White, Scott Ashwood, and Elizabeth Sloss, *Asbestos Litigation Costs and Compensation: An Interim Report* (Santa Monica, Calif.: Rand Corporation, 2002), www .rand.org/publications/DB/DB39/ (February 10, 2003).

11. Burke, "Shipbuilding's Deadly Legacy," Introduction.

12. Carroll et al., *Asbestos Litigation Costs and Compensation*.

13. Burke, "Shipbuilding's Deadly Legacy," Introduction.

14. Information on asbestos imports analyzed by Robert Virta, U.S. Geological Survey, "Re: Asbestos Product Import Data," forwarded e-mail (October 24, 2002), taken from http://dataweb.usitc.gov/scripts/tariff2002.asp (February 27, 2003). Also see James Alleman and Brooke Mossman, "Asbestos Revisited," *Scientific American*, July 1997, 70–75.

15. Brodeur, "Asbestos Tragedy."

16. Burke, "Shipbuilding's Deadly Legacy," Turning a Blind Eye.

17. Burke, "Shipbuilding's Deadly Legacy," Turning a Blind Eye.

18. Brodeur, "Asbestos Tragedy."

19. Burke, "Shipbuilding's Deadly Legacy," Turning a Blind Eye.

20. For a discussion of history of medical and legal understanding of asbestos-related disease, see Barry Castleman, *Asbestos: Medical and Legal Aspects* (Clifton, N.J.: Prentice Hall, 1990).

21. Charlotte Twight, "From Claiming Credit to Avoiding Blame: The Evolution of Congressional Strategy for Asbestos Management," *Journal of Public Policy* 11, no. 2 (1991): 153–86.

22. U.S. Congress, House of Representatives, "Failure to Regulate—Asbestos: A Lethal Legacy," Hearing before Committee on Government Operations, 98th Cong., 1st. sess. (June 28, 1983), 193.

23. Rajiv M. Rao, "End of the Line: Manville Is No More," *Fortune*, April 29, 1996, 42.

24. Johns-Manville Corporation, "Johns-Manville Corporate Chronology."

25. Carroll et al., *Asbestos Litigation Costs and Compensation*.

26. U.S. House of Representatives, Committee on Education and Labor, Subcommit-

tee on Elementary, Secondary, and Vocational Education, Oversight Hearings on Asbestos Health Hazards to School Children, 96th Cong., 1st. sess. (1979).

27. U.S. Environmental Protection Agency, *Asbestos Fact Book*, 4.

28. Asbestos Hazard and Emergency Response Act, 15 USC 2641 et seq., Sec. 201(a): 1 (1986).

29. Asbestos Hazard and Emergency Response Act, Sec. 209(a).

30. U.S. Environmental Protection Agency, Office of Air and Radiation, *The Asbestos Informer*, EPA 340/1-90-020 (Washington, D.C.: U.S. Environmental Protection Agency, 1990), 11.

31. U.S. Environmental Protection Agency, Office of Toxic Substances, *100 Commonly Asked Questions about the New AHERA Asbestos-In-Schools Rule* (Washington, D.C.: U.S. Environmental Protection Agency, 1988), 59.

32. U.S. Congress, Senate, "Implementation of the Asbestos Hazard Emergency Response Act," Hearing before the Committee on Environment and Public Works, Subcommittee on Superfund and Environmental Oversight, 100th Cong., 2d sess. (S.Hrg. 100-575, March 15, 1988).

33. U.S. Congress, House of Representatives, "Asbestos Dangers: Presence in Schools and Incompetent Disposal," Hearing before the Committee on Government Operations, 100th Cong., 1st sess. (August 3, 1987), 285.

34. U.S. Congress, "Implementation of the Asbestos Hazard Emergency Response Act"; the report is reproduced in U.S. Environmental Protection Agency, *EPA Study of Asbestos Containing Materials in Public Buildings* (Washington, D.C.: U.S. Environmental Protection Agency, 1988).

35. U.S. Congress, "Asbestos Issues," 7.

36. U.S. Environmental Protection Agency, Office of Pesticides and Toxic Substances, *Guidance for Controlling Asbestos-Containing Materials in Buildings*, EPA 560/5-85-024 (Washington, D.C.: U.S. Environmental Protection Agency, 1985), 1–5.

37. U.S. Environmental Protection Agency, "Asbestos Facts: Demolition and Renovation Regulations" (Washington, D.C.: U.S. Environmental Protection Agency, 1991), 2.

38. U.S. Environmental Protection Agency, *A Guide to the Asbestos NESHAP*, EPA-340/1-90-015 (Washington, D.C.: U.S. Environmental Protection Agency, 1990).

39. Peter Cary, "The Asbestos Panic Attack: How the Feds Got Schools to Spend Billions on a Problem that Really Didn't Amount to Much," *U.S. News & World Report*, February 20, 1995, 61–64.

40. Thomas Toch, "EPA Orders Asbestos Inspections for Public, Private Schools," *Education Week*, June 2, 1982, www.edweek.org/ew (January 15, 2003).

41. U.S. Environmental Protection Agency, *Guidance for Controlling Asbestos-Containing Materials in Buildings*, 1–5.

42. U.S. Environmental Protection Agency, *Asbestos Fact Book*.

43. U.S. Environmental Protection Agency, *Guidance for Controlling Asbestos-Containing Materials in Buildings*.

44. U.S. Environmental Protection Agency, *Guidance for Controlling Asbestos-Containing Materials in Buildings*, 4–10.

45. "40 CFR Part 763: Asbestos-Containing Materials in Schools, Final Rule, Supplemental Information" (October 30, 1987), *Federal Register* 52, no. 210: 41832.

46. U.S. Environmental Protection Agency, *Managing Asbestos in Place: A Building Owner's Guide to Operation and Maintenance Programs for Asbestos Containing Materials*, TS-799 (Washington, D.C.: U.S. Environmental Protection Agency, 1990).

47. U.S. Environmental Protection Agency, "The Asbestos Informer," EPA 340/1-90-020 (Washington, D.C.: U.S. Environmental Protection Agency, 1990).

48. U.S. Congress, Senate, "Asbestos Issues," Hearing before the Subcommittee on Toxic Substances, Environmental Oversight, Research and Development, Committee on Environment and Public Works, S.Hrg. 101-835, 101st Cong., 2d sess. (April 26, 1990), 50.

49. *Corrosion Proof Fittings v. EPA*, 947 F2d. 1201 (5th Cir. 1991).

50. U.S. Environmental Protection Agency, Office of the Administrator, *Asbestos, Sound Science, and Public Perceptions: Why We Need a New Approach to Risk*, address by William Reilly, 20Z-1006 (Washington, D.C.: U.S. Environmental Protection Agency, 1990), 4.

51. Education Week, *States News Roundup*, November 17, 1982, www.edweek.org/ew /(January 15, 2003.)

52. U.S. Congress, "Asbestos Issues," 6.

53. B. T. Mossman et al., "Asbestos: Scientific Developments and Implications for Public Policy," and B. T. Mossman and J. B. L. Gee, "Asbestos-Related Diseases," *New England Journal of Medicine* 320 (1989): 1721–30.

54. U.S. Environmental Protection Agency, *Asbestos, Sound Science and Public Perceptions*, 5.

55. See Lynn MacDonald and Jerod M. Loeb, "The Health Hazards of Asbestos Removal," *Journal of the American Medical Association* 267 (January 1, 1992): 52–54; and Jan Bone, "Custodial Workers Face Asbestos Hazards," *Safety and Health* 146 (July 1992): 70–75.

56. U.S. General Accounting Office, *School Facilities: Condition of America's Schools*, GAO-HEHS-95-61 (Washington, D.C.: U.S. General Accounting Office, 1995), 4.

57. U.S. General Accounting Office, *School Facilities*, 2.

58. U.S. General Accounting Office, *School Facilities*, 2.

59. U.S. Environmental Protection Agency, Office of Toxic Substances, *Asbestos in Schools: Evaluation of the Asbestos Hazard and Emergency Response Act (AHERA): A Summary Report*, EPA560/4-91-012 (Washington, D.C.: U.S. Environmental Protection Agency, 1991), p. 3-1.

60. Memorandum from John J. Neylan, director, Policy and Grants Division, Office of Compliance Monitoring, U.S. Environmental Protection Agency, June 13, 1994.

61. Memorandun from Sylvia Lowrance, principal deputy assistant administrator, Office of Enforcement and Compliance Assurance, U.S. Environmental Protection Agency, November 30, 1999.

62. Telephone interview with an asbestos staff member, March 1996.

63. Telephone interview with a U.S. Environmental Protection Agency AHERA enforcement specialist in January 2003.

64. Telephone interview with U.S. Environmental Protection Agency staff in December 2002 and January 2003.

65. U.S. Environmental Protection Agency, Office of Inspector General, *Final Report on Region III's Children's Health Initiative on the Asbestos Hazard and Emergency Response Act (AHERA)*, Report Number 2000-P-00024 (September 28, 2000), 7.

66. U.S. Environmental Protection Agency, *Final Report on Region III's Children's Health Initiative*, 9.

67. U.S. Environmental Protection Agency, *Final Report on Region III's Children's Health Initiative*, 9.

68. Comments made during telephone interviews in December 2002 and January 2003.

69. "Deaths in Montana Town Are Linked to Asbestos," *New York Times*, December 16, 2000, http://query.nytimes.com/search/article-printpage.html?res=9F07EFD91639 (December 15, 2002).

70. U.S. Environmental Protection Agency, Region 8, Background Document on Libby Asbestos, www.epa.gov/Region8/superfund/libby/lbybkgd.html (January 3, 2003).

71. U.S. Environmental Protection Agency, "Background Document on Libby Asbestos." For a discussion of the reporting on Libby, Montana, see Andrew Schneider, "Asbestos: The Forgotten Killer Rears Its Ugly Head," *IRE Journal* 24 (January–February 2001): 22–27.

72. Michael Janofsky, "Montana Town Grapples with Asbestos Ills," *New York Times*, May 10, 2000, http://query.nytimes.com/search/article-printpage.html?res=9D0DEFD C1E3 (December 15, 2002).

73. Office of the Governor, State of Montana, correspondence dated January 14, 2002, to Max Dodson, assistant regional administrator, U.S. Environmental Protection Agency, Region 8.

74. U.S. Environmental Protection Agency, Region 8, EPA Action Update 15, "Environmental News: Libby Added to National Priority List," press release dated October 23, 2002, www.epa.gov/Region8/superfund/libby/021023npllist.html (January 12, 2003).

75. Andrew Schneider, "EPA's Plan to Clean Up Insulation Is Too Limited, Some Say," *Saint Louis Post-Dispatch*, May 10, 2002, www.stltoday.com/stltoday/news/special /asbestos.nsf/ (March 10, 2003).

76. See Michael Moss and Adrianne Appel, "EPA Admits Shelving Report about Asbestos," July 22, 2000, http://query.nytimes.com/search/article-printpage.html?res = 9F01EFD6143; and "EPA Is Faulted on Asbestos Hazard," April 4, 2001, *New York Times*, http://query.nytimes.com/search/article-printpage.html?res=9B06E5D71F3 (January 8, 2003).

77. Moss and Appel, "EPA Admits Shelving Report about Asbestos."

78. Andrew Schneider, "White House Budget Office Thwarts EPA Warning on Asbestos-Laced Insulation," *Saint Louis Post-Dispatch*, December 27, 2002, www.stltoday .com/stltoday/news/special/asbestos.nsf/ (February 20, 2003).

79. Schneider, "White House Budget Office Thwarts EPA Warning."

80. U.S. Environmental Protection Agency, "National Consumer Awareness Campaign Launched on Vermiculite Insulation Used in Some Home Attics," May 21, 2003, http://www.epa.gov/newsroom/headline2_052103.htm (September 1, 2003).

81. S 1115, Ban Asbestos in America Act of 2003, introduced May 22, 2003.

82. U.S. Environmental Protection Agency, "EPA Response to 9-11: Benchmarks to Protect Public Health," www.epa.gov/wtc/benchmarks.htm (February 15, 2003).

83. U.S. Environmental Protection Agency, Office of the Inspector General, *EPA's Response to the World Trade Center Collapse: Challenges, Successes, and Areas for Improvement,* Report 2003-P-00012, August 21, 2003, www.epa.gov/oigearth/ereading_room/WTC_report_20030821.pdf (September 7, 2003), 13.

84. Office of the Inspector General, *EPA's Response to the World Trade Center Collapse,* 14.

85. Sandy Smith, "EPA Official: Lower Manhattan Should Be a Superfund Site," *Occupational Hazards* 64, no. 3 (March 2002): 18–20.

86. Office of the Inspector General, *EPA's Response to the World Trade Center Collapse,* 17.

87. Office of the Inspector General, *EPA's Response to the World Trade Center Collapse,* 17.

88. Carroll et al., *Asbestos Litigation Costs and Compensation.*

89. Carroll et al., *Asbestos Litigation Costs and Compensation,* 81.

90. Jeffrey H. Birnbaum, "Firms Unite to Leave Asbestos in the Dust," *Fortune,* December 30, 2002, 52.

91. Carroll et al., *Asbestos Litigation Costs and Compensation,* vii.

92. Global Environment & Technology Foundation, "Asbestos Strategies: Lessons Learned about the Management and Use of Asbestos," www.getf.org/asbestosstrategies /(January 15, 2003).

93. Conversation with an EPA official, January 2003.

94. U.S. Environmental Protection Agency, Office of Enforcement and Compliance Assurance, "Fiscal Year 95 TSCA Cooperative Agreement Guidance," unpublished and undated document, 9.

95. U.S. Environmental Protection Agency, "Fiscal Year 95 TSCA Cooperative Agreement Guidance."

96. Mid-West Regional Environmental Consortium, unpublished and undated document.

· 4 ·

The Survival of a Nonregulatory
Radon Program

The story of radon policy implementation is a story with a consistent theme: the continued struggle for survival amid competition from more familiar environmental hazards. Like the effects of asbestos, the negative health effects of exposure to radon have been known for decades. However, indoor radon as a policy issue rose from virtual obscurity to widespread public attention in 1985— not because of lawsuits (as in the case of asbestos), but because of a local human-interest event. This event captured the attention of the media and, for a while, publicizing radon as a health risk became a popular thing to do. Before 1985, few people had heard of radon; within the year, the U.S. Environmental Protection Agency (EPA) created an indoor radon program; by 1988, federal radon legislation was in place. Fifteen years after radon became widely recognized as a public health risk, state and EPA radon programs are up and running, but radon stories are no longer the darling of the media. Many state radon programs, established primarily through the "carrot" of federal grant money, have become relatively obscure as media interest in radon has waned.

This chapter presents the implementation story of the EPA and state radon programs, which rose like a phoenix from the depths of public and governmental inattention and now struggle to retain their place in the sun. The first sections provide a brief overview of the history of radon policy, the health effects associated with radon, and the passage of America's law dealing with radon exposure, the Indoor Radon Abatement Act. Then the chapter explores the current developments in the implementation story, along with the perceptions that EPA and state radon program officials have about their radon programs and federal–state working relationships.

Radon and Known Health Risks

Radon is an invisible, odorless, tasteless radioactive gas that occurs naturally because of the decay of uranium and radium. Because uranium is common in the earth's crust, radon is found virtually everywhere. Environmental exposure to radon becomes dangerous when radon gas is concentrated inside homes and buildings. Because radon is a gas, it readily travels through permeable soils and is easily drawn inside homes and other buildings through pathways such as cracks in the foundation or openings around sump pumps. Off-gassing of radon in water into indoor air is also possible. Once the gas seeps into structures, it can accumulate in high concentrations in unventilated areas. As radon breaks down, it produces particles charged with alpha energy. If inhaled, these alpha particles can damage lung cells, leading to cancer. The average person in the U.S. gets more radiation dose from exposure to indoor radon than from any other source of natural or human-made radiation.[1]

An understanding of the health risks associated with radon developed over several decades, largely by examining cancer deaths among underground miners. The first published review linking radon to mining-related cancers occurred in 1939.[2] Subsequent international and domestic epidemiological studies of miners in the 1940s and 1950s revealed correlations between levels of radon exposure and the incidence of lung cancer.[3] Between 1963 and 1988, twenty major epidemiological studies of various groups of underground miners led to the conclusion that radon could cause lung cancer.[4]

Health professionals began to link radon's health risk to residential settings when even low levels of radon in occupational exposures were associated with an increased incidence of lung cancer. Federal officials associated nonoccupational radon exposures with lung cancer in 1979, in an EPA report that attributed 10 to 20 percent of the U.S. incidence of lung cancer to radon.[5] The National Cancer Institute later agreed that 10 percent of all lung cancer deaths in the United States could be due to indoor radon.[6] However, radon exposure data in private homes was limited, and federal officials did not generally view radon exposure in nonoccupational settings as dangerous.[7] Not surprisingly, few federal–state cooperative efforts to reduce radon levels in private homes existed before 1980. Joint state–federal efforts before 1985 consisted of mitigating homes in a few well-defined geographic areas where radioactive materials had been used as part of the aggregate in home foundations or where homes had been built on disturbed mining lands, such as in Grand Junction, Colorado.[8]

Today, EPA considers radon a "Class A," or known, human carcinogen, and the second leading cause of lung cancer, next to smoking, in the United States.[9] EPA estimates that exposure to radon causes 14,000 deaths each year, making it one of the most dangerous environmental pollutants in terms of human health risk of all pollutants EPA seeks to control.[10] Perhaps the most definitive statement connecting radon to lung cancer was a series of reports released by the National Academy of Sciences. In its 1998 report, *Health Effects of Exposure to Indoor Radon* (also known as the *Biological Effects of Ionizing Ra-*

diation, or *BEIR VI*, report from the Committee of the same name), the academy concluded that radon causes between 15,000 and 22,000 lung cancer deaths per year, and that 12 percent of all lung cancer deaths are linked to radon.[11] The panel's mathematical models projected that indoor radon contributed up to 21,800 of the 157,400 lung cancer deaths reported in the United States in 1995.[12] To look at it another way, about sixty people a day die from lung cancer associated with radon exposure.

EPA uses a standard measure of radioactivity, the number of picocuries per liter (pCi/L), to measure the concentration of radon gas in the air. A quantity of 1 pCi/L means that there is enough radon in 1 liter of air to produce 2.2 radioactive decays per minute. Studies have shown that radon concentrations average about 0.4 pCi/L in the outdoor air and 1.3 pCi/L in the indoor air. EPA recommends that people take action to reduce radon levels above 4 pCi/L in homes and schools.[13] This action level is based on what was technologically possible in the early 1980s and does not necessarily represent a "safe" level of exposure to radon gas.

A Perfect Triggering Event

Despite mounting evidence about the connections between radon and lung cancer, few public health officials worried about the risks of radon exposure in homes. After all, most of the research between 1940 and 1980 involved miners, and there was little doubt that underground mines could harbor hazardous radon gas. Public health officials viewed radon as an occupational hazard. Indeed, radon might never have captured the attention of national policymakers, but for one remarkable incident. Radon's entry onto the systemic agenda of government came from the discovery of extraordinary levels of radon in a single Pennsylvania home in 1984.

This single event was so extreme and paradoxical that it stimulated an immediate response by state federal and local officials. Stanley Watras, a construction worker at the Limerick Nuclear Generating Station near Philadelphia, repeatedly triggered the plant's radiation alarms when he entered the building. This was puzzling, to say the least, because the plant was not yet generating fission products. After attempts to find Watras's radiation dose inside the plant proved fruitless, technicians from Philadelphia Electric Company performed a radiation survey in the Watras home.[14] Inside the home, they measured a radiation concentration so high that the senior health physicist immediately notified the Pennsylvania Department of Environmental Resources (PDER).[15]

After verifying test results of 2,600 pCi/L (remember that the average home has about 1.7 pCi/L), PDER hand delivered a recommendation that the Watras family immediately evacuate their home. The home's radioactivity levels exceeded by 100 times the level of radiation dose permitted for uranium miners, and the lung cancer risk to the Watras family was estimated by some scientists to be equivalent to smoking 135 packs of cigarettes a day.[16] A PDER literature review of radon concentrations in residential structures revealed that the Watras radon level was the highest level ever recorded for a private residence.[17]

PDER—stunned by the severity of the Watras home's radon contamination—immediately became concerned that other homes in the neighborhood could also have elevated levels of radon. The area in question was in Berks County in eastern Pennsylvania, along a geologic formation known as the Reading Prong. A PDER door-to-door survey revealed that about half of the 2,600 additional homes had elevated levels of radon, but none as high as the Watras home. The state agency established a Bureau of Radiation Protection office near the survey area and reassigned personnel to deal with radon concerns. Pennsylvania spent more than $2 million on radon testing and outreach in the eighteen months following the discovery of radon in the Watras home.[18]

Media coverage remained localized until a citizen's group formed to lobby for government aid to fix Pennsylvania homes. The group, Pennsylvanians Against Radon, eventually attracted more than 200 members and 3,000 signatures on a petition. It enlisted the assistance of Robert Yuhnke, a regional counsel for the Environmental Defense Fund. Yuhnke's involvement ultimately resulted in national media coverage by the *New York Times* on May 19, 1985—about sixteen months after PDER had been alerted to the radon dangers at the Watras home.

Largely in response to the discoveries in Pennsylvania, but also in response to burgeoning media attention to radon, EPA established a Radon Action Program in 1985. The agency was reeling. The Office of Radiation Programs staff had not anticipated that any home could have such extreme levels of radon. Nor did the agency fully anticipate the magnitude of nationwide radon contamination, the need to develop protocols for radon testing and mitigation, or the need for public communication about radon.[19] State input was solicited by the newly formed Radon Action Committee, but no systematic intergovernmental program was developed. Through the Superfund Amendment and Reauthorization Act in 1986, Congress endorsed an intergovernmental response to addressing radon, but it did not authorize a comprehensive grant program for the states. The House Subcommittee on Health and the Environment held hearings on radon in 1987 to determine the likelihood that the country had additional homes like those found in Reading Prong geological province.[20]

The Indoor Radon Abatement Act, 1988

The first formal intergovernmental effort to address radon exposure came with the passage of Public Law 100-551, the Indoor Radon Abatement Act (IRAA), on October 28, 1988. Like the Asbestos Hazard Emergency Response Act (AHERA), which established a goal of protecting children from asbestos regardless of costs, IRAA had an ambitious objective. Congressional architects declared that "the national long-term goal . . . is that the air within buildings in the United States should be as free of radon as the ambient air outside of buildings."[21] However, Congress provided few tools to EPA or to the states to meet this goal, and it rejected imposing any regulatory requirements. IRAA placed no requirements on homeowners, real estate professionals, building contractors, or schools. Instead, the law was primarily designed to characterize the incidence of high levels of radon and to provide initial support to state radon programs.

IRAA required EPA to implement a radon public information program and to determine the extent of public exposure to radon. The agency was also required to publish an updated version of its *Citizen's Guide to Radon* by June 1, 1989.[22] (Because of controversy over radon testing protocols, an updated document was not published until 1992; a second revision was published in 2002.) The guidance document was to include both testing protocols for homeowners and "action levels" for radon exposure.

More important for this study, Sections 305 and 306 of IRAA established a federal–state program to encourage testing of homes and schools, as well as mount public information campaigns. A key element of the initial federal–state program was the EPA–state radon screening survey. In conjunction with EPA, states were encouraged to participate in a survey of randomly selected homes to be tested for radon. Radon measurements were taken using short-term (three to seven days) testing devices placed in the lowest livable area of the home. From 1985 to 1990, thirty-four states agreed to participate.[23] By 1992, forty-two states had participated in joint EPA–state radon surveys, six states preferred to conduct their own surveys (to use long-term testing devices or for other reasons), and two chose not to participate due to funding or other constraints.[24]

A second nationwide study was conducted by EPA in 1992. The results of this National Residential Survey indicated that about 6 percent of U.S. homes had average radon levels greater than 4 pCi/L.[25] However, wide variations in residential radon exposure existed among states, depending upon geological features and housing stock, as confirmed by the state–EPA screening surveys and other data. For example, the eight states with the highest estimated radon concentrations in the livable spaces of homes accounted for about half of the U.S. homes with exposures greater than 20 pCi/L.[26]

IRAA encouraged state participation in alerting the public to the dangers of radon by establishing a three-year State Indoor Radon Grant (SIRG) program. The SIRG program divided federal funding among participating states according to criteria established by EPA.[27] States would match federal funding each year on a sliding scale: 25 percent in the first year, 40 percent in the second year, and 50 percent in the third year. Congress expected states to operate self-funded programs after the third year.

In the first year, states received SIRG funds to establish and maintain basic radon programs.[28] States enjoyed considerable latitude in establishing a basic program. Many states established toll-free radon hotlines, developed public information materials, and offered radon training for contractors, school officials, and real estate agents.[29] States also began evaluating home radon exposure by participating in the EPA survey program or by making radon test kits available to the public by other means. Beginning in 1993, EPA added performance criteria designed to measure environmental results. In addition to a qualitative assessment of program adequacy, states would be evaluated according to the increased number of homes tested for radon; the number of homes with high levels of radon that had been mitigated; and the extent to which residents knew about radon.

Radiation Program Branch staff in the ten EPA regional offices were given responsibility for soliciting and approving SIRG applications and overseeing state programs. Each regional office designated a SIRG contact to coordinate state radon programs and regional outreach efforts. Regional SIRG contacts were to serve as information conduits between the states and the EPA Radon Division. Radon staff within the Office of Air and Radiation at EPA headquarters retained responsibility for coordinating the public information campaign, including developing the *Citizen's Guide to Radon* and other outreach materials. Radon staff, though they did not make individual state grant decisions, determined SIRG allocations available to the regional offices.[30] Regional allocations of grant money were determined with a formula that calculated the number of homes likely to have exposures exceeding the action level of 4 pCi/L. Not all states were happy with the formula.

Early and Persistent Challenges to Implementing IRAA

Several implementation issues surrounded the implementation of IRAA during its early years. To use the vernacular of the framework given in chapter 2, the most influential extrinsic variables include the nature of the problem, the resources allocated to federal and state agencies, the demand for change, and national-level political support. Intrinsic factors include state agency culture and capacity, as well as state-level political support. Specifically, these issues

were (1) encouraging people to test and fix their homes through a nonregulatory apparatus, (2) determining the best orientation for the public information campaign, (3) resolving the debate regarding "safe" levels of radon exposure, and (4) ascertaining the availability of federal funding for state
programs. Each of these issues still presents challenges to the implementation
of IRAA today, and thus each is discussed in turn.

Unlike AHERA, IRAA established no federal regulatory mandates for controlling radon exposure. Absent federal regulations, any regulations governing radon exposures became the responsibility of the states. Using SIRG funds
as a carrot, Congress wanted to entice states to take up the regulatory reins
by licensing state radon professionals, requiring the disclosure of radon levels during real estate transactions, passing mandatory school testing legislation, and adopting radon-resistant building codes.

States legislatures, however, have often been as reluctant as Congress to regulate radon. Although most states have passed mandatory school testing legislation, few states have been willing to require schools with radon levels
above 4 pCi/L to mitigate radon. Only two states, Florida and New Jersey, required mandatory testing of day care centers for radon, but even they did not
force centers to reduce radon levels.[31] Nor have states rushed to embrace
radon-resistant building code requirements or mandatory real estate disclosure laws, although failure to disclose elevated radon levels during a real estate transaction may be cause for a court case.[32]

Unfortunately, the nonregulatory approach made little headway in convincing people to test their homes for radon. Between 1988 and 1992, only 9
percent of American homes were tested for radon.[33] To date, EPA estimates
that fewer than 15 percent of American homes have been tested for radon,
even though about 63 percent of Americans are aware that radon represents
a public health risk. More troubling is the fact that only about 500,000 out
of the 10 million homes with elevated radon levels have had mitigation
treatment.[34]

Most testing that occurs is the result of a pending real estate transaction.
In recognition of this trend, EPA published the *Home Buyers and Sellers Guide
to Radon* to assist in addressing radon during real estate sales. States with radon
disclosure requirements for real estate sales have higher rates of both testing
and mitigation.[35] As of 2002, thirty-seven states had some type of disclosure
requirement. Most of these states only have general disclosure requirements,
however, whereby every contract for a residential home purchase contains a
simple statement warning purchasers of the overall danger of radon. Only a
few states require that radon information about the particular home under
contract be given to the purchaser.[36] All states with specific disclosure requirements leave it up to the buyer and seller to decide whether or not to reduce

radon levels as part of the real estate sale. States that offer free or low-cost radon test kits have also increased the rate of home testing.[37]

A relatively easy way to control future exposures to radon is to build radon-resistant homes. Though mitigating high radon levels in an existing home may cost between $1,200 and $1,500, adding radon-resistant features to a new home during construction is easy to do, and much cheaper (costing about $300). However, most states have left the requirements for radon-resistant construction standards up to local governments. Relatively few counties and municipalities have imposed these requirements. In Colorado and Maryland, for example, only one county in each state has incorporated radon-resistant standards into its building codes. The total number of homes in the United States built with radon-resistant features is estimated to be about 1.8 million, or about 16 percent of all new single-family homes.[38]

Critics of radon policy implementation argue that all new homes in areas likely to have high levels of radon should be constructed with radon-resistant features. During Radon Action Month in January 2003, the executive director of the American Association of Radon Scientists and Technologists sharply criticized U.S. radon policy for its inability to achieve radon-resistant construction in new homes. Labeling radon policy a failure, he blasted the inability of EPA and state governments to prevent future radon exposures: "The national building rate results in new homes at risk [for high levels of radon] being constructed at twice the rate of mitigation. . . . Within 12 years, 11 million homes will exceed the safety standard, thus exposing 38 million Americans to unacceptable doses of radon. In those same 12 years, over a quarter million people will die from radon-induced cancer."[39]

Radon and Risk Communication

Implementing a nonregulatory policy, by definition, requires some voluntary movement on the part of the target group. In regulatory programs, members of a target group face sanctions for failing to comply. All of the other environmental programs examined in this book (asbestos, drinking water, and coal mining) give the implementing agency the ability to impose sanctions (usually in the form of a fine). Not so with radon policy. Advocates of voluntary programs may be pleased that governments (both state and federal) do not interfere with radon exposure in the home. Homeowners are free to choose what to do about radon. But, as the previous section suggests, few people act to protect themselves from elevated levels of radon—even though they may know it causes lung cancer. Why is this the case?

Research conducted in the late 1980s and early 1990s came to one conclusion: Most people do not believe that radon presents a serious health risk.[40]

Radon cannot be seen, smelled, or touched. If radon gas were pink or smelled bad, homeowners would be more likely to control it. Because it does not arouse any of the senses, however, it is hard for the public to believe it is a problem. Moreover, the consequences of radon exposure may not be manifest for two decades or more. Like smoking, radon-induced cancer takes years to develop and is a risk people take voluntarily.

Radon is naturally occurring. Unlike asbestos, no one manufactures radon and puts it into homes. There is no Johns-Manville to sue and no smokestack to blame. So even though radon causes more cancer-related deaths than industrial air pollutants, individuals are apathetic about radon at the same time that they actively contest human-made air emissions.[41] Moreover, the costs of mitigating radon in an existing home are borne by the homeowner. The costs of lowering radon levels in the home may be low-priority items for many household budgets. Absent immediate health effects, visible evidence, or a culprit on which to blame the pollution, radon as a health risk is hard to be taken seriously, except among radiation scientists.

Thus, the nature of the problem of radon presents a challenge for maintaining a viable public information campaign. EPA had never faced such a communication challenge, and it struggled with how to deliver the right message. Beginning in the late 1980s, EPA adopted a number of different approaches to encourage the public voluntarily to test residences for radon. In 1989, the Advertising Council and EPA developed the first radon public information campaign. It attempted to persuade people to test their homes out of fear. Public service announcements labeled radon the "deadly intruder." Print ads and public service announcements showed a chest X-ray and warned readers that "radon is deadly in this area."

The backlash was immediate. Some health physicists, state officials, and members of the media contended that EPA was trying to scare people into testing their homes. Some media outlets refused to air the public service announcements, accusing EPA of scaremongering. Negative reactions to the first series of announcements prompted EPA to adopt a light-hearted approach to communicating radon risk in the following year, as is shown in figure 4.1. This time, the radon ad showed people on stilts and posed the question, "What are you doing that is so important you can't test your home for radon?" With this strategy, EPA sought to create public awareness of radon with the hope that people would test their homes. The implicit message in the ad was that testing for radon was more important than other weekend activities. Subsequent radon campaigns have fallen somewhere in the middle of these two approaches, as is suggested by figures 4.2 and 4.3, but none has been dramatically successful in persuading people to test their homes. The television version of the ad, "Take the National Radon Test," won an Emmy in 2001.

WHAT ARE YOU DOING THIS WEEKEND THAT'S SO IMPORTANT YOU CAN'T TEST YOUR HOME FOR RADON?

Radon is a naturally occurring, deadly radio-active gas that finds its way into millions of homes all over the country. It's the second leading cause of lung cancer in America.

If you haven't tested for radon yet, pick up a kit this weekend. Testing is quick and easy. Or call for more information today.

CALL 1-800-SOS-RADON.

 A Public Service of This Publication

RADON AWARENESS CAMPAIGN
NEWSPAPER AD NO. RA-91-1801—2 COL. x 7"
Volunteer Agency: TBWA Advertising, Inc., Campaign Director: Stephen Kutler, Texaco, Inc.

Figure 4.1.   EPA / Advertising Council Radon Public Awareness Advertisement

Source: U.S. Environmental Protection Agency, Radon Division.

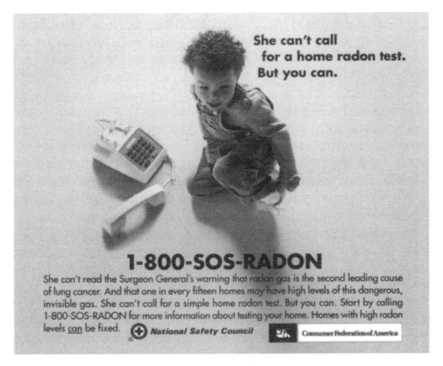

She can't call
for a home radon test.
But you can.

1-800-SOS-RADON

She can't read the Surgeon General's warning that radon gas is the second leading cause of lung cancer. And that one in every fifteen homes may have high levels of this dangerous, invisible gas. She can't call for a simple home radon test. But you can. Start by calling 1-800-SOS-RADON for more information about testing your home. Homes with high radon levels can be fixed. ⊕ *National Safety Council*   Consumer Federation of America

Figure 4.2.   EPA / National Safety Council Radon Awareness Advertisement

Source: U.S. Environmental Protection Agency, Radon Division.

Some scholars have criticized not only EPA's vacillating position on risk communication but also its attempt to reach everyone rather than focus on the areas of greatest risk. One could envision, for example, concentrating outreach efforts in parts of the country with the highest potential for elevated radon. A long-standing critic of EPA's radon program, Anthony Nero, commented, "In its zeal to spur millions of homeowners to act, EPA directed an alarmist—and often misleading or inaccurate—public information effort. The practical outcome has been a confused public, a frustrated EPA, and a large number of households that are still exposed to a very significant cancer risk."[42]

Another communication challenge for the agency involved choosing the appropriate testing protocol for the updated edition of the *Citizen's Guide to Radon*. The earlier version of the guide instructed homeowners to test in the lowest "livable" area of their residence. For many homes, this protocol suggested that people test their basements, whether they used them as a living space or not. Amid much debate between radon professionals, state radon program coordinators, relocation companies, and health physicists, EPA's Radon

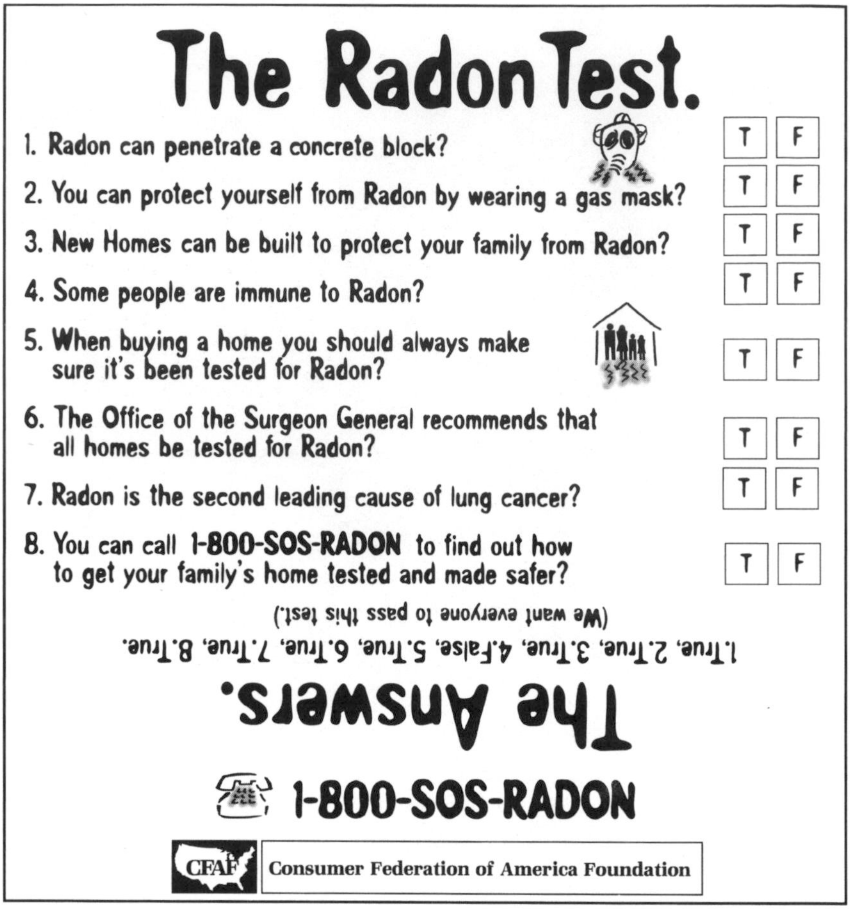

Figure 4.3. EPA / Consumer Federation of America Radon Awareness Advertisement

Source: U.S. Environmental Protection Agency, Radon Division.

Division changed the protocol to suggest testing in the lowest "lived-in" area.[43] The distinction was significant, because many homes have higher radon levels in the basement than in the ground or upper-level floors.

Perhaps the most challenging communication effort involved the dissemination of the EPA Map of Radon Zones, which was released in 1994. This map, created with the assistance of the U.S. Geological Survey, identified counties within states according to three levels, as is shown in figure 4.4. A county designated as Zone 1 has a predicted average indoor screening level for homes greater than 4 pCi/L; Zone 2 counties have a predicted average screening level between 2 and 4 pCi/L; and Zone 3 counties have a predicted average screen-

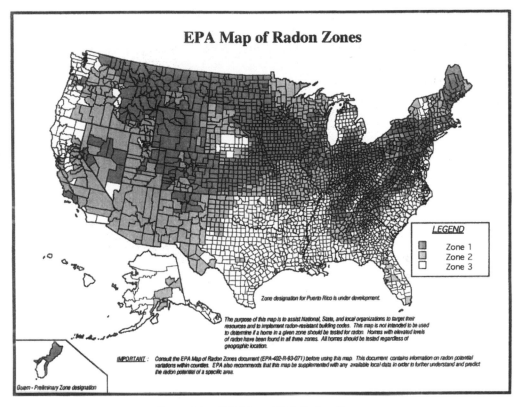

Figure 4.4.   EPA Map of U.S. Radon Zones

Source: U.S. Environmental Protection Agency, Radon Division.

ing level less than 2 pCi/L. The intended audiences for the radon map were state and local governments, and building code officials.

Although Sections 307 and 309 of IRAA directed EPA to list and identify areas of the United States with the potential for elevated indoor radon levels, state and EPA regional officials greeted the radon map was with skepticism. Concerns included designating a county based upon a paucity of available data (sometimes only a handful of test results were used to determine the zone for the entire county); EPA's preference for using EPA–state survey data rather than data generated through other sources; and a fear that Zone 2 and Zone 3 counties would feel that they were "off the hook" and not obliged to adopt radon-resistant building codes.[44]

Yet another issue that plagued IRAA implementation was the debate over the dose–response relationship.[45] Extrapolation of excess lung cancer deaths of uranium miners to American households presents uncertainty about the real extent of risk. Especially troublesome is EPA's assumption that the dose–response relation between radon and lung cancer is linear (i.e., there is no threshold tolerance or safe level of radon exposure). EPA set an action level of 4 pCi/L because it was thought to be the lowest level that could be achieved technologically, but it has steadfastly maintained that no level of radon exposure is safe. Although most scientists agree with the zero-tolerance threshold of radon exposure, some scientists reject the linear dose–response assumption and argue that people can be exposed to radon levels higher than 4 pCi/L and not face increased health risk. They argue that the exposure of miners to radon is not at all like residential exposures to radon, because miners were exposed to much higher levels of radon as well as to higher levels of dust and other contaminants.

The ongoing debate in the scientific community has translated into some mixed messages in the popular media. The following quote from the Berkeley Wellness Letter published by the University of California is a case in point: "How much radon would it take over what period of time to cause cancer, and how many people would it affect? In spite of years of research (19 more studies are currently underway) and millions of dollars spent, there's no answer to these questions. . . . Epidemiological studies concerning radon are good at detecting high risk, as in uranium mines, but not sensitive enough to detect low risks, such as may result from exposure in smoke-free homes."[46] Cassandra Chrones Moore, a Cato Institute adjunct scholar and author of *Haunted Housing: How Toxic Scare Stories Are Spooking the Public Out of House and Home*, accused EPA of conducting a "campaign of terror" that forces scientists to prove that radon does not cause cancer at levels below 4 pCi/L (as opposed to having EPA prove its zero threshold assumption).[47]

Compounding the issue of a threshold or "safe" radon level is the synergistic effect of cigarette smoking and radon exposure. EPA estimates that current smokers are at 20 times the risk of people who have never smoked and face about 70 percent of the total risk from radon. This led EPA to conclude that while radon represents a danger to all people, "any change in smoking patterns would have a dramatic impact on both the total and the radon-attributed lung cancer mortality rates."[48]

Thus, radon, like other environmental carcinogens, suffers from scientific uncertainty about acceptable risk. However, unlike other carcinogens that may be regulated under environmental laws, reducing radon exposure is primarily a voluntary activity. People may look at reports about scientific uncertainty as providing a reason to delay or avoid addressing elevated radon levels in their homes. This is especially true when the media attention to radon as a carcinogen has faded.

Regulatory and Nonregulatory Programs Collide: Radon in Drinking Water

An emerging issue involves the intersection of two laws: IRAA and the Safe Drinking Water Act (SDWA). As will be discussed in chapter 5, SDWA requires EPA to set maximum contaminant levels (MCLs) for pollutants in drinking water. These levels are designed to protect human health but are ultimately a risk management decision that does balance risk against the costs of treating drinking water. If attempts to identify the appropriate "action level" for radon have been controversial, efforts to regulate radon in water have been little short of the bureaucratic equivalent of war. At least two points of contention have prompted battle lines to be drawn. The first concerns the appropriate standard for radon; the second concerns the ability of states to pursue an alternative standard through reducing radon in the air.

In 1991, EPA drinking water staff proposed an MCL standard of 300 pCi/L of radon in water. This drew sharp criticism as being overly stringent—not only from public water suppliers but also from EPA staff and state officials implementing IRAA. Nearly half of all public water supply systems would not meet the standard, meaning that costly new equipment would be needed. States that draw drinking water supplies from groundwater and with geological conditions favoring uranium bearing rock were at greater risk of noncompliance. Some states, like Colorado, estimated that only 30 percent of public water suppliers would be in compliance with the 300 pCi/L standard.

More important, setting such a stringent standard for radon in water would do little to limit public health risks from radon exposure. For one thing, radon in water is primarily a danger only when it is released into the air, because the main health risk is lung cancer through inhalation, not ingestion, of radon. On the basis of a National Academy of Sciences report, EPA estimates that radon in drinking water causes about 168 cancer deaths per year (89 percent of those are from lung cancer; the remaining 11 percent are from stomach cancer).[49] This is a very small part of the 14,000 lung cancer deaths attributed each year to radon in the air.

A related argument centered on the process of setting the standard. Because radon in water is primarily a risk only when it is released into the air, the rate of radon transfer from water into air is important in determining the health-based standard. EPA uses a transfer factor of 10,000 pCi/L of radon in water to equal 1 pCi/L of radon in the air. (In other words, 40,000 pCi/L of radon in water would produce about 4 pCi/L of radon in the air, EPA's action level for radon.) This makes the 300 pCi/L standard seem absurd. Requiring public water supply systems to reduce radon in water to 300 pCi/L would be akin to setting a standard below background—or ambient air—levels of radon, and well below the EPA action level for radon. As one EPA radon official put it, "It's crazy. The radon standard for drinking water should be consistent with the national levels of radon in the indoor air. At 1.3 pCi/L, something like 13,000 pCi/L of radon in drinking water would be more like it."

The battle over the appropriate standard for radon in water would not easily be resolved. In enacting the 1996 Amendments to SDWA, Congress required EPA to withdraw its 1991 proposed regulation. It further required EPA to arrange for the National Academy of Sciences to analyze the risks associated with radon in water. The 1998 report cited above confirmed that the estimated risk posed by radon from drinking water was small, relative to the exposure to radon from indoor air.[50] EPA, in turn, was required to publish a radon health risk reduction and cost analysis for radon in water, propose an MCL goal and standard for radon by 1999, and finalize the standard by August 2000.[51]

In 1999, the EPA Office of Water proposed a compromise standard that could potentially merge the indoor air radon efforts with drinking water regulation. Essentially, through an alternative MCL, states would be allowed to adopt a less stringent standard for radon in drinking water, provided they develop "enhanced indoor air programs" that demonstrated they were taking action to reduce radon in air levels, including increasing their activities under IRAA. With these enhanced, or Multi-Media Mitigation (MMM), programs in place, public water suppliers in the state would have to provide water with radon levels no higher than 4,000 pCi/L. States that chose not to develop enhanced indoor air programs would have to meet the previously proposed MCL of 300 pCi/L. Public water suppliers, in the absence of state willingness to develop multimedia programs, could develop their own local MMM programs and then meet a radon standard for drinking water of 4,000 pCi/L.[52]

In June 2000, EPA sent a letter to all governors requesting them to commit to either implementing an indoor radon program that was consistent with the criteria in the rule or to notify EPA that the state preferred the 300 pCi/L standard. Subsequent public hearings soon found EPA in hot water, as vigorous debate surrounded both the 300 pCi/L MCL and the alternative MCL. Some state radon officials contended that this would shift a regulatory burden to their IRAA programs, making them do more with already paltry funds. They further argued that the indoor radon programs were set up as promotional, voluntary programs—not as regulatory programs. Conversely, some officials viewed this as an opportunity to leverage the small voluntary indoor radon program with the much more visible drinking water program. As one EPA official suggested, "No one knows the radon programs are even there. They have very little state-level support. With this standard in place, the public water suppliers would be a very strong ally."

Others suggested that EPA should forget the two-standard scenario altogether and instead set one standard somewhere between 300 and 4,000 pCi/L. One standard, albeit at a more appropriate level from the perspective of these participants, was important for two reasons. First, one standard would help private well owners make decisions about what to do. Private well owners, though not regulated under the Safe Drinking Water Act, often refer to standards for public water supplies in determining the safety of their water. Second, the alternative MCL provided no guarantee of risk reduction, because radon-reduction activities might have been undertaken anyway under the implementation of IRAA. Even more troubling was the possibility that states with MMM programs could choose to reduce radon levels in one community while ignoring radon risks in other parts of the state, because the requirements in the rule were for a state to show a reduction. Skeptics argued that while this might be good for a few citizens, it would not serve to reduce radon risk throughout the state in the same way as a single standard.

EPA, thus being in a difficult and contentious position, failed to meet its August 2000 deadline to finalize the radon in drinking water rule, and the rule was subsequently pulled back by the new administration of George W. Bush. As of this writing, the final rule is due out in December 2003, though several state and EPA radon officials interviewed continued to express the hope that the radon standard for drinking water would somehow be forgotten.

Funding State Programs and Leveraging with Partnerships

IRAA was not reauthorized when it expired in 1992, although several radon bills were introduced in 1993, 1994, and 1995. Many of these bills attempted to establish a national regulatory presence in real estate disclosure requirements, building codes, or school testing. Congressional attention to radon in subsequent years has been virtually nil—with only a handful of radon bills between 1996 and 2003. Absent new authorization, federal funds for state radon programs are tenuous, although state radon programs continue to be funded, and are in EPA's requested budget for fiscal 2004.[53]

Funding for state radon programs has been flat or decreasing since 1988. Initially, IRAA Section 306(j) authorized $10 million for three years (federal fiscal 1989, 1990, and 1991) to get state radon programs operational. Roughly $8.1 million was available to states annually under the SIRG program during those three years.[54] That amount has slightly decreased over time, even though additional states have opted to receive SIRG funds. Thirty-two states received smaller grants in 1993 than in previous years.[55] The average radon grant for 1993 was $139,000, down from $151,000 in 1992. For fiscal 2003, states requested more than $9.3 million in SIRG funding but received $7.8 million.[56]

Perhaps more important, states with the highest exposure risks do not necessarily receive large SIRG grants. South Dakota, which is ranked highest of all states in terms of radon concentration per unit of livable space, received only $30,000 in 1993. It received only half that ($18,500) in 2003. [57] North Dakota and Nebraska, ranked second and third in terms of percentage of homes over the EPA guidance level of 4 pCi/L, respectively received $100,000 and $40,000 in 1993 and $88,000 and $130,000 in 2003. In many cases, reduced grant awards are the result of a state's inability to meet escalating match requirements. In other cases, however, EPA headquarters or regional offices make decisions to reduce SIRG awards.

For example, Colorado's SIRG for fiscal 2003 was $305,000, down 20 percent from fiscal 2002. From a public health point of view, this is troubling, because Colorado has a high incidence of radon. Radon surveys predict that 44 percent of Colorado homes are in excess of 4.0 pCi/L, and some counties face much greater risks. Average pCi/L measurements for Clear Creek, Eagle, Gilpin, Pitkin, and Summit Counties exceed the EPA action level. In Clear Creek, more than 85 percent of all homes tested are above 4.0 pCi/L, with average readings of 6.4 pCi/L—dramatically higher than the nationwide average of 6 percent. [58] Even given this, federal funding for the Colorado program has decreased in recent years, and the state budget has not picked up the slack.

That radon is not a high-priority budget item for states or the national government seems clear. Radon fails to capture the attention of state legislatures or Congress, in large part because it fails to command much public attention. EPA and state budgets for radon are unlikely to increase anytime soon, given pessimistic forecasts for national and state government budgets. The paucity of resources has prompted EPA, states, and public health groups to pull together to extend radon outreach activities.

One intriguing part of the IRAA implementation story is EPA's ability to leverage its scare resources through partnerships with other organizations. The agency's outreach efforts increase through partnerships with the American Lung Association, the Consumer Federation of America, and the National Safety Council, among others. The Advertising Council partnered with EPA to develop public service announcements in the early years of IRAA implementation, and the Consumer Federation of America Foundation and National Safety Council partnered with EPA to produce public service announcements in later years.

To increase public outreach efforts, EPA launched Radon Action Week during the month of October. The week, which was designed to "jump-start" radon communication efforts, encouraged state and local governments to promote radon educational activities. In 2002, EPA changed Radon Action Week to Radon Action Month and moved it to January, which was chosen because radon levels can soar during the colder months when residents keep windows and doors closed and spend more time indoors.[59] (One official noted that as a practical matter, radon had less competition for the airwaves after the November elections.) An annual national poster contest sponsored by EPA, the U.S. Department of Agriculture Extension Offices, and the National Safety Council hopes to get children into the process of increasing awareness of radon.

When EPA decided to privatize the radon proficiency program, the National Environmental Health Association and the National Radon Safety Board took over national-level training and certification of radon testing and mitigation professionals. Though this action drew some sharp criticism from state radon program officials, as is noted in the next section, it did provide an opportunity for the agency to leverage another part of its program. EPA's partnering effort in radon is, as one official put it, "a key reason why the program succeeds at all, given the small staff devoted to radon at EPA."

In 1993, the Radon Program at EPA headquarters became part of the Indoor Air Quality programs (eventually to become the Indoor Environments Division). To some EPA officials interviewed, this move effectively leveraged scarce agency resources allocated to indoor air (compared with outside air, which is regulated by the Clean Air Act). Others, however, believed that the consolidation diluted the importance of radon, especially when public attention turned to other indoor air pollutants, such as mold and secondhand tobacco smoke.

In sum, a number of issues at the national level surround the continued implementation of IRAA, including the challenge of effectively communicating risk, requiring both radon testing during real estate transactions and radon-resistant construction standards for new homes, addressing scientific uncertainty about the 4 pCi/L action level, setting the standard for radon in drinking water, and continuing the program in the absence of IRAA reauthorization. Conversely, EPA has worked hard to leverage its resources through a wide array of partnerships, and its message that radon is the second leading cause of lung cancer has been supported by the National Academy of Sciences and other prestigious organizations. Additional state-level issues, as well as state perceptions of federal–state radon efforts, are also important. These are discussed in the next section.

Perceptions of State Radon Officials

In 2002, forty-six surveys were sent to officials identified by EPA as directing state radon programs. Thirty were returned, for a response rate of 65 percent. In 2002 and 2003, nine interviews were conducted with state radon officials and eight were conducted with EPA radon officials. In 1995, fifty-three surveys were sent to state radon officials. Forty-four were returned, for a response rate of 83 percent. In 1995 and 1996, twelve additional interviews were conducted in order to better understand the perspectives of state radon staff. One interview from an earlier survey mailed to state radon program directors in 1994 was used.[60]

State radon programs operate with small staffs. Ninety percent of state officials responding to the survey function with four or fewer full-time equivalent (FTE) personnel, and 53 percent of those have only one (or less than one) FTE staff member devoted to the radon program. Most state officials (67 percent) running a radon program have more than five years experience in the program. Unlike EPA headquarters, where radon was combined with other indoor pollutants, most states keep radon as a separate program, apart from any indoor air quality programs that may be operating at the state level. Most state radon programs are located within state health departments, usually in a bureau of radiological health, although a few are in environmental quality departments operating as an independent program or as part of an environmental health unit.

Most radon programs were created when states received their first SIRG grants. Eighty-seven percent of state radon programs depend upon federal grants for at least 50 percent of operational expenses, and 45 percent of these programs rely on federal funding for most or all of their programmatic expenses. Because states must contribute 50 percent of their own-source funds under current SIRG requirements, this suggests a heavy reliance by state radon programs on in-kind money. In other words, many state radon programs use federal monies for ongoing expenses and use staff time or other "soft dollars" to meet the SIRG matching requirements.

As matching requirements have increased and available federal funds have decreased, some states have opted out of the SIRG program. In 1996, Georgia, Maryland, and Texas indicated that they would not participate in the SIRG program.[61] For some states, radon programs are left to county governments. The state of Washington dropped its radon program in 1992, after providing minimal funding ($6,000) to support the radon consultation and referral services offered by the Spokane County Health District.[62] Other states have very few homes with elevated radon levels and are hard-pressed to find even soft money matches to continue their radon efforts. For example, only respectively 0.01 and 0.05 percent of the homes in Louisiana and Hawaii are estimated to have elevated radon levels.[63]

Factors That Facilitate or Hinder Implementation

When asked what hinders implementation, state radon program directors point to two things: first, inadequate funding; and second, lack of public or official interest in radon, as is shown in table 4.1. Some state officials suggest

Table 4.1. Factors That Hinder IRAA Implementation, as Ranked by State Officials, 2002

Factor	Percentage Identifying as an Issue (N = 30)
Insufficient resources	54
Public and state policymakers not interested in radon	46
Problems with regulatory or statutory language	21
Lack of agency or administrative support for program	13
Problems with certifying radon testing and mitigation personnel	13

Note: IRAA = Indoor Radon Abatement Act.

that the lack of funds prohibits expanding the program or doing effective outreach, as is indicated by this comment: "Our entire radon budget is less than $75,000 per year. It's difficult to run an effective program on such a limited budget." One official noted "we need to update the testing data collected over ten years ago. There are no funds to do this." Others suggest that limited funds hamper their ability to pass through money for county or local radon efforts. Others point to the lack of public funds to help people mitigate their homes: "We can get people to test, but we can't help them financially to get their homes fixed."

Several state radon directors observed that the SIRG funding provided by EPA is essential to continuing their state radon program. Commented one official, "Having the SIRG continues to be the biggest help [for the state radon program]. Keep the SIRG at the same level or greater, and we will continue to make significant progress." Indeed, two-thirds of all respondents to the 2002 survey indicated that the state would not replace SIRG funding with state revenues.

Funding state radon programs is so challenging that even coming up with the 50 percent match to receive the SIRG is difficult, according to some state officials: "Our state is not interested in supporting radon, even though many areas of the state exceed EPA guidance level." "Get rid of the match," suggested one official. Another agreed: "The way the law is written is a problem. The state has a tough time coming up with the match." A third comment was equally succinct: "Matching funds for SIRG is a big obstacle. State general funds for the match are scarce." An official from a state no longer receiving SIRG funding stated that the program is barely operational: "Our program consists only of answering phone calls and mailing information packets to individuals. . . . The majority of people are grateful for the information."

Interviews revealed a belief among state radon officials that their programs are in jeopardy. As one official noted, "We're concerned about potential negative impacts on state health agency funding for radon because of EPA block grants (performance partnerships) that may be targeted to another state agency, causing competition among departments and reducing or even eliminating our radon program." Another comment was quite similar: "I'd like to reduce the potential negative impact of 'hiding' radon grant support in block grants. If block grants come to our state, wave good-bye to the state radon effort." (Performance Partnership Grants are discussed in chapter 1.)

Public and policymaker lack of interest in radon also hampers implementation, as perceived by 46 percent of the survey respondents. In many cases, state officials point to the challenge of persuading people that radon is a serious health risk. "Since everything is voluntary, radon is easily perceived as unimportant," suggested a state program director. "Public apathy is still the biggest obstacle," stated a state official. Another noted the "public resistance (apathy) to test or mitigate," adding that "the same goes for school officials who say that if they test and there is a problem, there won't be any money to fix it anyway."

As is shown in table 4.2, only 10 percent of state officials agree that radon is a top priority, and only 23 percent believe that citizens are aware of the health risks of radon. Also intriguing is the interplay between state official perceptions of public concern about radon and radon risk communication. Most state officials are satisfied with EPA and state communication tools, such as the *Citizen's Guide* discussed above. State officials, for the most part, agree that they and their EPA counterparts deliver a clear and accurate message about radon, within the constraints of scarce resources. However, they do not believe that the public internalizes the message of potential risk to their health.

Some officials point to challenges within state bureaucracies, even their own agencies, such as this comment: "Management does not consider radon to be a significant health problem." Another concluded, "The lack of personnel and lack of full commitment by the state health department is the biggest obstacle. This lack of commitment is probably due to a lack of understanding of the magnitude of risks of radon." Suggested another official, "This is not a required EPA program, therefore it's not perceived as a 'real' environmental program." Another agreed, "Convincing upper management in the department of the seriousness of the problem. I believe this will be a new challenge with the incoming administration." Another comment held the same sentiment: "The state radon program needs to be supervised by someone who can give it a high priority, or any priority, in the department."

State radon officials are also concerned about the lack of regulatory muscle behind their radon efforts, as is illustrated by these comments: "Aside from a school testing requirement, the radon effort is voluntary in this state. One county requires radon-resistant construction, as does one municipality. [In-state] competition for funding has been a critical factor the past two years, and

Table 4.2. Perceptions of State Radon Officials about State Radon Programs (percentage indicating that they strongly agree or agree), 1995 and 2002

Perception	1995 (N = 44)	2002 (N = 30)
Program is effective	75	63
Program is stronger than three years ago	41	56
Program is adequately funded	48	26
Staff is adequately trained	n.a.	77
Citizens are aware of risks of radon	43	23
Radon is a top environmental priority	11	10
Local officials are actively protecting public from radon	n.a.	13
I am satisfied with the way radon risk is communicated	n.a.	70

Note: n.a. = not available.

all counties have had to scale back their programs." Radon officials are also concerned about the apparent lack of attention directed toward radon when compared with other environmental pollutants. "Radon is not treated like lead or asbestos. It gets no respect. That means low public support for initiatives, which results in low administrative support, which means that radon is a 'stealth public program,'" commented one state official. Another agreed: "Schools don't see radon as a problem. They see mold as a problem."

When asked about factors that facilitate implementation, state officials perceive the expertise of the staff, the array of partnerships, and the existence of federal funding (even if it is not a large amount) as key factors. As table 4.2 shows, state radon directors believe (77 percent) that their staff is adequately trained to run the radon program, and most officials believe that their program is effective (63 percent). Many state radon staffs have long histories with the program, and training in public health. Noted one state radon official: "We have a dedicated and professional staff and management that solidly support the radon program. Even though we face obstacles at times and since we have a large program to run, these [dedicated staff and managers] make our job and the issue of radon easier to deal with." As one official put it, "Our radon program runs very well as a community involvement program at the local level (due mostly to our efforts at the state level), but this happens with little middle and top-level management support. This is true even though over three-fourths of our citizens live in Zone 1 and Zone 2 counties."

The EPA Radon Program and Working Relationships

Another dimension of IRAA implementation emerges when state officials express their opinions about their working relationships with EPA regional and

Table 4.3. Perceptions of State Radon Officials about Working Relationships with the EPA (percentage indicating that they strongly agree or agree), 1995 and 2002

Perception	1995 (N = 44)	2002 (N = 30)
I have a positive relationship with EPA regional radon staff	88	83
I have a positive relationship with EPA headquarters	58	43
EPA staff has a high degree of technical expertise	60	57
EPA regional radon program is adequately funded	48	23
Oversight is flexible	90	73
Regional and headquarters officials view program similarly	42	10
EPA clearly communicates goals and requirements	44	40
Without the EPA, the state would not be as serious about running a radon program	44	43
EPA is concerned about protecting the public from radon	74	60

Note: EPA = U.S. Environmental Protection Agency.

headquarters staff, as is shown in table 4.3. Several state officials were quick to express very positive views about their EPA colleagues, noting "excellent" working relationships. Eighty-three percent of state officials believe that EPA regional staff are supportive of the state radon program, and 73 percent believe they have sufficient flexibility to run their programs. Though state officials view working relationships as positive, they seem less synergistic than six years ago. States and EPA are still "pulling together" (to use the language of the typology), but they are not pulling with quite the same intensity as in the past. What concerns state officials?

First, state radon officials perceive that EPA is not as involved with the state programs as in the early years, and that it may not be as interested in assisting states maintain viable programs. One official returned the survey with this comment: "Even though EPA claims differently, they are not involved nearly as much as before radon got lost in the Indoor Air Quality programs. Our EPA regional radon contact is mostly involved in the 'Tools for Schools' program, with mold being the dominant issue." Other officials mirrored that comment closely: "We need more involvement by our regional coordinator." "Our interaction with EPA is minimal." "They [EPA] should show more interest in radon in general, like in the early years. This would result in new materials for distribution and new training opportunities. My staff and I feel like we are fighting a losing battle all by ourselves. Management does not seem to care about the program, and neither does EPA. It is hard to stay enthusiastic about the issue. The only reward is a weekly paycheck."

Several commented that their EPA regional radon coordinator continued to cut SIRG funds to the state, with apparent disregard for state needs. "We've recently been reduced by 22 percent by EPA. It looks to me like bad decision making from some folks from EPA headquarters." Like state asbestos program officials, state radon officials perceive that the EPA regional offices are inadequately funded. Only 23 percent agreed that the EPA regional office had enough funds to adequately run the radon program (down from 48 percent in 1995).

A related perception is that EPA does not effectively communicate program goals and requirements. When asked why this perception was held, one state official commented that EPA should understand that states with small programs are not able to as easily meet the reporting requirements. In this case, state officials feel overly burdened with preparing quarterly reports and the annual request for radon funding under SIRG. A few officials noted the duplication between reporting requirements under the National Environmental Performance Partnership (NEPPS) and those required under the SIRG program. One result for states that have included radon as part of their performance agreement is that state radon officials have to prepare two reports (one for NEPPS and one for the EPA regional radon coordinator). They may choose to ignore the request of the regional radon coordinator—eroding positive working relationships as a result. In some regions, such as Region 5, all states within the region had opted not to include the radon program in the Performance Partnership Grants.

Issues of working relationships include a perceived failure of EPA to alert state officials of pending EPA- or EPA partner–sponsored activities. States noted that it was difficult to get EPA to provide information about radon activities. As one interviewee put it: "EPA should be a readily available source of information or research if needed. There are many questions we would like solid answers to and at times it seems difficult to get the answers or to get assistance."

Finally, the radon proficiency programs have gone awry, from the perspective of some state radon officials. The radon measurement proficiency program and the radon contractor proficiency program were shifted out of the auspices of the federal government and moved to the National Environmental Health Association and the National Radon Safety Board. In 1995, state officials were also concerned about the proficiency programs, but the concern was primarily with the dwindling number of radon contractors. As the interest in radon has waned, so too has the radon business. In 1994, when increased fees for radon professionals were established, the number of organizations and individuals listed on EPA's proficiency list fell by 17 percent. In 1995, a state official commented: "EPA is destroying an already dying radon industry. No one wants to do radon work anymore, yet EPA makes it more expensive to be a radon professional. [EPA should] make the radon proficiency programs more cost-effective for participants so that we can be assured of an adequate list of service providers in various areas of our state."

More frequently, comments about communication dealt with improving communication between states and EPA headquarters. In 1995, state officials believed that EPA headquarters consulted them too late in the evolution of the national radon map or in the development of the *Citizen's Guide* and other EPA radon documents. This perception was even more prevalent in 2002, but for different reasons. In part, the perception of less positive working relationships between EPA headquarters and state radon officials is related to the radon in drinking water standard; it also may be connected to perceived disparities in funding at the EPA regional level or the SIRG funding formula. It also may be connected to state officials' view that the EPA radon program has been lost in the Indoor Environments Division.

Conclusions about the Radon Program

Although their working relationships are not perfect, state and federal radon officials seem to be "pulling together," with high levels of mutual trust and involvement. EPA regional and state radon staffs share the belief that elevated radon levels present a serious risk to the public; they also tend to feel neglected when compared with other environmental programs. Radon is like the Rodney Dangerfield of environmental programs—it gets "no respect," even though radon is one of the most serious public health risks under the auspices of EPA.

Because of this lack of public and policymaker attention, state and federal radon officials seek to pull together to maintain a viable program. Several state radon program directors interviewed have the attributes of policy champions, with zeal to protect the public from high levels of radon. Others have become discouraged. Nearly all state staff feels that they occupy tenuous positions—especially as state budgets decrease and radon no longer is a favorite of the media. This coupling of shared consensus about policy goals with nervousness about the continued fiscal health of the program works to increase the cooperative spirit of intergovernmental relationships.

What is troubling is that federal–state relationships are not as cordial as in previous years. From the perspective of the states, EPA is still "pulling" for radon, but with attention diverted to other indoor air pollutants. Instead of a stand-alone division, radon is now "just another" indoor air pollutant in the Indoor Environments Division. When this relationship change is coupled with flat or decreasing levels of SIRG funding, state officials are somewhat less inclined to see synergistic federal–state relationships, though they still pull together.

Figure 4.5.   Radon Cartoon, Published in 1988

Source: Copyright Stuart Carlson, *Milwaukee Sentinel*; used by permission.

Extrinsic variables that influence implementation of the radon program include the nature of the problem. IRAA relies on the public to respond voluntarily to health risks associated with radon exposures in the home. The public, in turn, cannot smell, see, or taste radon. It is an invisible, naturally occurring intruder. Absent another Watras event, media attention toward radon has waned, with few cartoons like the one in figure 4.5. Though the medical and scientific communities agree that radon is a carcinogen, debates remain about the merits of the 4 pCi/L action level and testing protocols. EPA, in turn, has found persuading people to test their homes for radon a continued hard sell. It is likely that most future radon mitigation will be the result of policy change at the state level (e.g., requiring disclosure during real estate transactions) rather than at EPA.

Also complicating IRAA implementation is the standard for radon in drinking water. If the final standard is published as currently proposed, it may put state radon programs on more solid financial footing. However, it may also have the opposite effect, if no new funds to implement the alternative MCL are forthcoming. In any event, it will prove costly to small public water supply systems, as is discussed in chapter 5.

However, radon does continue to get some attention and support. Radon Action Month commanded a spot on the home page of EPA's website and a statement from EPA administrator Christine Whitman. Partnerships, moreover, continue to exist and even expand. Perhaps most important, the science behind the risks of radon continues to connect radon to lung cancer, and the number of critics of the risk assessment is decreasing.

At the state level, many radon state officials see limited support for radon programs. State funds are seldom directed toward radon (with a few notable exceptions). Most state radon officials rely on SIRG, and only on SIRG, to operate their programs. Moreover, state laws or local policies on real estate disclosures of radon or on radon-resistant building codes have been rare. In short, the story of implementing IRAA is a prime example of the struggles of non-regulatory programs to remain viable.

Notes

1. American Association of Radon Scientists and Technologists, "Radon Risks and Health Effects," www.aarst.org/radon_risk.shtml (February 25, 2003).

2. William R. Field, "Radon Occurrence and Health Risk," Virtual Hospital, University of Iowa Health Care, June 1999, www.vh.org/adult/provider/preventivemedicine /Radon/HealthRisk.html (February 25, 2003).

3. National Research Council, Committee on the Biological Effects of Ionizing Radiation, *Health Risks of Radon and Other Internally Deposited Alpha-Emitters: BEIR IV* (Washington, D.C.: National Academy Press, 1988).

4. U.S. Environmental Protection Agency, Office of Radiation Programs, *EPA's Radon Program: Reducing the Risk of Indoor Radon* (Washington, D.C.: U.S. Environmental Protection Agency, 1991), 2–3.

5. Richard Guimond, W. Elliott, J. Fitzgerald, S. Windham, and P. Cumy, *Indoor Radiation Exposure Due to Radium-226 in Florida Phosphate Lands* (Washington, D.C.: U.S. Environmental Protection Agency, 1979).

6. American Association of Radon Scientists and Technologists, "Radon Risks and Health Effects."

7. Margo Oge, acting director of the Office of Radiation Programs, U.S. Environmental Protection Agency, "Overview of the U.S. Environmental Protection Agency's Radon Action Program," speech given to the International Symposium on Radon and Radon Reduction Technology, Philadelphia, April 1991.

8. Denise Scheberle, "Radon and Asbestos: A Study of Agenda Setting and Causal Stories," *Policy Studies Journal* 22 (spring 1994): 74–86.

9. Office of Radiation Programs, *EPA's Radon Program*, ES-1.

10. Office of Radiation Programs, *EPA's Radon Program*, ES-1. For a discussion of relative risk, see U.S. Environmental Protection Agency, "Unfinished Business: A Comparative Assessment of Environmental Problems" (Washington, D.C.: U.S. Environmental Protection Agency, 1987).

11. U.S. Environmental Protection Agency, "BEIR VI Report-Public Summary," June 5, 2002, www.epa.gov/iaq/radon/public.html (September 23, 2002).

12. Warren E. Leary, "Research Ties Radon to as Many as 21,800 Deaths Each Year," *New York Times*, February 20, 1998, http://query.nytimes.com/search/article-printpage .html?res=9E06EFDC103 (January 8, 2003).

13. U.S. Environmental Protection Agency, Indoor Environments Division, *A Citizen's Guide to Radon*, EPA 402-K02-006 (Washington, D.C.: U.S. Environmental Protection Agency, 2002), 2.

14. Thomas M. Gerusky, "The Pennsylvania Radon Story," *Journal of Environmental Health* 49 (January–February 1987): 197.

15. Allan Mazur, "Putting Radon on the Public's Risk Agenda," *Science, Technology and Human Values* 12 (summer–fall 1987): 84–98, at 89.

16. Susan L. Rose, "Radon: Another Perspective," *Forum for Applied Research and Public Policy* 4 (spring 1989): 12; Kathryn Harrison and George Hoberg, "Setting the Environmental Agenda in Canada and the United States: The Cases of Dioxin and Radon," *Canadian Journal of Political Science* 24, no. 1 (March 1991): 3–27.

17. Gerusky, "Pennsylvania Radon Story," 197.

18. Thomas M. Gerusky, Pennsylvania Department of Environmental Protection, "The Pennsylvania Radon Story," October 15, 2001, www.dep.state.pa.us/dep/deputate /airwast/rp/radon_division/PA_Radon_Story1.htm (February 20, 2003).

19. Margo Oge, "EPA's Radon Program and the Indoor Radon Abatement Act," speech presented at the Fourth National Environmental Health Conference, San Antonio, June 20, 1989.

20. U.S. House of Representatives, Subcommittee on Health and the Environment, Hearings on Radon Exposure: Human Health Threat, November 5, 1987.

21. Public Law 100-555, Sec. 301.

22. Public Law 100-551, Sec. 303.

23. U.S. Environmental Protection Agency, Office of Air and Radiation, *1989 Summary of State Radon Programs*, EPA 520/1-91-015 (Washington, D.C.: U.S. Environmental Protection Agency, 1990), 3.

24. U.S. General Accounting Office, *Air Pollution: Actions to Promote Radon Testing*, GAO/RCED-93-20 (Washington, D.C.: U.S. General Accounting Office, 1992), 19. Delaware, Florida, New Hampshire, New Jersey, New York, and Utah conducted independent surveys; Oregon and South Dakota declined to participate in the state–EPA residential survey.

25. U.S. Environmental Protection Agency, Office of Policy, Planning, and Evaluation, *Radon Program Review*, draft report (Washington, D.C.: U.S. Environmental Protection Agency, 1992), III-5.

26. U.S. Environmental Protection Agency, Radon Division; data provided from a memorandum dated March 1, 1993. The states, in rank order based upon radon concentrations in the livable spaces of homes, are South Dakota, Iowa, Pennsylvania, North Dakota, Montana, Nebraska, Colorado, and New Hampshire.

27. U.S. Environmental Protection Agency, Office of Indoor Air and Radiation, *Administrative Guidance for the State Indoor Radon Grants Program* (Washington, D.C.: U.S. Environmental Protection Agency, 1992), 2.

28. Office of Indoor Air and Radiation, *Administrative Guidance for the State Indoor Radon Grant Programs*.

29. Office of Air and Radiation, *1989 Summary of State Radon Programs*.

30. Office of Air and Radiation, *Administrative Guidance for the State Indoor Radon Grants Program*, 2.

31. Andy Newman, "Radon Testing Bill Passed," *New York Times*, February 27, 1997, http://query.nytimes.com/search/full-page?res=9B01e5DB1331f93BA1575 (January 8, 2003).

32. For example, a case in Pennsylvania charged Howard Hanna Real Estate Company and Prudential Preferred Realty with two counts of fraud and one count of negligent misrepresentation and violation of the state's consumer protection law, as reported in the article "David Takes on Goliath in Real Estate Test Case," *Emanations: Newsletter of the Regional Radon Training Centers* 5, no. 4 (September 1995): 7.

33. U.S. General Accounting Office, *Air Pollution*, 3.

34. Brian Gregory and Philip P. Jalbert, U.S. Environmental Protection Agency, "National Radon Results: 1985 to 1999," October 21, 2002, www.epa.gov/iaq/radon/images/radonresults85-99.pdf (March 2, 2003).

35. Office of Policy, Planning, and Evaluation, *Radon Program Review*, III-15.

36. Environmental Law Institute, *State Radon Legislation: Issues and Options* (Washington, D.C.: Environmental Law Institute, 1993), 4–5.

37. U.S. Environmental Protection Agency, Office of Air and Radiation, *Activities and Factors Contributing to Effective State Radon Programs, Final Draft* (Washington, D.C.: U.S. Environmental Protection Agency, 1994), 13.

38. Gregory and Jalbert, "National Radon Results," 5.

39. Peter Hendrick, American Association of Radon Scientists and Technologists, "U.S. Radon Policy Borders on Failure," January 2003, www.aarst.org/index.shtml (February 12, 2003).

40. Examples include Neil D. Weinstein, Mary Lou Klotz, and Peter M. Sandman, "Optimistic Biases in Public Perceptions of the Risk from Radon," *American Journal of Public Health* 78, no. 7 (July 1988): 796–800; and Peter M. Sandman, Neil D. Weinstein, and M. L. Klotz, "Public Response to the Risk from Geological Radon," *Journal of Communication* 37, no. 3 (summer 1987): 93–108.

41. For early governmental efforts to alert the public to radon, see Anne Rickard Jackowitz, "Radon's Radioactive Ramifications: How Federal and State Governments Should Address the Problem," *Environmental Affairs* 16 (1988): 329–81.

42. Anthony V. Nero Jr., "A National Strategy for Indoor Radon," *Issues in Science and Technology* (fall 1992): 33–40, at 33. See also Leonard A. Cole, *Element of Risk: The Politics of Radon* (Washington, D.C.: AAAS Press, 1993).

43. Indoor Environments Division, *Citizen's Guide to Radon*, 5.

44. These concerns are ones identified through conversations with radon staff in two different EPA Regions.

45. For a critique of EPA's radon dose–response relationship see Susan L. Rose, "Radon: Another Perspective," *Forum for Applied Research and Public Policy* 4 (spring

1989): 12–15; and Phillip H. Abelson, "Radon Today: The Role of Flimflam in Public Policy," *Regulation* 14, no. 4 (1991): 95–100.

46. University of California, Berkeley, "Reassessing Radon Risk," *Berkeley Wellness Letter* 11, no. 5 (1995): 4–5, at 4.

47. Quoted in Sandra Fleishman, "Radon: It's Still Here," *Washington Post*, January 25, 2003, www.washingtonpost.com/ac2/wp-dyn/A36378-2003 (January 28, 2003).

48. Office of Policy, Planning, and Evaluation, *Radon Program Review*, III-7.

49. U.S. Environmental Protection Agency, Office of Water, *Radon in Drinking Water: Questions and Answers*, EPA 815-F-99-007 (Washington, D.C.: U.S. Environmental Protection Agency, 1999), 1.

50. U.S. Environmental Protection Agency, "Initial EPA Perspectives on NAS Report: "Risk Assessment of Radon in Drinking Water," September 16, 2002, www.epa.gov /safewater/radon/nasdw.html (September 23, 2002).

51. U.S. Environmental Protection Agency, "Drinking Water Priority Rulemaking: Radon," November 26, 2002, www.epa.gov/safewater/radon/stat.html (January 16, 2003).

52. Office of Water, *Radon in Drinking Water*, 2.

53. U.S. Environmental Protection Agency, chief financial officer, budget documents, February 21, 2003, www.epa.gov/ocfo/budget/budget.htm (February 23, 2003).

54. Many states began SIRG cooperative agreements in fiscal 1990; thus, funding was available through fiscal 1992.

55. U.S. Environmental Protection Agency, Office of Indoor Air and Radiation, internal memorandum listing state radon grant allocations.

56. Charles Gasque, "Regional Summary," March 17, 2003, personal e-mail (March 29, 2003).

57. U.S. Environmental Protection Agency, Office of Indoor Air and Radiation, "State Indoor Radon Grants Policy Priorities for 1993," unpublished document given to SIRG recipients.

58. National Environmental Health Association, "Short-Term Test Results for Pikes Peak Region," www.nehacert.org/Coilo%20area%20slides_files/slide0006.html (March 2, 2003).

59. U.S. Environmental Protection Agency, EPA Newsroom, "EPA Administrator Whitman Urges Home Testing for Radon, Commemorates National Radon Action Month," January 14, 2003, www.epa.gov/epahome/headline_011403.htm (February 26, 2003).

60. The results of the first survey of state radon program directors were reported in "Pesticides and Radon: State Perceptions of EPA and Administrative Support," paper presented at the Midwest Political Science Association meeting, April 1994.

61. U.S. Environmental Protection Agency, Region 5, memorandum dated March 6, 1996.

62. Personal correspondence with the Spokane County Health District, June 27, 1995.

63. U.S. Environmental Protection Agency, Radon Division, "Cumulative Ranking of States by Radon Concentration in the Livable Space," unpublished report, July 1993.

· 5 ·

Implementing Drinking Water Regulations in a One-Size-Fits-All World

Understanding the implementation of the Safe Drinking Water Act (SDWA) and federal–state working relationships within drinking water programs requires taking a hard look at the wide range of public water suppliers, the intensely emotional and complicated process of setting standards, and the aging pipes and other infrastructure. These have prompted not only environmental groups but also government agencies at all levels to foresee a "crisis" on the drinking water horizon. At one level, the law is clear: Provide water for human consumption that is as safe as feasible, given technological limitations. However, as the saying goes, the devil is in the details. The U.S. Environmental Protection Agency (EPA) must first promulgate national standards, which involves the challenge of determining levels of contaminants that pose acceptable risk. Then, more than 160,000 public water supply systems must implement these standards, usually by employing the appropriate technological controls. Meeting these standards is required of all public water suppliers—whether they supply drinking water to a few dozen taps or a few million. The safe drinking water program provides a perfect illustration of what happens in a one-size-fits-all regulatory environment when the target group is anything but one size.

This chapter begins by exploring the implementation of SDWA, considering its key provisions and major amendments. Congress made major changes to SDWA in 1996. Special attention is directed toward the obstacles that challenge its successful implementation, including the diversity of the target group, the standard-setting process (its technical, intergovernmental, and political aspects) and the costs associated with implementing the law now and in the future. The chapter also explores new challenges, including the intersection of national security and safe drinking water. The last part of the chapter examines the perceptions that state drinking water administrators have about implementing SDWA and the nature of federal–state working relationships. Finally, the chapter offers an assessment and conclusions about both federal–state relationships and the future of SDWA.

Key Elements of the Safe Drinking Water Act

SDWA, enacted in 1974, forever changed federal involvement in providing safe drinking water supplies to the public.[1] Federal regulation of drinking water began when the U.S. Public Health Service first established standards for the bacteriological quality of drinking water in 1914.[2] These standards, however, applied only to drinking water on interstate carriers, such as ships or trains, and then only to contaminants capable of causing contagious disease. The Public Health Service expanded these standards three times during the next fifty years. By 1962, the Public Health Service regulated twenty-eight contaminants, and all states had adopted these standards as requirements or guidelines for local public water supply systems.

However, the inadequacy of this arrangement soon became apparent. In 1969, the Public Health Service conducted a Community Water Supply Survey that showed only 60 percent of public water systems surveyed met the standards. Less than half of the systems had adequate disinfection, clarification, and pressure in the distribution system to provide proper treatment. A study four years later detected thirty-six chemicals in treated water taken from treatment plants in Louisiana, showing that chemical, as well as biological, contaminants threatened drinking water supplies.[3] In the early 1970s, EPA (which assumed responsibility for the federal role in drinking water after its creation in 1970) conducted evaluations of public water supply systems and identified shortcomings in state drinking water programs. These studies helped to focus congressional attention on the need for a stronger national regulatory role in drinking water protection and resulted in the passage of SDWA.[4]

After SDWA's passage, the federal role became one of overseer and standard setter. Not unlike other major environmental laws, SDWA required EPA to set national standards that protect human health and then required public water suppliers to meet those standards. The Public Water Supply Supervision program established under SDWA became the base regulatory effort protecting the nation's water supplies.

Unlike the Asbestos Hazard and Emergency Response Act, which offers states the opportunity to seek waivers for programmatic responsibility for asbestos but does not delegate primary enforcement to the states, or the Indoor Radon Abatement Act, which is a nonregulatory program providing radon grants to states, SDWA is a highly regulatory law that depends upon delegating programmatic and enforcement authority to states. Like the Clean Water Act or the Clean Air Act, SDWA is implemented with a delegated program. States may seek primacy to operate the safe drinking water program, including the inspection and enforcement components. Primacy states are required to have programs that include statutory and regulatory enforcement authority ade-

Table 5.1. Public Water Systems by Type and Size, 2002

Type	No. of People Served	No. of Systems
Community	253 million	53,694
Nontransient noncommunity	7 million	20,221
Transient noncommunity	13 million	91,325
Total	273 million	165,240

Source: U.S. Environmental Protection Agency, Office of Enforcement and Compliance Assurance, Providing Safe Drinking Water in America: 2000 National Public Water Systems Compliance Report, EPA-305-R-02-001 (Washington, D.C.: U.S. Environmental Protection Agency, 2002), 3.

quate to compel compliance with national primary drinking water regulations; a system for conducting inspections of public water supply systems, called sanitary surveys; a process to certify laboratories that test for contaminants; and, provisions for other management and oversight activities.[5] SDWA authorizes EPA to pay up to 75 percent of the costs of administering the drinking water program to primacy states. However, the actual EPA contribution in the 1980s and 1990s was closer to 35 percent of the state's total program costs, because federal dollars were insufficient to cover 75 percent of program costs.[6] As of 2000, all states except Wyoming had primacy for managing their drinking water programs.[7]

Public Water Supply Systems

Public water supply (PWS) systems provide drinking water to at least fifteen service connections (e.g., households, businesses, and schools) or regularly serve at least twenty-five people for at least sixty days a year.[8] There are three types of systems: community, nontransient noncommunity, and transient noncommunity systems. Table 5.1 shows the distribution of types of PWSs. As is shown in the table, of the 273 million consumers of public water supplies, all but 20 million use community water systems.[9]

Nontransient noncommunity water systems include schools, factories, and other large facilities that provide drinking water to their students or employees from their own water supplies. Historically, these systems were required to meet only those standards designed to prevent short-term health problems, such as standards for bacteria, nitrates, and turbidity.[10] Since the 1986 amendments were made to SDWA, however, these systems have had to meet many of the same standards as community systems. Transient noncommunity systems serve transitory customers in areas such as campgrounds, gas stations, or highway rest stops, using their own water sources. These systems are required to meet only those standards designed to prevent short-term, or acute, health effects, primarily bacterial contaminants (i.e., total coliform content).

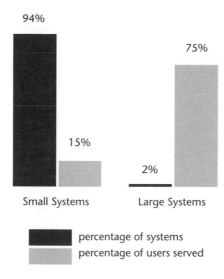

Figure 5.1.   Small and Large Public Water Supply Systems (percentage of systems and users served)

Source: U.S. Environmental Protection Agency, Office of Enforcement and Compliance Assurance, *Providing Safe Drinking Water in America: 2000 National Public Water Systems Compliance Report*, EPA-305-R-02-001 (Washington, D.C.: U.S. Environmental Protection Agency, 2002), 3.

Another way to look at PWS systems is to consider the vast differences in size, as shown in figure 5.1. Ninety-four percent of America's PWS systems are small, serving fewer than 3,300 users. Though representing the vast majority of all systems, these 156,120 systems provide service to just 15 percent of all users. In contrast, only 2 percent, or 3,812, of PWS systems serve more than 10,000 users. Yet that represents 75 percent of all users.[11] (Medium-sized PWS systems serve the remaining 10 percent of the population.) The diversity of the target group has staggering implications for implementing the law. Small systems lack technical capacity and resources to comply. Nevertheless, comply they must. With few exceptions, regardless of their size, the primary regulatory task for these public water suppliers under SDWA is to control contaminants in drinking water.

Not surprisingly, small systems are the ones most likely to violate regulatory requirements. According to data from the Safe Drinking Water Information System, 42,000 health-based or significant monitoring violations of SDWA occurred in 2000.[12] For every 1 million customers of community PWS systems serving 500 or fewer people, there were approximately 800 health-based and 7,164 total violations. In contrast, large systems had only 2 health-based and 10 total violations per million users.[13] To look at it another way,

95 percent of the 15,434 PWS systems designated as significant noncompliers by EPA in 2000 served fewer than 3,300 users.

Primacy states and EPA employ a variety of techniques to foster compliance with SDWA. Though the law provides for civil and criminal penalties, rarely do primacy states move to formal sanctions. Usually, a series of warning letters, visits, or telephone calls is enough to remind the drinking water supplier of regulatory obligations. It is easy to understand why. Small PWS systems operate with miniscule budgets that could not bear the added expense of fines or sanctions. A study by EPA found that the median total water revenue collected in PWS systems serving 25 to 100 people was zero, and that revenues for small systems (those serving fewer than 3,300 users) were low.[14] In 2000, states issued 1,266 formal enforcement actions against the 42,000 significant violations; only 44 were referred to the state attorneys general for civil prosecution. EPA issued 1,921 formal enforcement actions, 3 of those required penalties.[15]

To establish regulatory obligations, EPA must identify contaminants, determine the public health risk they pose, and then establish acceptable standards for the levels at which they may be present in public water supplies. The next section briefly describes the process of setting drinking water standards.

Setting National Drinking Water Standards

Drinking water standards are regulations that EPA sets to control the level of contaminants in drinking water supplies.[16] EPA first identifies a contaminant that is present or may be present in drinking water and then conducts a risk assessment to determine whether to regulate the contaminant, and what levels represent acceptable risk. A contaminant is defined by SDWA as "any physical, chemical, biological, or radiological substance or matter in water."[17] Before 1986, SDWA required EPA to propose and then promulgate a recommended maximum contaminant level (RMCL).[18] The RCML was then used as the basis for setting the maximum contaminant level (MCL).

As part of the 1986 amendments to SDWA, Congress removed the RCML term and replaced it with the maximum contaminant level goal (MCLG), which is a nonenforceable public health goal "set at the level at which no known or anticipated adverse effects on the health of persons occur and which allow[s] an adequate margin of safety."[19] Establishing MCLGs involve animal toxicity and epidemiology studies and other exposure data to determine concentration thresholds for particular hazardous and toxic substances. EPA, however, assumes no safe level of exposure for carcinogens. Therefore, the agency sets MCLGs of zero for cancer-causing contaminants.[20]

After the risk assessment determines the proposed MCLG, EPA sets National Primary Drinking Water Regulations (NPDWR, or primary standards), and secondary standards for drinking water. Secondary standards are guidelines for contaminants that may cause cosmetic effects (e.g., skin or tooth discoloration) or that affect aesthetic qualities of drinking water (e.g., taste, odor, or color). These guidelines are not enforceable by EPA.

Primary standards are established either as MCLs for individual contaminants or as general requirements for treatment techniques. An MCL is set as close to the MCLG as "feasible."[21] The concept of feasibility allows EPA to consider technological limitations and costs of treatment, recognizing the difficulty of achieving in practice the MCLG, especially because many of these goals are set at zero. The MCL frequently translates into requiring the use of the best available technology. Once set, MCLs are enforceable standards that water supply systems must meet. When the agency cannot issue MCLs, Congress authorized the EPA administrator to promulgate an NPDWR that requires the use of a treatment technology (e.g., the use of granular activated carbon filters) in lieu of establishing an MCL. Primary standards go into effect three years after being finalized.[22]

After determining an MCL or treatment technique, EPA must complete an economic analysis to determine whether the benefits of that standard justify the costs associated with implementing it. As one might imagine, each point in the process (identifying a contaminant, choosing which contaminants to regulate first, setting the MCL, and conducting the cost–benefit analysis) is highly controversial. In the first twelve years of the law, EPA struggled to set MCLs. Congressional frustration at the slow pace of standard setting prompted the 1986 amendments.

Amendments of 1986 and 1996 to the Safe Drinking Water Act

SDWA has been amended ten times, but the two most significant groups of amendments were passed in 1986 and in 1996.[23] The 1986 amendments sharply reduced EPA's discretion in both choosing contaminants to regulate and in the pace at which primary standards are set. The 1996 amendments changed yet again the congressional approach to achieving safe drinking water goals. Table 5.2 highlights some of the provisions of each group of amendments.

According to one longtime EPA drinking water official, the 1986 amendments caught the agency off guard because the amendments made the agency's "wish list" of contaminants to regulate a "to-do" list. Before 1986, EPA had issued interim primary drinking water regulations for only twenty-three contaminants, though it had attempted to set standards for many others.[24] Section 1412 of the 1986 amendments took EPA's wish list of eighty-three contaminants and required EPA to establish standards by June 1989.

Table 5.2. Major Provisions of the 1986 and 1996 Amendments to SDWA

1986 Amendments	1996 Amendments
• Required EPA to set MCLGs and MCLs for 83 named contaminants	• Required EPA to conduct a cost–benefit analysis for every new standard
• Required EPA to establish regulations beyond the 83 specified contaminants, and to regulate 25 additional contaminants every three years	• Removed the 1986 requirement to regulate 25 contaminants every three years
	• Required the EPA to publish a list of high-priority contaminants based upon a risk-assessment process
• Required disinfecting of all public water supplies	• Created a Drinking Water State Revolving Fund
• Required additional programs to protect groundwater and created the Wellhead Protection Program	• Required states to conduct source water assessments to determine susceptibility of drinking water to contamination
• Required EPA to implement a new ban on lead-based solder, pipe, and flux in distribution systems	• Greatly expanded public notification provisions through Consumer Confidence Reports, Annual Compliance Reports, and a publicly accessible database

Note: EPA = U.S. Environmental Protection Agency; MCLGs = maximum contaminant level goals; MCLs = maximum contaminant levels; SDWA = Safe Drinking Water Act.
Source: U.S. Environmental Protection Agency, Office of Water, *25 Years of the Safe Drinking Water Act: History and Trends*, EPA-816-R-99-007 (Washington, D.C.: U.S. Environmental Protection Agency, 1999), 7–13.

Congress specifically listed the contaminants in statutory language, allowing EPA the ability to substitute only seven contaminants.[25] The list of eighty-three included twenty-two of the twenty-three contaminants currently regulated. However, that meant MCLGs and national primary drinking water regulations had to be set for sixty-one new contaminants in the span of three short years.

EPA did make remarkable progress. By 1992, the agency had issued regulations for seventy-six of the eighty-three contaminants. (Arsenic, radium, radon, two classes of radionuclides, and sulfate remained.)[26] The seventy-six contaminants are represented by four rule categories: the Total Coliform Rule, the Surface Water Treatment Rule, the Chemical Rules, and the Lead and Copper Rule. EPA set an MCL and MCLG of zero for total coliform content. Coliforms are a group of bacteria that when found in drinking water may indicate the presence of pathogens. The Surface Water Treatment Rule seeks to reduce the occurrence of unsafe levels of disease causing microbes such as *Legionella* bacteria and the protozoan *Giardia lamblia*. Surface water is especially susceptible to microbial contamination from sewage treatment plant discharges and polluted runoff from farms. EPA set the MCLG for *Legionella* and

Giardia lamblia at zero, and required all surface water systems to filter and disinfect their water to provide a minimum of 99.9 percent combined removal and inactivation of microbes.

Even more overwhelming than the list of eighty-three was the newly created timetable for setting drinking water standards. Section 1412 directed the EPA administrator to publish a list of contaminants that may require regulation every three years, called the Drinking Water Priority List. EPA published the first list in the *Federal Register* in 1988. To ensure the continued adoption of drinking water standards, the 1986 amendments required EPA to propose regulations for not less than twenty-five of these contaminants every three years, starting in January 1991.[27]

In addition to dramatically altering the SDWA standard-setting process, the 1986 amendments also established requirements for other types of treatment, such as disinfection and filtration, and required public water systems to monitor for unregulated contaminants. The amendments further sought to protect drinking water taken from groundwater supplies by establishing the wellhead protection program and requiring EPA to promulgate monitoring regulations for hazardous waste underground injection operations.

The new implementation landscape for SDWA after the 1986 amendments was challenging, to say the least. Before the amendments, the agency had to identify contaminants and proposed health-based standards—but could make decisions about which contaminants to regulate and how quickly to set the standards. Perhaps most troubling was the congressional direction that EPA regulate twenty-five contaminants every three years, a grueling pace that soon proved unworkable. Testimony from Robert Perciasepe, a former EPA assistant administrator, that the 1986 amendments created a "regulatory treadmill [that] dilutes limited resources on lower priority contaminants" helped Congress recognize the Herculean task it had asked EPA to perform. It changed the law in 1996.

The 1996 amendments replaced the 1986 requirement to regulate twenty-five contaminants with a new selection process that allowed EPA to identify contaminants that warrant regulation based upon risk, as was discussed in the previous section. Congress still, however, held EPA to a standard-setting schedule. It required EPA to publish, by February 1998, a list of high-priority contaminants not currently regulated and then to determine through its standard-setting process whether to regulate at least five of the contaminants on the list. Beginning in 2001, and every five years thereafter, EPA would review its determinations about the list of candidate contaminants for regulation.[28]

It is important to note that Congress required EPA to complete the development of regulations that were in process. Specifically, that meant finalizing standards for disinfection by-products and that a new radon and updated arsenic standards would have to be issued.[29] In 1998, EPA issued its first new drinking water standards in six years, the Interim Enhanced Surface Water Treatment Rule and the Disinfection By-Products Stage 1 Rule.[30]

Arsenic: A Case Study of the Politics of SDWA

On January 22, 2001, EPA adopted a new standard for arsenic in drinking water at 10 parts per billion (ppb), replacing the old standard of 50 ppb. The rule became effective on February 22, 2002, and systems must comply by January 23, 2006. Though perhaps not as contentious as the radon rule described in chapter 4, the arsenic rule has led to an intense political battle, prompting nothing less than a constitutional challenge to SDWA by a Western state. A quick review of the arsenic rule reveals all the intersections between national and state political actors, strained federal–state relationships, and legislative and executive branch posturing. It also reveals the challenge of implementing a one-size-fits-all regulatory standard.

Though many people associate arsenic with industrial processes, it is a naturally occurring, widely distributed element in the Earth's crust. Western states have the highest levels of naturally occurring arsenic, especially in small water systems that rely on groundwater. EPA adopted the 50 ppb standard for arsenic in 1975, based upon a standard set by the Public Health Service in 1942.[31] Congress, however, considering the 50 ppb outdated and not protective of human health, directed EPA in its 1996 SDWA amendments to propose a new standard for arsenic by January 2000, with a final standard to be issued by 2001. Congress also directed EPA, in cooperation with the National Academy of Sciences, to study arsenic's health effects, thereby reducing uncertainty about risks associated with low levels of arsenic exposure.

In 1999, the National Academy of Sciences concluded that the 50 ppb standard represented an unacceptable health risk, but it did not specify what level would be safe. In June 2000, EPA proposed a standard of 5 ppb, though it asked for public comment on several alternatives: 20, 10, and 3 ppb. In January 2001, during the final days of Bill Clinton's administration, and after months of regulatory development and debate, EPA proposed a standard of 10 ppb. Three months later, George W. Bush's administration signaled its willingness to depart from the environmental policies of the previous administration. The new EPA administrator, Christine Whitman, withdrew the new arsenic standard, saying that it was not supported by the best available science.[32]

Meanwhile, political forces were gathering around the arsenic standard. PWS systems and some states argued that the costs of compliance with the 10 ppb standard far outweighed any potential health risk. The states of Nebraska and New Mexico, the cities of El Paso and Albuquerque, the National

Mining Association and the Western Coalition of Arid States together sued EPA in March 2001, but they agreed to stay their lawsuit pending the outcome of health and cost reviews. At the same time, the Natural Resources Defense Council argued that 3 ppb instead of 10 ppb represented an appropriate health-based standard for arsenic. In June 2001, the council filed a lawsuit arguing that EPA had violated the SDWA requirement to set the arsenic standard. With lawsuits pending on both sides, Congress took matters into its collective hands. Both the House of Representatives and the Senate approved arsenic amendments to the appropriations bill. The House prohibited EPA from using funds to delay the rule or to issue a rule above 10 ppb.[33] In a dramatic reversal in October 2001, EPA announced that it would adopt the 10 ppb standard originally set by the Clinton administration.

Facing a firm 2006 deadline for implementing the arsenic standard, Nebraska attorney general Jon Bruning, the city of Alliance, Nebraska, and the Competitive Enterprise Institute (which represents five water utilities) have filed a legal brief challenging EPA on constitutional grounds. They argue that the SDWA unconstitutionally interferes with states' rights and that Congress does not have authority to regulate a local enterprise, such as the intrastate delivery of drinking water.[34] The case was heard by the U.S. Court of Appeals for the District of Columbia Circuit on April 15, 2003.

The 1996 SDWA amendments also address the costs associated with complying with drinking water standards by establishing a new multiyear Drinking Water State Revolving Fund (DWSRF). Congress authorized $9.6 billion to establish the DWSRF program. Under DWSRF, which operates like the revolving fund program authorized under the Clean Water Act, EPA provides grants to states, which in turn identify investment priorities for infrastructure improvements among public water suppliers and manage the loan program. Loan repayments replenish the fund, and monies are then made available to other public water suppliers.[35] By 1998, every state had a DWSRF program approved by EPA and had received a first commitment for capitalization grants. (Congress appropriated $2.8 billion for the DWSRF through fiscal 1999.)[36]

Congress strengthened public notification requirements. Though the original SDWA required water system operators to notify customers when they violated drinking water standards, many operators ignored or did not fully address the notification requirement.[37] Believing that an informed public was a powerful enforcement tool, Congress required PWS systems to provide customers with an annual Consumer Confidence Report on delivered water quality. EPA issued its final Consumer Confidence Report Rule in 1998. The first reports were due in October 1999. As is illustrated in the public service announcement shown in figure 5.2, EPA was eager to tell the public that these reports were available. Most community PWS systems complied with the

Now It Comes With A List Of Ingredients.

A short new report from your water supplier will tell you what's in your tap water. Look for your report and read it. When it comes to your drinking water, the most important ingredient is you.

⊕EPA **Drinking Water. Know What's In It For You.**
Call your water supplier or the Safe Drinking Water Hotline at 1-800-426-4791. Or visit www.epa.gov/safewater/

Figure 5.2.   EPA Advertisement for Consumer Confidence Reports

Source: U.S. Environmental Protection Agency.

right-to-know requirement. By 2000, 84 percent of community water systems distributed reports. However, 8,470 systems failed to produce Consumer Confidence Reports.[38]

A final element of the 1996 SDWA amendments worth noting is the provision for protecting source water. Congress recognized that it is often less expensive and more environmentally sustainable to prevent pollution from getting into drinking water supplies than it is to remove contaminants through treatment. This is especially true for groundwater, which is difficult to clean up once contamination occurs. Because approximately 80 percent of community water systems draw their supplies from underground sources, protecting source water is critical to maintaining safe drinking water.[39] EPA has approved Source Water Assessment Programs for all states. A state program includes delineating the source water protection area, inventorying all contaminant sources, determining the susceptibility of the public water supply to contamination, and releasing the results of the assessments to the public. Assessments were due by May 2003.

Implementation Challenges and the Conceptual Framework

As the brief overview of its provisions indicates, SDWA is a complex law presenting numerous implementation challenges. Within the framework developed in chapter 2, several variables present barriers to its implementation.

Statutory Language

Clearly, statutory language has complicated SDWA's progress. At the national level, the process of developing drinking water standards proved cumbersome and time consuming for EPA. As was mentioned above, frustration with EPA's regulatory pace prompted Congress to spur the agency into action by first creating a list of contaminants to be regulated (the list of eighty-three) and then requiring it to set twenty-five new standards every three years. Though Congress replaced the 1986 timetable, it still mandated that EPA promulgate standards for specific contaminants.

An additional problem related to the statutory and legal context is that all drinking water contaminants are treated as though they are equally dangerous. In other words, with few exceptions, PWS systems must monitor and control for contaminants in drinking water regardless of relative risk. By EPA's own admission, the need for public water suppliers to comply with all of the standards diverts federal, state, and local resources away from focusing on contaminants that may pose the greatest risk.[40]

One example of the failure to address the highest priority risks has been EPA's focus on toxic substances rather than on microbiological contaminants, such as *cryptosporidium*. In 1992, EPA estimated that roughly 79 percent of all MCL violations were violations of microbiological contaminant standards, a figure that has not changed much in the intervening years.[41] In its most recent compliance report, EPA estimated that 70 percent, or 13,645, of violations were for the Total Coliform Rule.[42] EPA's focus on chemical rather than biological contaminants became painfully clear in 1993, when 403,000 people became ill due to a *cryptosporidium* outbreak in Milwaukee. The microbe made it through the city's water filtration system into the water system, even though the city was in compliance with drinking water standards. Eventually, *cryptosporidium* was a factor in the deaths of more than 100 people.[43] This was the largest incident of illness and fatalities due to drinking water contaminants in the United States.

Litigation and Politics around Standards

Setting standards for drinking water contaminants embroils EPA in wide-ranging political and legal battles. As is illustrated by the arsenic example, public water suppliers and state and trade or professional associations are willing to sue EPA, in the hope that courts will be sympathetic. The most recent attempt was a lawsuit brought by several PWS systems, the National Mining Association, and the Nuclear Energy Institute challenging the radionuclides standard (*City of Waukesha v. EPA*). The petitioners argued that EPA had not met its requirement under the 1996 SDWA amendments to employ sound science and conduct a cost–benefit analysis in setting the standard. The D.C. Circuit Court of Appeals disagreed and upheld EPA standards for uranium, radium-226, radium-228, and certain beta/photon emitters in its decision on February 25, 2003.[44]

Nature of the Problem: Costs and Small Systems

Although the pace of standard setting may be troublesome to congressional representatives and to environmental and public health groups, the cost of operating a monitoring and treatment program for contaminants has been overwhelming, especially for small PWS systems. The cost of compliance for small systems (which represent nearly 90 percent of community water suppliers) has been widely acknowledged, including in several reports by the U.S. General Accounting Office (GAO) and EPA in the 1990s.[45] In the early 1990s, EPA estimated that the annual cost of compliance would rise to $1.4 billion by 1995 and would likely double with the addition of new drinking water standards and the upcoming disinfectants and disinfection by-products rule.[46] The costs of complying with SDWA regulations were a central concern of local governments in calling for relief from unfunded mandates, as was discussed in chapter 1.

Recent estimates of the costs of compliance range in the billions of dollars. Political debates intensify as infrastructure needs become more evident. The 1996 SDWA amendments required EPA to determine the infrastructure needs of PWS systems. In its first Drinking Water Infrastructure Needs Survey, published in 1997, EPA estimated that total infrastructure need nationwide for the

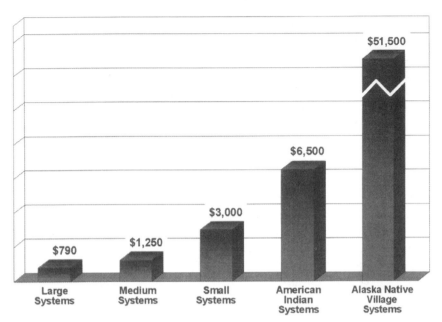

Figure 5.3.   Average Twenty-Year Cost per Household of Safe Drinking Water
(in 1999 dollars)

Note: Does not include costs associated with proposed and recently promulgated Safe Drinking
Water Act regulations.

Source: U.S. Environmental Protection Agency, Office of Water, *Drinking Water Infrastructure
Needs Survey: Second Report to Congress*, EPA 816-R-01-004 (Washington, D.C.: U.S. Environmental Protection Agency, 2001), 41.

next twenty years was $138 billion, with nearly $77 billion needed immediately to protect public health and maintain existing distribution and treatment systems."[47] Four years later, the news was the same. EPA projected the need at more than $150 billion, with $102 billion needed now.[48] Most of the costs are for replacing aging infrastructure such as pipes, many of which are more than fifty years old. A total of $83 billion was projected to be needed for transmission and distribution projects. However, $31 billion, or 21 percent of this total need, was allotted to comply with SDWA regulatory requirements.[49]

The numbers are even more disturbing when viewed from the lens of the PWS customer. As figure 5.3 illustrates, the cost per household of safe drinking water is almost four times higher for small systems than for large systems. Small systems lack the economics of scale that allow large systems to spread the costs associated with infrastructure improvements or SDWA regulations among their many customers. Each household serviced by a small system could pay more than $3,000 in addition to its regular water bill, and EPA reports that as a conservative estimate because it does not include proposed or recently promulgated regulations.[50] Households within Alaskan native villages could face costs of more than $51,000.

One way for small PWS systems to comply is to restructure, such that groups of small systems share services or contract with private companies or large systems for services such as operation and maintenance, meter reading and billing, and sample collection and analysis. As part of its review, the Science Advisory Board recommended that a "greater consolidation of small systems should occur" whenever it is necessary to provide monies to upgrade the treatment systems.[51] EPA has also promoted restructuring through a brochure and manual on restructuring, but there are limits to how effective restructuring can be at reducing the costs of SDWA compliance.[52] Small PWS systems may not want to consolidate with other systems for political or logistical reasons. In some cases, restructuring may not be feasible due to the ownership or location of the water supplier.

For example, not all small PWS systems are public entities. Many are run by mobile home parks, investor-owned facilities, or homeowners' associations. Others serve small clusters of homes in rural areas or are suburban systems that lie within the standard metropolitan statistical areas defined by the U.S. Census Bureau. Indeed, a recent EPA study found that 60 percent of all small systems are privately owned.[53]

As the federal funding share of state drinking water programs continues to erode, some states may opt to return authority for the drinking water program to EPA. Connecticut and Massachusetts narrowly avoided returning the program after the funding for each state's share of the drinking water program was eliminated in its fiscal 1993 budget. Ultimately, these states and others may find the drinking water program on precarious budgetary ground.[54]

By EPA's own estimate, "no state, even after receiving a fee increase, has sufficient funding to meet all the requirements of the SDWA."[55] In 1992, the agency moved to allow states five additional years to comply with all aspects of the regulations. Meanwhile, many states have attempted to supplement federal funding with increased fees for water supply customers. However, between 1992 and 1994, only twenty-eight states successfully raised revenues within the state; twenty-one passed user fee increases, and seven made additional appropriations.[56]

Drinking Water Security

The September 11, 2001, terrorist attacks in New York and Washington, D.C., have influenced the implementation of SDWA. Securing the nation's drinking water supplies always posed a substantial challenge, but the attacks brought the challenge to the forefront of political debates about national security. Previous efforts recognized the need to protect water supplies but were limited in scope. In 1998, President Clinton issued Presidential Decision Directive 63 that designated EPA as the lead agency in ensuring that the nation's water supply was safe from attack. However, efforts in response to the directive focused on cyber security, not on physical or biological attacks.[57]

In the aftermath of September 11, Congress wanted a more aggressive approach to protecting water resources. The Public Health Security and Bioterrorism Preparedness and Response Act of 2002 (Public Law 107-188) requires community water systems that serve more than 3,300 people to review their vulnerability to terrorist attack or other acts intended to disrupt the drinking water supply. Congress provided EPA with $175 million in emergency supplemental appropriations for counterterrorism activities. EPA dedicated $89 million of that amount in an effort to reduce the vulnerability of PWS systems to terrorist attacks. Large PWSs could apply for grants up to $115,000 to develop a vulnerability assessment and emergency response plan. No grant monies were available in 2002 for PWSs serving fewer than 100,000 people.[58] Though the costs of complying with the new antiterrorism requirements are not as large as those of replacing infrastructure or meeting drinking water standards, this is one more responsibility that must be borne on the shoulders of PWS systems.

Intergovernmental Relationships

The problem of how small PWS systems can comply with new drinking water standards not only presents the political dimension of implementation but also illustrates intergovernmental tensions. Clearly, concern over the costs of compliance may increase the amount of animosity in relationships between federal, state, and local actors. Also troubling, however, is the tension in the federal–state relationships that occurs when states are criticized for failing to enforce the requirements of the safe drinking water program.

Several GAO studies have identified ongoing deficiencies in state programs. In a 1990 report, GAO noted that the six states it studied failed to take "timely and appropriate enforcement action against significant non-compliers."[59] A study by EPA found that 28 percent of all community water suppliers were in violation of SDWA.[60] State regulators, in turn, undertook formal enforcement action for less than 9 percent of these systems.[61] Troubling the issue of enforcement is fact that the majority of significant noncompliers tend to be small systems. State officials are reluctant to adopt strong compliance postures toward systems that lack the ability to add new treatment technologies or monitoring staff. Thus, not only were PWS systems failing to comply but states also were failing to report these violations to EPA or to take action to address the problem. In 1992, EPA initiated action to withdraw the primacy status of three states, Alaska, Maine, and Washington.[62] Although these states ultimately retained primacy, this action illustrates the tenuous nature of the federal–state relationship in the drinking water program.

Perceptions of State Drinking Water Officials

Although the previous discussion suggests a number of challenges confronting SDWA's implementation, it is also important to explore the perceptions of state drinking water administrators. In 1995, fifty-six surveys were mailed to state drinking water program directors. Forty-three were returned, for a response rate of 77 percent. In 2002, eighteen surveys were mailed to state drinking water administrators.[63] Eleven were returned, for a response rate of 61 percent. The small number of responses indicates caution in exploring opinions. Still, the opinions give insights into state drinking water programs. The following sections identify the range of perceptions among state officials regarding the safe drinking water program. Eight interviews were conducted in 2002; six were conducted in 1995.

As was described in the opening section of the chapter, forty-nine states have primacy for implementing SDWA. This federal–state arrangement provides states with funding, but it also comes with the responsibility for running all aspects of the drinking water program. State drinking water programs are much larger than the asbestos and radon programs discussed in chapters 3 and 4. All respondents to the 1995 and 2002 surveys report having at least sixteen full-time equivalent personnel in the drinking water program, and nearly all state officials have been involved with the program at the state level for more than five years.

Factors That Hinder Implementation

When asked about factors that constrain the implementation of their programs, directors of state drinking water programs identify several factors, some of which mirror observations discussed in the previous section. Seventy-three percent of state drinking water administrators believe that funding is inadequate to operate their programs (see table 5.3). Many administrators point to an insufficient flow of federal dollars to support the program. They also, however, identify state budgetary constraints, especially when state hiring freezes take effect. As one put it, "We can't do it all effectively, because of limited staffing. We have to prioritize resources for the greatest needs. We've come a

Table 5.3. Factors That Hinder the Implementation of SDWA, as Ranked by State Officials

Factor	Percentage identifying as an issue in 2002 (N = 11)
Insufficient resources	73
Difficult, cumbersome, or ineffective regulatory process	64
Challenge for public water suppliers to comply with regulations	54
State policymakers not interested in drinking water	45
Lack of agency or administrative support for program	36
Problems with data system or data management	27

Note: SDWA = Safe Drinking Water Act.

long way in implementing the 1996 [SDWA] amendments." Another observed, "No resources have been added at either the state or public water supply system level for this immense workload. Everyone has to absorb the new requirements along with their previous duties. We're getting by now, but the strain is starting to show."

State administrators also point to the nature of the standard-setting process as being an obstacle to running an effective drinking water program, with 64 percent describing it as overwhelming, difficult, inefficient, or cumbersome. One state official observed, "There are too many regulations, too fast, and without adequate assessment of risk." Another agreed: "We have an uphill battle persuading public water suppliers that all of the new regulations are needed." Another described the process this way: "There's a growing sentiment that the new regulations are like 'going after microbes with an elephant gun.' There are too many of them that simply don't make sense for small systems." One official put it this way: "The rule by rule approach EPA chooses to take in carrying out the provisions of the SDWA is the biggest constraint to implementation. The agency has no sense of priorities, no acknowledgment of resource limitations, and no acknowledgment of the cumulative impact these rules have on states or water systems."

An EPA official agreed: "The agency tends to look at each rule as unique and separate. They don't add the costs of the other rules to their analysis, even though most of the standards require new technologies. Moreover, EPA imposes a ruling, and states have a one-time opportunity to comment. The regulation becomes one more thing for states to do with little or no more money to do it."

More than half of state drinking water administrators believe that public water suppliers find it challenging to comply with the regulations. State administrators believe that many small public water suppliers lack the resources to mount the monitoring program and/or to update their facilities. Some drinking water program directors worry about the ability of small PWS systems to perform their obligations under SDWA, as illustrated by this comment:

> Monitoring for contaminants should be performed by the state regulatory agency (or our contractor) and not the water systems, so that we can truly determine the quality of the drinking water. Many systems do not perform monitoring as required due to the costs involved, therefore we know little about their current water quality. Additionally, some systems do not use appropriate sampling protocols, thus making results questionable. The reality is that opportunities for fraud are great with a self-monitoring program.

Thus, resources at both the local and the state levels appear to be limited, according to the respondents in this study. This perception has not changed in the past six years. Limited state resources hamper the ability of the state to conduct sanitary surveys; limited resources at the local level encourage noncompliance with monitoring requirements.

Table 5.4 presents the perceptions that state officials have about their drinking water programs. The table lists data from both study years. It is not surprising that no state administrator responding to the 2002 survey agrees that program funding is adequate (compared with 29 percent in 1995). Similarly, no administrator agrees that PWS systems are adequately funded.

Political support outside the agency is somewhat mixed. Though about half of the drinking water officials agree that state administrators support their program (65 percent in 1995; 45 percent in 2002), they are less likely to agree that drinking water is a top environmental priority in the state. One official noted that "support for the program is lacking from agency management, regulated suppliers, the state legislature and the general public. If there was an outbreak, that would all change—but as long as there's no perceived problem, the drinking water program is not valued." One state director commented that citizens assume that public drinking water supplies are safe and only pay attention to drinking water regulation after a highly publicized drinking water problem, such as the *cryptosporidium* scare in Milwaukee in 1993.

Several state officials noted the need to better coordinate implementing SDWA with the Clean Water Act. They fear that state environmental administrators are more attentive to Clean Water Act implementation, especially that of Total Maximum Daily Loads. These officials see missed opportunities for collaboration with staff working on watershed initiatives and their efforts to identify source water contaminants.

Despite these concerns, state administrators believe that the state drinking water program is effective (84 percent in 1995; 64 percent in 2002). They believe that the public is more protected from contaminants in drinking water

Table 5.4. Perceptions of State Drinking Water Administrators about Drinking Water Programs (percentage indicating that they strongly agree or agree), 1995 and 2002

Perception	1995 (N = 43)	2002 (N = 11)
Program is adequately funded	29	0
Public water systems are adequately funded	n.a.	0
Drinking water is a top environmental priority	n.a.	18
Drinking water in my state is secure from attacks	n.a.	28
Need a stronger state program	72	45
Administrators are supportive	65	45
Program is effective	84	64
Staff is adequately trained	70	73
Public is more protected from contaminants now	n.a.	73

Note: n.a. = not available.

now than six years ago (73 percent agree). They also agree that their personnel are adequately trained to run a drinking water program (70 percent in 1995; 73 percent in 2002).

Perceptions about Working Relationships

Many state drinking water officials perceive a maze of federal regulations, inflexible and complicated EPA policy, and inappropriate or even overwhelming compliance requirements. In 1995, only 12 percent of state drinking water directors believed that EPA drinking water program was effective (see table 5.5), compared with 84 percent who perceived the state program to be effective, as was shown in table 5.4. In part, officials link this to their perception that funding for the EPA drinking water program is inadequate. Only 12 percent of the 1995 and 27 percent of the 2002 respondents agree that their EPA regional office has enough money to run the drinking water program. In part, officials liken EPA's perceived ineffectiveness to a lack of appreciation for the "real world" of PWS systems.

No state official responding to the study or interview questions agrees that EPA understands the concerns of small public water suppliers. They express their frustration through comments such as "EPA now wants to protect everyone from everything, no matter what the cost is to public water systems; we have systems reverting to private ownership because they can't afford to meet the PWS requirements" and "They have a one-size-fits-all mentality for setting rules, and seemingly don't care what the effect is on small systems."

These comments are also suggestive of a common opinion of state program directors about EPA: "Constantly changing and excessively complicated fed-

Table 5.5. Perceptions of State Drinking Water Administrators about Working Relationships with EPA (percentage indicating that they strongly agree or agree), 1995 and 2002

Perception	1995 (N = 43)	2002 (N = 11)
I have a positive relationship with EPA regional staff	86	91
I have a positive relationship with EPA headquarters	30	45
EPA staff has a high degree of technical expertise	19	18
EPA regional program is adequately funded	12	27
Oversight is flexible	19	36
Regional and Headquarters officials view program similarly	0	0
EPA clearly communicates goals and requirements	21	18
EPA reporting requirements are appropriate	9	0
EPA regional officials evaluate program fairly	58	82
Without EPA, the state would not be as serious about program	30	18
EPA is concerned about drinking water contaminants	67	55
EPA understands the concerns of small public water suppliers	n.a.	0
EPA program is effective	12	n.a.

Note: EPA = U.S. Environmental Protection Agency; n.a. = not available.

eral regulations and a one-size-fits-all enforcement approach by the federal government ensure that we [the state agency] won't get to cleaner water. Moreover, this approach results in excessive costs for small [PWS] systems, often with no or little impact on public health risk." And: "New and changing requirements and priorities from EPA, some of which do not make a great deal of sense for our state, inhibit our ability to run an effective program."

State administrators are not likely to perceive EPA staff as having a high level of expertise (only 19 percent agreed in 1995, and 18 percent in 2002). As one state director commented, "EPA should provide more technical assistance to state programs such as having staff epidemiologists and other experts we can turn to for help and advice. In our [EPA] region, they call on us for help in understanding their own regulations." Another put it more sharply when asked what one thing she would change about EPA's involvement in safe drinking water: "Have technically competent EPA staff at regional and headquarters levels. The lack of this competence is appalling and results in bad rule making and interpretation of rules, and expensive, yet ineffective requirements for PWS systems."

Perhaps most remarkable is the fact that no state drinking water director believes that the staff at EPA regional offices and the staff at EPA headquarters view the state programs in the same way. No official agreed that the regions and headquarters are on the same page in either 1995 or in 2002. Many state officials direct their frustration with the intergovernmental implementation process at actions that occur at EPA headquarters, as is illustrated by these comments: "EPA resources should be shifted from enforcement of regulations to research and development. EPA's role should focus on developing scientifically sound standards which the states enforce," and "EPA's responsibilities should be more focused on conducting necessary scientific research to establish appropriate MCLs and associated treatment technologies and states should be responsible for implementation of program. Why spend so much [federal] money on enforcement when the EPA can't set reasonable standards?"

Another state director suggested that "those [EPA staff] in Washington, D.C., writing the rules should have field experience so they would understand what it takes to implement the rules and how those rules impact water suppliers, especially the small water suppliers." Another commented about the role orientation of EPA headquarters staff: "EPA is legalistic and this must be changed. EPA should be a service to states, not the states a service to EPA. Regional EPA offices should have more autonomy from EPA headquarters because they have a better idea of what is going on."

The data in table 5.5 support this dichotomy in state perceptions of EPA regional and headquarters staff in another way. Every respondent in both study years perceives a better working relationship with their EPA regional contact than with EPA headquarters staff. State officials overwhelmingly agree that their relationship with EPA regional staff is positive (86 percent in 1995; 91 percent in 2002). However, many fewer state officials would agree that working relationships with EPA headquarters are positive (30 percent in 1995; 45 percent in 2002). Certainly, proximity to and frequent interaction with EPA regional contacts is a major reason why state officials perceive more positive relationships with EPA regional offices than EPA headquarters. However, state officials also perceive EPA headquarters as having a different mindset, as is evident in this comment: "EPA headquarters is too large and too detached from implementation issues, specifically the rule drafters." State officials also feel that they have little significant input into the rule-making process. As one state director noted, "EPA should include states right from the very beginning on rule development. States can provide better input on what the implementation problems will be because we live it every day. Right now, though, it seems like they ignore us."

EPA has some room to improve the oversight activities associated with SDWA's implementation, from the perspective of several state officials. Most notably, state directors express concern with unreasonable and inconsistent reporting requirements, as is shown in table 5.5. Only 9 percent of state directors agreed in 1995 that their reporting requirements were reasonable—and no respondent agreed that reporting requirements were reasonable in 2002. Only 19 percent agreed that they had sufficient oversight flexibility to run the state program in 1995, though 36 agreed in 2002. "EPA should butt out and leave implementation to the states! They should throw up fewer barriers and be an assistance to states rather than a hindrance." Finally, fewer than one in five state administrators in either study agrees that EPA clearly communicates program goals and requirements. A regional EPA official compared the EPA guidance document for complying with the arsenic standard to a Sears catalog in size, wondering "what small system [operator] is going to have time to read that?"

Some of the earlier frustrations of the state staffs with EPA could more appropriately have been directed toward Congress and the congressional instructions given to the agency in the 1986 amendments to SDWA. As was discussed earlier in the chapter, EPA was under both congressional directive and court order to promulgate new primary standards for eighty-three different contaminants and to add new standards every three years. This directive is far more conducive to a "command-and-control" regulatory style than to a cooperative approach geared toward sound science and regulatory negotiations. Though some state officials seem to believe that the standard-setting process was something that could be controlled by EPA, others noted the effect of the 1986 amendments: "Setting standards every three years seems to me to be a ludicrous policy. Why doesn't Congress acknowledge that one public water supply system may have a unique, but terribly important, contaminant that needs to be addressed from a public health point of view? We'd go farther [in protecting the public] with less money."

In sum, officials of state drinking water programs overwhelmingly feel that their programs are effective and have improved in the past few years. When compared with other environmental program officials, they perceive higher amounts of state-level administrative and political support for maintaining their programs. The most challenging extrinsic factor for implementing their programs is limited funding, especially for small PWS systems.

Officials of state drinking water programs agree that EPA regional drinking water staffs are supportive of state programs and that they enjoy positive federal–state working relationships. What concerns the state officials as they implement their programs is the EPA staff's lack of technical expertise, cumbersome and unnecessary reporting requirements, and a lack of communication with EPA headquarters staff. They also share a common sentiment that EPA officials in Washington are less interested and aware of the state's implementation obstacles and the challenges faced by PWS systems.

Many state officials perceive EPA headquarters staff as being overly "top-down" and less interested in helping states run their programs than in developing ill-conceived and inflexible program requirements. Though state directors agree that they have good working relationships with the EPA regional staffs, they are less convinced that drinking water personnel at EPA headquarters are interested in helping them run a good state program that results in protecting the public from contaminants in drinking water.

EPA Responses

EPA was not insensitive to the criticisms levied against the drinking water program in the mid-1990s. On March 29, 1995, EPA administrator Carol Browner released the agency's "white paper" on the drinking water program, *Strengthening the Safety of Our Drinking Water: A Report on Progress and Challenges and An Agenda for Action.*[64] The report highlighted five action items for EPA: providing more public information about drinking water issues; focusing on the most serious health risks; providing technical assistance to protect source water and help small PWS systems; reinventing federal–state partnerships to improve drinking water safety; and investing in community drinking water facilities to protect human health. The report represented EPA's response to President Clinton's environmental reinvention initiative, which was issued on March 16, 1995.[65]

The initiative, part of the Clinton administration's broader governmental reform effort under the auspices of the National Performance Review, identified twenty-five high-priority actions for the agency. Among them was a directive for EPA to cut costs and increase flexibility for states and water suppliers by targeting regulations on substantial health risks, seeking a delay for court-ordered schedules for drinking water, and reducing monitoring burdens for chemical contaminants.[66]

The combined impetus of the EPA drinking water report and the president's initiative prompted the EPA Office of Ground Water and Drinking Water to undertake a reassessment of the drinking water program and create a new approach toward federal–state relationships. This effort culminated in the *National Drinking Water Program Redirection Strategy*, which was published in 1996.[67] The strategy has four principles: engage in sound science with adequate data in determining the need for regulation and other agency actions; establish risk-based priorities for setting high-quality standards; establish strong flexible partnerships with state and local governments for implementation; and have community-based source water protection.

As is shown in table 5.6, the transformation of the drinking water program appears headed in the right direction, at least when compared with the im-

Table 5.6. Transformation of the Drinking Water Program Proposed by the EPA Office of Ground Water and Drinking Water

Old Approach	New Approach
Many new regulations	Fewer new regulations (priorities based on risk)
Measure activities	Measure environmental results
Source water protection and public water supply programs separate	Integrate prevention and implementation
Extensive oversight of regional/state programs	Empowerment/state partnerships
Rely on mandates	Balance mandates and voluntary approaches
"Do It" ourselves	Leverage stakeholders and energize communities
Intermittent coordination with stakeholders	Early, comprehensive stakeholder involvement
Detailed program reporting	Reporting simplified
Technical jargon	Plain English

Note: EPA = U.S. Environmental Protection Agency.
Source: U.S. Environmental Protection Agency, Office of Water, National Drinking Water Program Redirection Strategy, EPA-810-R-96-003 (Washington, D.C.: U.S. Environmental Protection Agency, 1996), 14.

plementation challenges perceived by most state drinking water program directors. For example, the "new" oversight approach taken by EPA will measure environmental results rather than state activities and seek to empower state drinking water programs. Moreover, the strategy's principle to engage in sound science and set regulations based on the highest priority reflects the sentiments of the 1996 amendments to SDWA. The provisions to increase flexibility for states, simplify reporting requirements, and employ greater use of partners are also very similar to the goals of the National Environmental Performance Partnership System discussed in chapter 1. However, from comments of both state and EPA drinking water officials, this transformation is not complete.

Conclusions about the Safe Drinking Water Program

When the intergovernmental safe drinking water program is considered within the policy implementation framework (see figure 2.1), extrinsic and intrinsic factors seem to influence its implementation. Most influential are the statutory requirements and the fiscal challenges faced by small PWS systems.

SDWA requires EPA to set standards protective of human health. When EPA fails to set such standards, environmental groups sue EPA to perform a nondiscretionary duty. Once a standard is proposed, political forces prepare for battle over the final standard, as is suggested by the arsenic example. As one EPA official noted, "We get to be the good guys and the bad guys, all at the same time."

Moreover, statutory shifts, first to the 1986 SDWA amendments and then to the 1996 amendments, have certainly changed the way the law is implemented. Congress abandoned its highly prescriptive approach to standard setting in the 1986 amendments when it drafted the 1996 amendments. However, Congress left intact its expectation that EPA would continue to regulate drinking water contaminants.

The intrinsic factors that help explain implementation include mixed levels of political support for drinking water programs and a state agency culture with high levels of empathy for community water systems. Their empathy with small suppliers makes state officials reluctant to cite monitoring violations. Agency capacity, as viewed by survey respondents, is sufficient, but the capacity of the target group (public water suppliers) to comply with regulatory requirements varies, largely depending on the size of the system. The high costs of complying with unnecessary monitoring and treatment requirements prompt local politicians to voice their opposition to fully implementing SDWA. And state drinking water officials see missed opportunities to work with EPA staff to implement the Clean Water Act, especially to protect source water.

When the federal–state working relationship typology is considered, the relationship in the drinking water program seems to fall in the "coming apart and contentious" category, though the relationship has somewhat improved from six years ago. Working relationships between EPA regional and state staffs are positive, but other measures of the federal–state relationship are troubling.

Perhaps most telling is the fact that the state officials do not perceive EPA as fully understanding public water suppliers, despite the agency's concerted effort to reach out to stakeholders. From the viewpoint of state drinking water staff, role orientations of EPA headquarters staff may hinder the implementation of state programs. They view EPA headquarters officials as detached from the daily business of protecting public water supplies. Efforts to redirect the drinking water program at EPA and continued scrutiny by GAO and other agencies seem to be moving the program in the right direction—albeit slowly. These perceptions suggest that though EPA as the federal oversight agency is highly involved in the drinking water program, the nature of that involvement could still be improved (e.g., by providing more technical support).

With every glass of water, one should recall the intricate implementation story that has brought safe water to the taps of most Americans since the first

Safe Drinking Water Act in 1974. Keeping potable water supplies involves more than 160,000 water systems and governments at all levels. Each new national drinking water standard brings the promise of litigation and intergovernmental acrimony. Drinking water infrastructure needs in the future, coupled with new drinking water standards, guarantee that this will be a very interesting story for a long time to come.

Notes

1. Public Law 93-523, December 16, 1974.

2. U.S. Environmental Protection Agency, Office of Water, *Twenty-Five Years of the Safe Drinking Water Act: History and Trends*, EPA-816-R-99-007 (Washington, D.C: U.S. Environmental Protection Agency, 1999).

3. Office of Water, *Twenty-Five Years of the Safe Drinking Water Act*, 2.

4. U.S. Environmental Protection Agency, Office of Water, *Technical and Economic Capacity of States and Public Water Systems to Implement Drinking Water Regulations: Report to Congress*, EPA-810-R-93-001 (Washington, D.C.: U.S. Environmental Protection Agency, 1993), 3.

5. 63 *Federal Register* 23363 (April 28, 1998). A description of primacy requirements can also be found at www.epa.gov/ogwdw/pws/primacy.htm.

6. U.S. General Accounting Office, *Drinking Water Program: States Face Increased Difficulties in Meeting Basic Requirements*, GAO/RCED-93-144 (Washington, D.C.: U.S. General Accounting Office, 1993), 3.

7. U.S. Environmental Protection Agency, Office of Enforcement and Compliance Assurance, *Providing Safe Drinking Water in America: 2000 National Public Water Systems Compliance Report*, EPA-305-R-02-001 (Washington, D.C.: U.S. Environmental Protection Agency, 2002), 1.

8. SDWA, Sec. 1401(4), 42 USC Sec. 300f(4); Office of Water, *Twenty-Five Years of the Safe Drinking Water Act*, 3.

9. U.S. Environmental Protection Agency, Office of Enforcement and Compliance Assurance, *Providing Safe Drinking Water: 1997 National Public Water Systems Compliance Report and Update on Implementation of the 1996 Safe Drinking Water Act Amendments*, EPA-305-R-99-002 (Washington, D.C.: U.S. Environmental Protection Agency, 1999), 3.

10. Office of Water, *Technical and Economic Capacity of States and Public Water Systems*, 4.

11. The figures appear in Office of Enforcement and Compliance Assurance, *Providing Safe Drinking Water: 1997 National Public Water Systems Compliance Report*, 3. However, the large number of small public water supply systems is widely reported as an implementation obstacle. See, e.g., U.S. General Accounting Office, *Safe Drinking Water Act: Progress and Future Challenges in Implementing the 1996 Amendments*, GAO/RCED-99-31 (Washington, D.C.: U.S. General Accounting Office, 1999).

12. Office of Enforcement and Compliance Assurance, *Providing Safe Drinking Water in America: 2000 National Public Water Systems Compliance Report*, 4.

13. U.S. Environmental Protection Agency, Office of Water, *National Characteristics*

of *Drinking Water Systems Serving Populations under 10,000*, EPA 816-R-99-010 (Washington, D.C.: U.S. Environmental Protection Agency, 1999), iii.

14. Office of Water, *National Characteristics of Drinking Water Systems*, iii.

15. Office of Enforcement and Compliance Assurance, *Providing Safe Drinking Water in America: 2000 National Public Water Systems Compliance Report*, 6.

16. U.S. Environmental Protection Agency, Office of Ground and Drinking Water, "Setting Standards for Safe Drinking Water," November 26, 2002, www.epa.gov /ogwdw/standard/setting.html (December 18, 2002).

17. SDWA, Section 1401(6), 42 USC Section 300f(6).

18. Stephen E. Williams, "Safe Drinking Water Act," in *Environmental Law Handbook*, 13th ed., ed. Thomas F. P. Sullivan (Rockville, Md.: Government Institutes, 1995), 203–24, at 204.

19. SDWA, Sec. 1401(3), 42 USC Sec. 300f(3).

20. U.S. Environmental Protection Agency, *The Safe Drinking Water Act: A Pocket Guide to the Requirements for the Operators of Small Water Systems* (San Francisco: U.S. Environmental Protection Agency, Region 9, 1993), 8.

21. SDWA, Sec. 1412(b)(5), 42 USC Sec. 300g-1(b)(5).

22. U.S. Environmental Protection Agency, Office of Ground and Drinking Water, "Setting Standards for Safe Drinking Water."

23. The Safe Drinking Water Act Amendments of 1986 are contained in Public Law 99-339.

24. Office of Water, *Technical and Economic Capacity of States and Public Water Systems*, 26.

25. Lawrence Jensen, "Safe Drinking Water Act," in *Environmental Law Handbook*, 12th edition, ed. Thomas F. P. Sullivan (Rockville, Md.: Government Institutes, 1993), 253.

26. Office of Water, *Twenty-Five Years of the Safe Drinking Water Act*, 7.

27. Office of Water, *Technical and Economic Capacity of States and Public Water Systems*, 26.

28. EPA refers to this list as the Contaminant Candidate List.

29. U.S. General Accounting Office, *Safe Drinking Water Act*, 6.

30. Conventional techniques to control microbial contaminants in drinking water require the addition of disinfectant chemicals. These chemicals may themselves produce adverse health effects. The disinfection by-products standard seeks to minimize the adverse health effects of disinfectants while still controlling microbial contaminants in drinking water.

31. Mary Tiemann, "Arsenic in Drinking Water: Recent Regulatory Developments and Issues," Congressional Research Service Report to Congress, RS20672, August 23, 2001, www.ncseonline.org/nle/crsreports/water/h2o-40.cfm?&CFID=535 (December 18, 2002), Summary.

32. Douglas Jehl, "EPA to Abandon New Arsenic Limits for Water Supply," *New York Times*, March 21, 2001, http://query.nytimes.com/search/article (March 2, 2003).

33. Tiemann, "Arsenic in Drinking Water."

34. Darren Samuelsohn, "Nebraska Brings Constitutional Challenge against Rule, SDWA," *Greenwire*, October 24, 2002, www.eenews.net/Greenwire/searcharchive (March 3, 2003).

35. U.S. General Accounting Office, *Safe Drinking Water Act*, 15.

36. Office of Enforcement and Compliance Assurance, *Providing Safe Drinking Water: 1997 National Public Water Systems Compliance Report*, 32.

37. U.S. General Accounting Office, *Drinking Water: Consumers Often Not Well-Informed of Potentially Serious Violations*, GAO/RCED-92-135 (Washington, D.C.: U.S. General Accounting Office, 1992).

38. Office of Enforcement and Compliance Assurance, *Providing Safe Drinking Water in America: 2000 National Public Water Systems Compliance Report*, 6.

39. Office of Water, *Twenty-Five Years of the Safe Drinking Water Act*, 13. Also see U.S. Environmental Protection Agency, "Source Water Assessment Program," May 30, 2003, www.epa.gov/safewater/protect/swap.html (September 6, 2003).

40. U.S. Environmental Protection Agency, Office of Water, *Strengthening the Safety of Our Drinking Water: A Report on Progress and Challenges and an Agenda for Action*, EPA 810-R-95-001 (Washington, D.C.: U.S. Environmental Protection Agency, 1995), 11.

41. Office of Water, *Technical and Economic Capacity of States and Public Water Systems*, 117.

42. Office of Enforcement and Compliance Assurance, *Providing Safe Drinking Water in America: 2000 National Public Water Systems Compliance Report*, 6.

43. Jeff Cole, "City Confident of Success in Crypto Lawsuit: Attorneys to Argue for Dismissal, Claiming Immunity," August 29, 1999, *Milwaukee Journal Sentinel*, www.jsonline.com/news/metro/aug99/water30082999.asp (March 6, 2003).

44. U.S. Environmental Protection Agency, "U.S. Court Upholds Drinking Water Standards," press release, February 26, 2003, http://yosemite.epa.gov/opa/admpress.nsf/0/325746c0bb8a922285256cd900515a09?OpenDocument (September 15, 2003).

45. E.g., see U.S. General Accounting Office, *Drinking Water: Key Quality Assurance Program Is Flawed and Underfunded*, GAO/RCED-93-97 (Washington, D.C.: U.S. General Accounting Office, 1993); U.S. General Accounting Office, *Drinking Water Program: States Face Increased Difficulties in Meeting Basic Requirements*, GAO/RCED-93-144 (Washington, D.C.: U.S. General Accounting Office, 1993); U.S. General Accounting Office, *Drinking Water: Combination of Strategies Needed to Bring Program Costs in Line with Resources*, GAO/T-RCED-94-152 (Washington, D.C.: U.S. General Accounting Office, 1994); U.S. Environmental Protection Agency, Office of Water, *Technical and Economic Capacity of States and Public Water Systems to Implement Drinking Water Regulations*, EPA 810-93-001 (Washington, D.C.: U.S. Environmental Protection Agency, 1993).

46. U.S. General Accounting Office, *Drinking Water*, 7.

47. Office of Water, *Drinking Water Infrastructure Needs Survey: First Report to Congress*, EPA 812-R-01-004 (Washington, D.C.: U.S. Environmental Protection Agency, 1997), 8.

48. Office of Water, *Drinking Water Infrastructure Needs Survey: Second Report to Congress*, EPA 816-R-01-004 (Washington, D.C.: U.S. Environmental Protection Agency, 2001), 12.

49. Office of Water, *Drinking Water Infrastructure Needs Survey: Second Report to Congress*, 15.

50. Office of Water, *Drinking Water Infrastructure Needs Survey: Second Report to Congress*, 41.

51. U.S. Environmental Protection Agency, Science Advisory Board, *An SAB Report: Safe Drinking Water, Future Trends and Challenges*, EPA-SAB-DWC-95-002 (Washington, D.C.: U.S. Environmental Protection Agency, 1995), 13.

52. U.S. Environmental Protection Agency, Office of Water, *Helping Small Systems*

Comply with the Safe Drinking Water Act: The Role of Restructuring, EPA/812-K-92-001 (Washington, D.C.: U.S. Environmental Protection Agency, 1992).

53. Office of Water, *Technical and Economic Capacity of States and Public Water Systems*, 81.

54. U.S. General Accounting Office, *Drinking Water: The Widening Gap between Needs and Available Resources Threatens Vital EPA Program*, GAO/RCED-92-184 (Washington, D.C.: U.S. General Accounting Office), 7.

55. Office of Water, *Technical and Economic Capacity of States and Public Water Systems*, 110.

56. Office of Water, *Technical and Economic Capacity of the States and Public Water Systems*, 109.

57. Mary Tiemann, "Safeguarding the Nation's Drinking Water: EPA and Congressional Actions" Congressional Research Service, CRS Report RL31294 (Washington, D.C.: Library of Congress, 2002), 5.

58. Tiemann, "Safeguarding the Nation's Drinking Water."

59. U.S. General Accounting Office, *Drinking Water: Compliance Problems Undermine EPA Program as New Challenges Emerge*, GAO/RCED-90-127 (Washington, D.C.: U.S. General Accounting Office, 1990), 3.

60. Office of Water, *Technical and Economic Capacity of the States and Public Water Systems*, 113.

61. Office of Water, *Technical and Economic Capacity of States and Public Water Systems*, 121.

62. U.S. General Accounting Office, *Drinking Water Program*, 4.

63. Not all states were surveyed because a mailing list was not available from EPA, and obtaining the names of drinking water administrators through other sources (e.g., professional associations) proved difficult. Thus, the researcher developed a shorter mailing list of administrators by searching state websites and making telephone calls to state agencies. In addition, the researcher reviewed position statements of professional water associations (e.g., the Association of State Drinking Water Administrators) to augment and/or support the primary observations.

64. U.S. Environmental Protection Agency, Office of the Administrator, *Strengthening the Safety of Our Drinking Water: A Report on Progress and Challenges and an Agenda for Action* (Washington, D.C.: U.S. Environmental Protection Agency, 1995).

65. Bill Clinton and Al Gore, *Reinventing Environmental Regulation*, report issued by the White House, March 16, 1995.

66. Clinton and Al Gore, *Reinventing Environmental Regulation*, 21.

67. U.S. Environmental Protection Agency, Office of Water, *National Drinking Water Program Redirection Strategy*, EPA-810-R-96-003 (Washington, D.C.: U.S. Environmental Protection Agency, 1996).

· 6 ·

High Stakes, Small Wins, and Big Coal in the Surface Mining Program

The Surface Mining Control and Reclamation Act (or SMCRA; Public Law 95-87) has a simple purpose: "to establish a nationwide program to protect society and the environment from the adverse effects of surface coal mining operations."[1] However, the implementation of SMCRA has been anything but simple. The story of this law illustrates many facets of implementation. From high-stakes politics, to the disposition of the federal overseers, to changes in the national political climate, to the various permutations of state-level performance, to the wide variations in the targeted regulatory population and the precision and significance of statutory language, SMCRA exhibits all of the difficulties involved in putting a regulatory framework into practice.

More than a quarter-century after the passage of SMCRA, political battles ensnarl its implementation. The coal mining law stands out as the most politically charged among the laws studied in this book for several reasons. First, though the drinking water and asbestos programs largely look at changing the behaviors of public entities (public water suppliers or schools) and the radon program is completely nonregulatory, the surface mining program regulates the behavior of private coal companies. In turn, the survival of these private companies depends upon their maintaining a competitive edge. Since the enactment of SMCRA, coal production has surged, but the number of coal companies and people working in the coal mining industry has plummeted. The remaining coal companies, by their sheer size alone, are potent political forces at the state level. The same is true at the national level. When the National Mining Association speaks, politicians listen.

The nature of mining offers a second reason that SMCRA is so politically volatile. Many people never see a mining operation up close. However, it is something to see. Most mines are gigantic and use equipment that makes normal bulldozers seem Lilliputian. The operation may disturb thousands of acres at a time—something that catches public attention. When people associate this land disturbance with a public health or safety risk or environmental disaster, they react—and strongly.

That is not the case with drinking water, asbestos, or radon. Drinking water is a part of the public infrastructure almost everywhere in the country. Absent an event like the *cryptosporidium* outbreak in Milwaukee (chapter 5), citizens expect water that is safe to drink every time they turn on the faucet. Despite its significant health risk, we see no visible evidence of radon and are not very worried about it, as was discussed in chapter 4. Asbestos in schools policies backfired in the 1990s when too many schools engaged in costly and unnecessary asbestos removal projects. Except for recent incidents such as that in Libby, Montana, most people consider asbestos risk obsolete (chapter 3).

SMCRA stands apart from the other laws in the book for another reason. It is both a natural resource and pollution control law. This chapter begins with a brief review of the partial preemption regulatory scheme and the history of surface mining policy formulation. Subsequent sections detail the key provisions of the law and the evolving oversight role of the Office of Surface Mining (OSM). The chapter concludes with a discussion of the perceptions that state and federal surface mining officials have about the implementation process.

Wrestling with Issues of Control: The Primacy Approach

When U.S. president Jimmy Carter signed SMCRA into law on August 3, 1977, undoubtedly jubilant members of Congress cheered. Legislation regulating the environmental effects of coal mining, the product of a tortuous decade-long congressional battle, had finally become a reality. For environmentalists, residents of coal mining areas, and many federal policymakers, SMCRA provided a much-needed national regulatory presence in a long-ignored environmental area. Nevertheless, although the political skirmishes surrounding the adoption of this national policy were over, a new battle was about to begin. SMCRA, after twenty-five different bills and two presidential vetoes (both by President Gerald Ford), was on paper; now, it had to be put into practice in the coalfields.

In implementing SMCRA, the political struggles over coal would take place on new battlefields. Congress formulated policy in a national arena; the implementation of SMCRA would take place in each coal-producing state. This shift of the locus for battle from a national to state arena was not by chance; it was by design. Like many environmental laws, congressional architects chose a partial-preemption regulatory approach for implementing SMCRA. As was discussed in chapter 1, this approach returns regulatory control to the states, but only after the states adopt enforcement programs that meet national standards.

Like federal–state arrangements in other environmental laws, the federal agency could approve a state's program in whole or in part. In SMCRA, states had eighteen months to develop regulatory programs, and sixty days to respond to any programmatic deficiencies noted during the approval process. Congress required states assuming "exclusive jurisdiction over the regulation of surface coal mining and reclamation operations" to pass state laws, promulgate rules and regulations, and identify a state authority to implement the law, among other requirements.[2] In turn, OSM was required to hold at least one public hearing and obtain the concurrence of the U.S. Environmental Protection Agency (EPA) with respect to water or air quality standards before granting primacy.

Under primacy, states had leeway to implement their laws and design their enforcement strategies, provided they were as stringent as applicable federal requirements. If state officials chose not to shoulder implementation responsibility for the coal mining regulatory program, the federal government remained as implementer. If a state's approved programs proved inadequate in enforcing national standards, Congress authorized OSM to preempt the state's authority and institute a federal program in the state. The states' acceptance of primacy for a surface mining regulatory program was not an abdication of national control.

Once a state received primacy, a tumultuous in-state implementation process began. State regulators now practiced a federally prescribed "hands-on" enforcement strategy, including inspections of mining operations. State inspectors frequently found themselves in uncomfortable adversarial relationships with coal operators. State inspectors found that a more accommodating enforcement style alleviated the mutual discomfort felt by both mine operators and themselves.[3] Conversely, discomfort often increased when citizens' or environmental groups pushed for stricter enforcement. SMCRA required reclamation despite the costs or behavioral change required of coal operations. Substantial compliance costs squeezed the profit margins of regulated companies, prompting their active interest in state enforcement activity. They expressed this interest through interactions with agency personnel and administrators, political appointees, or state politicians. In turn, state legislators and executive sovereigns are inclined to listen to economically important industries within state boundaries. Thus, the nature of regulatory policy under primacy creates an environment with mixed local pressures on state officials charged with implementation responsibilities.

Simultaneous with local pressures, however, were national pressures. Federal oversight of state surface mining programs exerted countervailing pressures on primacy states, because such states serve as implementers of national policy goals. State enforcement programs are constrained by policy decisions made at the federal level: States must conform to the operative framework established by the federal oversight agency.[4] These bottom-up and top-down pressures set the stage for federal–state conflict over SMCRA enforcement.

This presents pressures that are both similar and different from those faced by implementers of the Safe Drinking Water Act (SDWA) discussed in chapter

5. Clearly, both sets of state officials operate on middle ground, needing to please federal overseers while mediating the concerns of the regulatory target group. State inspection and enforcement personnel operating under SMCRA and SDWA will encounter resistance from groups targeted in the regulations. However, state coal mining inspectors will face a different kind of political pressure in implementing the law because the mining industry represents an economic presence in the state or local community. Mining concerns operate under considerable pressure to produce competitively priced coal and are therefore reluctant to incur costs associated with that production that would price them out of the market. Public water supply systems are a utility, often part of the community's public infrastructure.

Federal regulatory programs embodying national goals but administered by state agencies almost inevitably create tensions between the two levels of government over the nature, timing, and scope of implementation. This chapter seeks to explain these pressures and their relative effects on implementing the surface mining program and on developing state–federal relationships.

Coal Mining: East versus West

Although it is common to talk about scarce natural resources, this term should not be applied to U.S. coal. Coal is by far America's most abundant fossil fuel, with nearly 19 billion short tons of estimated recoverable coal reserves at active mines.[5] In the United States, there are twenty-four coal-producing states in three major coal-producing regions: the Appalachian, the Interior (Illinois Basin), and the Western (see figure 6.1). About 503 billion tons of demonstrated reserves exist in the U.S., according to government estimates.[6] The U.S. Department of Energy estimates that these reserves are the largest in the world and are enough to supply America's energy demand for several hundred years.[7] Given this abundance, it is little wonder that solons recognized the redeeming qualities of "King Coal," especially when supplies of other fossil fuels became precarious shortly before the passage of SMCRA in 1977.

Historically, the U.S. demand for coal as an energy source expanded slowly. It was not until 1885 that the nation relied on its coal more than on abundant trees for it energy supplies.[8] Coal production, fueling industrial development, soon escalated, reaching 200 million tons before 1900. As is shown in figure 6.2, coal production has steadily increased since the mid-1900s. Much of the increase has come since 1970, with increased reliance on coal to provide electricity. The electric power industry accounts for almost 90 percent of domestic coal consumption.[9] Production of coal in 2001 reached a record 1.12 billion short tons, nearly a million tons more than in 1998.[10]

U.S. total: 1,118.1

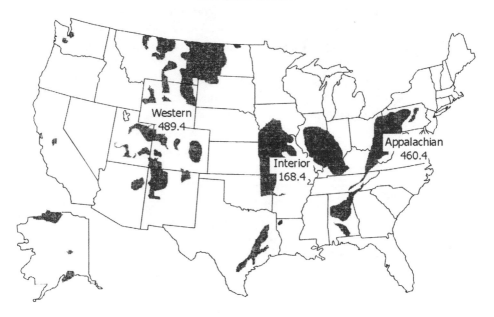

Figure 6.1.   Map of Coal Production by U.S. Region (millions of short tons)

Source: U.S. Energy Information Administration, "U.S. Production by State, July–December 1998," *Weekly Coal Production* summary, May 7, 1999, www.eia.doe.gov/cneaf/weekly/weekly_html/wcpdecem.htm (March 3, 2003).

Increases in America's coal production accompanied dramatic changes in the geographic distribution of coal mining and in the number and size of mines. Coal mining in the West before 1970 represented a relatively minor contribution to overall U.S. coal production. In 1965, for example, only 4 percent of America's coal came from Western mines.[11] However, the dominance of Eastern coal companies steadily eroded. By 1998, states west of the Mississippi River produced more coal than states east of the Mississippi River.[12] This trend is likely to continue.[13]

Several factors explain the rapid rise of Western coal production. Perhaps the most significant is related to the timely joining of energy demand and environmental policy. In response to political directives in the wake of the Arab oil embargo to increase domestic energy use, coal became the energy source of choice for the generation of electricity. Power plants became the major consumers of U.S. coal, accounting for more than 8 out of every 10 tons of coal produced.[14] At about the same time, concerns about sulfur dioxide emissions

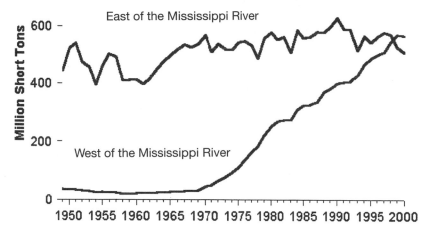

Figure 6.2.   Trends in U.S. Coal Production (millions of short tons), 1950–2000

Source: U.S. Department of Energy, Energy Information Administration, "Energy in the United States: 1635–2000," www.eia.doe/gov/emeu/aer/eh/images/figure22.jpg (March 4, 2003).

that caused acid deposition prompted Congress to pass the Clean Air Act in 1970. Amendments in 1977 and 1990 required power plants to reduce sulfur emissions.[15] The Clean Air Act Amendments of 1990 set a threshold for sulfur dioxide emissions by power plants but left it up to the plant how to meet the requirement. Many power plants opted to reduce emissions by burning Western coal—a cost-efficient alternative to installing pollution control systems or scrubber technologies for power companies. In assessing changes in coal production in the 1990s, the Department of Energy asserted, "The Clean Air Act Amendments, along with earlier clean air regulations, constitute the single most significant factor driving a continuing growth in demand for western coal. With solid markets already assured and vast reserves of coal, western surface mines, especially in the low-sulfur, thick coal deposits of the Powder River Basin were well positioned . . . to win over new customers."[16]

The last part of the quote points to a second factor. Western coal is abundant and cheap to produce. Increased Western coal production had profound effects on the composition of mining firms and on the relative productivity of coal firms nationwide. Many small Eastern coal operations—faced with the arduous task of competing with the tremendous economies of scale of Western coal—simply disappeared. Before the expansion of Western mining, these

Table 6.1. Comparison of 2001 Coal Mining Data by Location (East or West of the Mississippi River)

Location	No. of Mines	Production[a]	Productivity[b]
Western states	92	598,908	21.78
Eastern states	1,386	527,027	4.26
Total	1,478	1,125,935	6.04

[a]Thousands of short tons.
[b]Short tons per miner per hour.
Sources: U.S. Department of Energy, Energy Information Administration, "Coal Production and Number of Mines by State and Mine Type," www.eia.doe.gov/cneaf/coal/page/acr/table1html; and Richard Bonskowski, "The U.S. Coal Industry in the 1990's: Low Prices and Record Production," U.S. Energy Information Administration, www.eia.doe.gov/cneaf/coal/special/coalfeat.htm.

operators could hold onto narrow profit margins and move in and out of the coal mining business. In 1967, there were more than 7,000 mines, most of them in Appalachia; by 1987, there were fewer than 4,000. By 2001, only 1,386 coal mines operated east of the Mississippi River, as is shown in table 6.1. The table also shows the sharp contrast between Eastern and Western coal mining operations. Just 92 mines in the West produced more coal than all the Eastern mines combined, with a productivity rate more than five times that of their Eastern counterparts.

Moreover, most coal comes from one state—Wyoming—which is home to the nation's nine largest surface mines. The three largest coal mines in the country—the Powder River Coal Company, Thunder Basin Coal Company, and Codero Mining Company—all in Wyoming, mined nearly 190 million short tons of coal in 2001—an amount that dwarfs the coal production of every other state. For example, in 2001 Kentucky mines produced 133 million tons, Pennsylvania mines 74 million tons, and Virginia mines a paltry 33 million tons. Only mines in West Virginia came close, producing 162 million tons.[17]

To retain some competitive vitality, Eastern mining operations responded by increasing the size of the mine and utilizing cheaper mining methods. At the same time, mining companies reduced the number of employees. In a paradoxical and inverse relationship, the inexorable move to increase productivity resulted in fewer workers even as the quantity of coal mined increased. Between 1986 and 1997, companies cut employment by 47 percent overall, and by more than 68 percent at operations mining fewer than 100,000 tons of coal per year.[18] In West Virginia, the largest coal-producing state in the Appalachian region, mining jobs have dropped precipitously since the late 1940s. In 1999, about 15,000 citizens found work in the coal mines, compared with almost ten times that number (125,000) employed as coal miners in 1948.[19]

A final factor contributing to the decline of coal production in the Eastern United States is that mining has depleted coal reserves. Many parts of the Appalachian region are in the mature phase of the resource life cycle, with economically viable coal reserves diminishing or gone. According to U.S. Geological Survey estimates, Georgia, Maryland, and Tennessee are virtually "mined out." Declining coal production in Ohio and Pennsylvania suggests that these states are well past peak production. Alabama and Virginia, according to government estimates, may soon enter a phase of general decline. Only eastern Kentucky and West Virginia produce coal in increasing amounts, and both states appear to be some years away from maximum production.[20]

Coal Mining Techniques and Potential Environmental Consequences

Different techniques exist to mine coal, based on regional variations in the terrain and in the coal bed size. Many people typically think of coal as being mined underground, as indeed it is. In 2000, more than half of the mines in Appalachia were underground mines, and these mines accounted for over half of coal produced. In contrast, less than 10 percent of Western coal and slightly more than a third of coal from the Interior region is extracted underground.[21]

One of several underground mining methods usually mines coal beds 200 feet beneath the surface. The traditional "room and pillar" mining technique is still practiced. With this method, miners cut a series of "rooms" into the coal bed and extract the coal, leaving pillars of coal to support the mine roof. Mining advances to new rooms, forming an undersurface grid pattern. Once mining is completed, these underground rooms are left behind, with the hope that the pillars will continue to support the ground above the room. Should the pillars give way, the ground may collapse.

A more recent underground mining technique is longwall mining, a form of high extraction underground mining incorporating planned subsidence. In longwall mining, a machine moves back and forth across the face of the underground coal seam. Self-advancing hydraulic jacks support the underground roof as the coal face is sheared by the machine. As mining advances into the coal bed, the jacks follow—allowing the roof above the previously mined area to fall (hence, the term "planned subsidence"). A longwall panel is larger than the "room and pillar" mined area, averaging 800 feet wide and up to two miles in length.[22] Longwall mining is generally more efficient than conventional underground methods because the operation is continuous and larger and requires fewer workers.[23]

Figure 6.3. Mountaintop Removal of Coal in West Virginia

Source: Courtesy of Vivian Stockman, Ohio Valley Environmental Coalition; used by permission.

Surface mining, sometimes referred to as strip mining, is employed when coal is located within 200 feet of the land surface. Surface mining, a large-scale earth-moving operation, scrapes away soil above the coal, called overburden, and removes the underlying coal. The efficiency of a surface mine in part is determined by the overburden ratio, or the amount of overburden excavated per ton of coal recovered. The lower the ratio, the more productive the mine. Most low-ratio mining operations are in the West. Coal-recovery rates at these large open-pit surface mines, such as the most productive American mines in the Powder River Basin area of Wyoming, often exceed 90 percent.

Coal mined on hilly or mountainous terrain requires that the miner reach the coal and control the overburden. Traditionally, surface mining operations employed a technique called contour mining, whereby mining followed the natural shape of the terrain. More recently, coal companies in the East have employed large-scale mountaintop removal, a technique that, as the name suggests, maximizes efficiency by simply removing large parts of the mountain (figure 6.3). The overburden is often deposited in valleys, a technique referred to as "valley fills."

Regardless of the method used, coal mining can have profound consequences on the environmental quality of postmined land as well as associated surface and ground water. A major concern is the ability of mining companies to reclaim the land to its "approximate original contour" (a term used in SMCRA and discussed below). Environmental concerns also associated with surface mining include soil erosion, reestablishment of wildlife and native vegetation, and depletion and/or contamination of groundwater supplies. Groundwater supplies, once contaminated or lost, are difficult or impossible to restore or recharge. Reestablishing vegetation is especially difficult in the arid climate of the West, where massive operations disturb thousands of acres of land. Environmentalists worry that even if reclamation is possible, it will take decades to reestablish native plants and grasses. Although inadequate reclamation of postmined lands continues to dominate discussions of potential environmental damage due to coal mining, other environmental issues are also of concern.

Environmental groups, such as the Ohio Valley Environmental Coalition, sharply criticize the practice of mountain top removal and valley fill—not only for destroying the natural contour of the mountain but also for destroying the valley. Valley fill alters the course of surface water and contributes to flooding. Flooding, in turn, creates a public health and safety hazard. A recent example is Lyburn Hollow, West Virginia, where the collapse of a sediment pond above a valley fill flooded twelve homes in July 2002.[24] Other major types of environmental impact associated with underground mining are the subsidence of overlying and adjacent land, the loss of surface water and groundwater, and discharge of acid mine drainage. Subsidence is particularly troublesome when miners employ high extraction techniques such as longwall mining. Subsidence is rapid and inevitable and covers large areas.

To summarize, the U.S. coal industry is etching an ever-increasing presence in America's energy mosaic. U.S. coal production has increased steadily since the passage of SMCRA and has shown no sign of slowing down. However, the continued health of the coal industry has not guaranteed success for all individual coal operators. Indeed, since the passage of SMCRA the number of coal mines has been cut in half as small Eastern miners have lost their competitive edge to monolithic Western concerns and larger local Eastern corporations. Thus, the advent of surface mining regulation occurred just as Western mines were being positioned to challenge the dominance of Appalachian mines. In addition, the ability of Western coal miners, especially in Wyoming, to operate colossal coal mines by taking advantage of low overburden ratios and generous coal bed deposits would dictate the shape of regulatory enforcement in both regions, as is discussed later in the chapter.

Formulating Federal Surface Mining Policy

After more than 100 bills on surface mining had been introduced in the 93rd, 94th, and 95th Congresses alone, followed by two presidential vetoes, SMCRA finally became law on August 3, 1977. Understanding the turbulent history of the law helps explain the painful implementation of SMCRA. A tragic event helped muster the political will to deal with the environmental consequences of coal mining. In 1972, erosion instability due to mining caused the collapse of a coal waste dam in Logan County, West Virginia, killing 125 people. News coverage of the disaster brought the specter of uncontrolled mining into American homes and triggered congressional action.[25]

Congress was not of one mind, however, as to what a federal coal mining law should look like. One side of the debate sought to ban surface mining. Representative Ken Hechler (W.Va.) introduced one of the first bills dealing with surface mining, H.R. 15000, the Strip Mining Abolition Act, in 1973. His bill called for gradually phasing out surface-mined coal. In an interview for this book, Hechler described his motivations: "I've always felt, and history has proven me correct, that any law attempting to regulate a powerful industry like coal mining is bound to be skewed by political pressures. Federal and state authorities are primarily interested in production and in speeding up the permitting process, and only putting 'band-aids' in environmental protection."[26]

Other congressional representatives argued that surface mining should be controlled, not abolished. They argued that surface mining operations were very much in concert with Western coal mining. Representative Morris Udall (Ariz.) introduced H.R. 2, the Surface Mining Control and Reclamation Act, on the first day of the 95th Congress. It overwhelmingly passed both houses in August 1977. SMCRA ultimately represented an uneasy merger of two political camps: persons inside and outside government who pushed for increased domestic coal production, and environmental and grassroots citizens' groups who sought to curtail the ecological degradation caused by surface and underground mining.

Inside the federal bureaucracy, however, a chorus of voices sang the "gloom and doom" song of the potential effects of federal legislation on coal production. In congressional testimony after the second presidential veto in 1975, administrators from the Federal Energy Administration, the Department of the Interior, and the Department of Commerce, among others, predicted the demise of smaller coal companies and the attendant rise of America's dependence on foreign energy supplies. Frank Zarb, then head of the Federal Energy Administration, took the most strident position in justifying President Ford's veto: "The facts and figures . . . demonstrate that the responsible, if perhaps not the politically popular, course has been taken. We have estimated that from 40 to 162 million tons of annual coal production would be lost during the first full year of implementation. We are talking about locking away billions of tons of coal and we consider our estimates to be conservative."[27] Other testimony pointed to the loss of mining jobs: "Not only would American consumers pay more (for energy) . . . many thousands would lose their jobs . . . we have concluded that from 9,000 to 36,000 jobs would in fact be lost."[28]

Another administrative argument against a federal surface mining law was the impact it would have on national security, as is suggested by this testimony: "The loss of even 40 million tons of coal per year could increase imports by more than 450,000 barrels [of oil] per day . . . with additional costs of $1.9 to $7.8 billion a year for energy. Because of the gravity of our energy situation, this nation cannot afford to reduce the availability of our one abundant energy resource unless we have another to replace it. Coal is the only major domestic resource upon which we can rely as a secure source of energy in the coming decades."[29]

Mining interests divided on their support of SMCRA. Large Western coal firms tacitly supported federal surface mining legislation. They believed that the legislation would end uncertainty about the "rules of the game" for U.S. coal production. Moreover, because these firms invariably would mine coal on public lands, they needed the security of one set of mining regulations. Finally, SMCRA, because it regulated but did not abolish surface mining, posed no threat to company profit margins.

Moreover, Western coal operators preferred to position themselves to shape the character of subsequent regulations rather than lose the opportunity at hand by blocking the passage of SMCRA.[30] By nominally supporting what appeared to be an inevitable federal presence in coal regulation, these large coal firms were able to direct their political resources toward ensuring that the final law would be flexible enough to accommodate their interests. Their interests included the allowance of site-specific mining variations, mining on alluvial valley floors, and less stringent restrictions on the length of mining permits.

Many coal firms in the East, however, were vehemently opposed to SMCRA.[31] Eastern operators were fearful that the bill's provisions for requiring that mined land be returned to its approximate original contour would make mining Eastern coal virtually impossible. Smaller operators in Appalachia were especially vociferous in their opposition because compliance costs posed significant economic hardships for their marginally profitable mines. Underground mining interests—still reeling from the effects of the Mine Health and Safety Law (1969)—supported SMCRA as a political trade-off for their recently incurred economic costs in complying with federal mine safety standards.

National environmental groups, such as the National Wildlife Federation, Sierra Club, Environmental Defense Fund, and Friends of the Earth, directed public concern for the environment toward surface mining. They joined forces with a growing number of state-based citizens' groups, such as the Citizens for Better Reclamation in Virginia and the Northern Great Plains Resource Council in Montana and Wyoming, to lobby for federal regulation of surface mining. With its chances having been buoyed by national media attention to vast acres of unreclaimed land, the federal legislation seemed certain to pass eventually.[32]

Organized labor initially supported federal environmental controls on surface mining. Contrary to the administration's predictions, members of the United Mine Workers (UMW) felt the passage of SMCRA would secure current employment and even provide more jobs. Because SMCRA was directed toward surface mining operations (and the UMW membership was composed of less than 10 percent surface miners), it had the potential to solidify the position of labor-intensive deep coal mines.[33] Furthermore, SMCRA potentially would remove the small operators from Appalachia, many of whom were able to avoid operating with unionized employees. However, as SMCRA evolved to include regulation of the "surface effects" of underground mining, the UMW's formal position changed to oppose the law, although local groups continued to support federal intervention in surface mining.[34]

In addition to these political battles, yet another key political issue was raised in an attempt to thwart federal legislation: the contention by coal-producing states and the coal industry that state regulations were adequate and, therefore, federal regulations would be an unnecessary encumbrance to proper state regulatory operations. In fact, however, many states had not addressed surface mining problems. The majority of coal-producing states passed legislation after Congress directed national attention toward surface mining; 32 out of 38 states implemented state regulatory programs between 1970 and 1975.[35]

Though most coal-producing states had regulatory programs in place by 1975, there were widely disparate degrees of program effectiveness and state enforcement.[36] This perceived lack of uniformity, coupled with the problem of interstate competition, eventually determined the need for federal legislation. As the situation was described in a U. S. Senate Committee Report, "The primary problem alleged with individual states regulating mining for coal is that a uniform set of regulations is lacking. This . . . arrangement allows the states to regulate mining activities according to their unique conditions. However, when one state passes stringent rules and enforces these rules when a neighboring state does not, it creates a condition of unfair competition for mine operators."[37]

In short, passing an acceptable federal coal mining law designed to protect the environment was fraught with complex political alliances and obstacles. This contentious and protracted development of federal surface mining legislation guaranteed that implementation would be as tortured a process as policy formulation had been. Each time Congress went back to the legislative "drawing board," it emerged with bills that, while granting some additional variances to the coal industry, were more precise in regulatory requirements. This increasingly detailed articulation of legislative intent resulted in a longer list of major provisions and performance standards for both state and federal regulatory agencies. Furthermore, recurring delays in the enactment of a federal surface mining bill produced more—rather than less—stringent requirements for the coal industry. Public Law 95-87 offered little flexibility for regulators in developing a regulatory program to implement the act or to the targeted industry in complying with its provisions.

Moreover, some of SMCRA's detailed provisions embodied conflicting requirements, such as section 516, which requires operators to "prevent subsidence causing material damage to the extent technologically and economically feasible . . . except in those instances where mining technology used requires planned subsidence in a controlled manner . . . provided that nothing in this section shall be construed to prohibit the standard method of room and pillar mining."[38] This section is mystifying; it simultaneously allows and prevents subsidence and leaves ambiguous the terms "planned subsidence" and "material damage." This section also illustrates the deference given to underground mining of coal compared with surface mining.

In addition, congressional and administrative debates directed SMCRA toward dual national goals: coal production and environmental protection. SMCRA Section 101(b) states that it is "essential to the national interest to insure the existence of an expanding and economically healthy" underground coal industry.[39] Therefore, only the surface effects of underground coal mining are regulated under SMCRA.

Yet another effect apparent from the development of federal coal mining legislation is that it opened wide the arena of federal–state mistrust. Ongoing debates regarding which level of government to entrust with primary regulatory authority, federal or state, and then how much authority to allow, were major parts of congressional deliberations. Ultimately, SMCRA delegated responsibility to states—but only after significantly constraining state regulatory power.[40]

The legislative testimony indicates that Congress considered environmental performance standards too important to be rendered meaningless through lax state enforcement (which had prompted federal regulation in the first place). Thus, whereas SMCRA tacitly recognizes the need for "site-specific" implementation, the statute offers little opportunity for regulatory flexibility. The fact that Congress specified the state–federal relationship in great statutory detail would preclude federal regulators from deviating too far from a narrowly prescribed oversight role.

Finally, the passage of SMCRA left a chasm within the targeted industry— not only between Eastern and Western coal concerns but also between underground and surface operations. Political realities dictated the sacrifice of marginal Appalachian coal companies, which lacked both the expertise and production levels to readily incur compliance costs. At the same time, it provided protection for large Eastern underground and Western surface operations, both of which could accommodate compliance costs. Congress attempted to maintain the viability of the small Appalachian coal miner by establishing a 2-acre exemption, where mining operations that disturbed less than 2 acres would not be required to comply with SMCRA's requirements. However, this opened wide the opportunity for unethical coal operators to circumvent SMCRA by mining the same seam of coal from multiple sites (all under 2 acres) or by establishing shell corporations of separate mining companies that would share common equipment, personnel, and offices. (The 2-acre exemption was repealed in 1987.)[41]

Struggles to enact a surface mining bill set the stage for continued conflict during implementation, as states sought regulatory control and various components of the coal industry pursued mutually exclusive agendas. The next sections highlight the major elements of the surface mining law and OSM's response to SMCRA.

SMCRA's Provisions and the Implementation Story

Some stories of SMCRA implementation struggles are as old as the original law. Indeed, as the previous section suggests, statutory language has produced a number of implementation hurdles. SMCRA created OSM within the Department of the Interior. The sole purpose of this new agency was to implement the major provisions of SMCRA. The law has two major components, which are known as Title IV and Title V.

Title IV establishes a program to reclaim lands mined before August 3, 1977 (the date SMCRA was enacted), and abandoned without reclamation. The Title IV abandoned mine land (AML) program is funded by a tax on current producers of coal. Production fees—35 cents per ton of surface-mined coal, 15 cents per ton of coal mined underground, and 10 cents per ton of lignite—are collected from all active mining operations. Fees are deposited in the Abandoned Mine Reclamation Fund and are used to reclaim abandoned mines. More than $6.6 billion in fees were deposited in the fund between 1978 and 2002.[42]

SMCRA specifies that at least 50 percent of the revenue collected within the state is reserved for that state, provided it has a federally approved AML program.[43] This is the state share. OSM uses the remaining 50 percent, or federal share, for high-priority or emergency reclamation projects and to support the Small Operator Assistance Program. However, getting the state's "fair share" of this coal tax or even the federal share is not automatic, due to a peculiar federal budget idiosyncrasy. Monies from the AML go into the general treasury of the U.S. government. Once there, the money may be used to help lower the appearance of federal budget deficits, even though it cannot be allocated for any other purpose but to reclaim abandoned mines.[44]

By the end of 2002, the fund had an unappropriated balance more than $1.5 billion, and nearly $1 billion of that was the state share. It is easy to see why. In 2001, AML fees generated about $284 million. Congress allocated only $82 million to the twenty-three states and three Native American tribes with AML programs, far short of the 50 percent promised by SMCRA. The balance stayed in the general treasury of the U.S. government. State governments have begun to complain. Wyoming officials' irritation shows on the state's environmental website, which dedicates a page to explaining the gap between what the state is due under the law and what Congress has authorized. According to the website, Wyoming's coal industry has paid $1.51 billion in AML fees since 1977. Through 2001, Wyoming received a total of $435 million, which is only about 29 percent of the total fees collected from Wyoming coal producers. In 2001 alone, Wyoming's coal industry paid $112 million in AML fees but received $28.7 million, or about 24 percent of the coal tax.[45] Over time, such large discrepancies add up. The balance for Wyoming's state share was nearly $371 million at the end of 2002.

This, however, is about more than just who gets the money. Abandoned mines are dangerous. In the past two years, seventy-eight people have died in accidents involving abandoned mines.[46] Several states, primarily in the Appalachian region, have a large number of abandoned mines. West Virginia, with 1,629 abandoned coal mines, faces a huge reclamation challenge. However, the state cannot access its $120 million state share of AML fees because Congress has not authorized the expenditure—a situation not likely to improve in the near term. The George W. Bush administration is proposing to cut spending from the fund to just $174 million, even though the proceeds from coal taxes and interest will exceed $350 million.[47]

Title V of SMCRA established the regulatory program, which allows for state assumption of inspection and enforcement duties upon federal approval. To receive approval, state programs must be "no less stringent" than federal provisions.[48] Regulatory requirements for coal mining operations begin with premining activity. Coal operators are required to submit detailed mining plans, which are used by state regulators to identify potential environmental problems before a permit to mine is issued. Permits are issued for five years, subject to renewal. In addition to detailed permitting provisions, SMCRA also requires that reclamation bonds be posted by coal firms before mining begins. These bonds ensure that mine sites will be fully reclaimed, even if operators fail to undertake reclamation activity. Often, however, these bonds are insufficient to pay for reclamation if a mining company files bankruptcy or just walks away from a mine.[49] In 1995, the West Virginia Highlands Conservancy filed suit in federal court to require OSM to take over SMCRA enforcement in the state. In its lawsuit, the group maintained that the failure of the state's Division of Environmental Protection to require sufficient reclamation bonds could ultimately cost taxpayers more than $60 million.[50]

Once a mine is operating, the state enforcement system contains four interlocking components: performance standards, inspections, enforcement actions, and penalties. SMCRA sets detailed performance standards for surface mining and the surface effects of underground mining.[51] These include requirements that the land be restored to its approximate original contour (referred to as AOC), that it be revegetated, that acid mine drainage be prevented, that subsided lands be restored, that "prime farmland" be restored to productivity, that hydrological disturbance be minimized, and that erosion be controlled. Other provisions include a requirement that reclamation proceeds "as contemporaneously as practicable" and that highwalls (exposed vertical rock faces) be limited in height during mining and ultimately eliminated.

Not all areas can be surface mined. SMCRA prohibits mining in national parks; federal lands within national forests; areas within 100 feet of a public road or cemetery; and land within 300 feet of a public building or occupied dwelling, unless waived by the owner. These prohibitions may be relaxed if a coal operator can establish "valid existing rights."[52] Finally, states can declare areas where successful reclamation is unlikely, or areas with particular historical or environmental value, as "off limits" to mining operations.

Section 523(a) of SMCRA requires OSM to establish a regulatory program that applies to surface coal mining operations on federal lands. The federal land program is especially important in the West, where the federal government owns 60 percent of identified coal reserves. Using cooperative agreements, OSM may delegate most of the Federal Land Program to primacy states. Fourteen states had cooperative agreements in 2001.[53]

State inspections are conducted at coal mines to ensure compliance with the performance standards and other SMCRA provisions.[54] Every mine must be inspected monthly, and at least one full inspection must be carried out each calendar quarter. Inspections must occur on an irregular basis without advance notice to the operator.[55] Inspectors must cite any observed violations. Usually, the coal operator is given a notice of violation (NOV), which specifies the methods for abatement and sets a reasonable time limit (ninety days or less) for correcting the violation.

Operators that do not abate the violation within the NOV time frame must receive a failure-to-abate cessation order (FTACO). However, if a violation is serious enough to constitute an imminent danger to public health and safety or can reasonably be expected to cause significant environmental harm, then a cessation order (CO) must be issued immediately and the operator must cease mining activity until the violation is addressed.

Two elements of the enforcement system make SMCRA prone to a strong command-and-control approach. First, inspectors must take action on every violation they observe, regardless of its perceived environmental impact. SMCRA provides for no exceptions; inspectors cannot legally substitute written or verbal warnings for formal enforcement actions (NOVs or COs). Second, NOVs must be issued immediately on-site. These two requirements place the onus of enforcement squarely on the shoulders of field inspectors, which was just what Congress intended. As was explained by the congressional authors, "By mandating primary enforcement authority to field inspectors, this bill recognizes that inspectors are in the best position to recognize and control compliance problems."[56]

Civil penalties are also part of the state's enforcement arsenal. COs and FTACOs have mandatory monetary penalties; state inspectors may attach monetary penalties to NOVs at their discretion. Typically, fines are determined on the basis of four criteria: seriousness, negligence, violation history of the coal company, and the company's good-faith abatement effort. Once fined, the operator may pay the penalty or request an informal hearing. During the hearing, the operator and the inspector make presentations to state agency administrators, who decide to abate the violation or enforce the penalty. A formal administrative hearing is held if the operator is not satisfied with the decision, and the resulting decision may be appealed to the courts.

SMCRA also authorizes criminal penalties for willful violations and, in some cases, where a pattern of abuse is evident; mining permits may be suspended or revoked. Criminal penalties apply to company executives as well as corporate officers and directors. Individual punishments for convicted chronic violators may be fines as high as $10,000 or imprisonment for up to one year.

In creating SMCRA, Congress relied on citizen participation for enforcement. Citizens can request that state or federal regulatory authorities conduct inspections, and citizens have the right to accompany regulatory personnel on site. Permits, permit revisions and proposed reclamation bond releases are all subject to public comment and must be publicly advertised for citizen review. Citizen complaints received by OSM require a response. In 2002, OSM received 147 complaints. This resulted in the agency conducting 21 initial and 49 follow-up inspections, which led it to find 207 violations of SMCRA requirements by coal companies. OSM issued 111 ten-day notices (TDNs) to state regulatory programs.[57] Citizens may also seek legal redress by suing either federal or state regulatory authorities for failure to enforce SMCRA. They may sue coal operators for permit or regulatory violations. Finally, citizens may petition states to designate certain areas as unsuitable for mining.

In 2002, the organization Kentuckians for the Commonwealth scored a major victory when it successfully sued to stop the disposal of mountaintop mining wastes into streams. It argued that the U.S. Army Corps of Engineers had violated Clean Water Act requirements when it issued a permit to fill a valley stream in Martin County, Kentucky. The Bush administration asked U.S. district judge Charles Haden II to suspend his ruling, which enjoined all coal companies from sweeping wastes in mountain streams, but he refused.[58] The Fourth Circuit Court of Appeals overturned Haden's ruling in January 2003, calling it overly broad, and lifted the injunction. Undaunted, environmental groups filed a notice of intent to sue, this time for the federal government's failure to protect endangered species.

Primacy states receive federal grants to run the surface mining regulatory program. Federal grants require a 50 percent state match. In 2001, OSM gave $55.5 million in grants to primacy states. OSM calculates grant awards on the basis of the number of mines, not the amount of coal produced, which means that a state with many mines receives much larger regulatory program grants. In 2001, Kentucky received nearly $13 million; West Virginia, $8 million; and Wyoming, nearly $2 million.[59]

The Evolution of OSM Oversight

OSM serves two functions as federal overseer: it evaluates a primacy state's performance in carrying out its approved program; and it provides backup enforcement against violating operators in the event that a state fails to enforce SMCRA provisions.[60] Sixteen OSM field and area offices conduct complete inspections of coal mines; respond to citizen complaints by conducting on-site inspections; issue TDNs to state agencies when a violation is observed during an inspection; and issue NOVs to coal operators when a state does not respond to TDNs and cite the violation. OSM inspectors also must issue COs directly to a coal operator when they observe a violation that creates an imminent danger to public health or safety or will significantly damage the environment. Finally, OSM field office staff annually evaluate each primacy state's inspection and enforcement program. Unless federal inspectors feel an operator's violation represents "imminent harm," states are given the first oppor-

Table 6.2. Evolution of OSM Oversight, Selected Years

OSM Phase and Period	No. of Inspections	No. of Enforcement Actions[a]	OSM Actions
Regulatory enthusiasm, 1977–81 (1981 data)	29,639	3,957	Permanent program regulations published after 15,000 pages of comments from 600 sources
Regulatory retrenchment, 1981–85 (1985 data)	5,088	982	Regulatory reform task force created; 91 percent of all regulations rewritten
Regulatory realignment, 1985–94 (1989 data)	4,241	687	Two-acre exemption eliminated; Applicant Violator System begins
Shared commitment, 1995 through the present (1995 data)	3,722	210	REG 8 Directive, OSM reorganization, and staff reduction
Shared commitment, (2001–2 data)	2,221	20	25th anniversary (2002); OSM sued over mountaintop removal

Note: OSM = U.S. Department of the Interior, Office of Surface Mining. SMCRA = Surface Mining Control and Reclamation Act.
[a]Includes Notices of Violation and Cessation Orders.
Sources: U.S. Department of the Interior, Office of Surface Mining, *Annual Reports* for 1981, 1985, 1989, 1995, and 2002.

tunity to interact with the coal operator. To start the process, a federal inspector who observes a violation during an oversight inspection issues a TDN to the state agency. Only after a TDN expires and the state has failed to respond can OSM inspectors issue a NOV to the coal operator.[61]

Primacy states and coal operators have challenged the legality of the direct enforcement by OSM, but several court decisions have upheld the agency's authority.[62] However, OSM's changing role orientations have been just as important as court decisions. A review of the history of SMCRA since its enactment suggests that there have been four "implementation phases," which can be associated with different styles of federal oversight: regulatory enthusiasm (1977–80); regulatory retrenchment (1981–84); regulatory realignment (1985–94); and shared commitment (1995 through the present), as shown in table 6.2.[63]

OSM's first task as a fledgling oversight agency was to ensure that adequate state programs developed through its own initial regulations. To accomplish this, OSM chose to adopt an ambitious and vigorous posture toward implementing oversight. This regulatory enthusiasm reflected not only a desire to curtail immediately environmental abuses but also a general distrust of states' regulatory ability to control the coal industry. Few operations wanted the new regulations. OSM received more than 15,000 pages of comments from more than 600 entities after the proposed rules were published in the *Federal Register*.[64] OSM began its regulatory program with the dual goals of minimizing state discretion and ensuring programmatic consistency among primacy states. For example, reclamation standards developed by OSM typically employed design and performance criteria.[65] Although the coal industry challenged some of these early standards, the permanent program rules contained many more design criteria than those of any existing state program.

Another example of the enforced compliance strategy embodied in the initial rule-making process was the narrowing of state discretion, or the "state window." The state window permitted states to employ alternative regulatory standards and procedures upon OSM approval. Although originally conceived as a way of accommodating legitimate state interest in regulatory flexibility, the final OSM state window provision was viewed by states as effectively precluding their authority and as counterproductive to a partial-preemption regulatory partnership.[66]

Finally, OSM inspectors were recruited for their commitment to a strict "go by the book" enforcement strategy.[67] The agency put coal operators on notice that it intended to enforce the letter of the law. Headquarters staff, not field office personnel, developed inspection and enforcement guidelines that directed federal inspectors to "ticket" every observed violation.[68]

The detailed regulations coupled with OSM's regulatory enthusiasm were destined to invoke the wrath not only of most coal firms but also of most primacy states. By 1979, coal mining states and mining interests had captured the attention of Congress, where a bill was introduced to sharply curtail OSM's rule-making and enforcement authority.[69] Thus, OSM began to come under scrutiny not for being too lax in its enforcement effort but for being overzealous in its pursuit of regulatory goals.

The second phase, regulatory retrenchment, began with the new administration of Ronald Reagan. To undo what administrative critics of OSM termed its "regulatory excesses," the administration radically altered its organizational mission, structure, and purpose. Perhaps the most ominous signal that the implementation of SMCRA would pursue a different course was the appointment of three pro-industry institutional leaders: the secretary of the interior, James Watt; the OSM director, James Harris; and the OSM assistant director, J. Steven Griles. Under this leadership, OSM moved from vigorous to accommodating oversight.

The Reagan administration based this regulatory retrenchment on three notions. First, OSM's regulatory pendulum had swung too far toward environmental concerns, failing to recognize the law's mandate to balance environmental protection with the nation's need for coal production. Second, OSM in its earlier regulatory zeal had overstepped its legislated authority, to the detriment of legitimate state regulatory discretion. Third, many OSM regulations violated the tenets of Executive Order 12291, which required the elimination of unnecessary or overly burdensome regulations.

OSM director Harris argued, "The measure of a good regulation is its effectiveness, not its stringency. Some definitions of stringency connote punishment. The proper mission of OSM is to regulate the coal industry, not punish it."[70] Accordingly, OSM reviewed all its regulations for their inclusion of "unnecessary design criteria" and impracticality to "actual field situations."[71] OSM's review of its regulatory program was swift; within two years, it had rewritten 91 percent of its regulations. Nearly 60 revisions to original rules were approved by 1983.[72] Among those revisions was a new policy for issuing NOVs. As of April 1983, a new oversight policy advised OSM inspectors that "issuing a NOV serves no useful purpose" if the mine operator can take remedial action during the inspection.[73]

The strongest rationale for a new OSM mission came from the agency's relationship with the states. OSM administrators argued that the federal government had "grown out of proportion," becoming "a ponderous burden on the states" and promised to restore regulatory balance. Citing state primacy as the main objective of the law, OSM director Harris criticized the agency's "heavy-handed" approach in its regulatory scheme and state program approval process.[74]

Two tactics were employed to effectively increase reliance on state rather than federal regulatory activity. First, OSM staffing levels were decreased. In 1980, OSM employed 891 full-time equivalent (FTE) personnel; by 1982, FTE staff had been reduced to 742, a decrease of 20 percent. Furthermore, almost all of the decrease was due to the elimination of federal oversight inspectors (from 210 in 1980 to 69 in 1983).[75] A second tactic aimed at restoring regulatory responsibility to the states was a major reorganization of the agency. All five regional field offices and twenty out of forty-two established OSM state offices were eliminated. In the West, the former Region V Office was dissolved and its regulatory duties were split among three field offices: the Casper Field Office, the Albuquerque Field Office, and the Western Technical Center.[76]

Yet another indicator of OSM's changing regulatory posture was its inability or unwillingness to employ alternative enforcement techniques, such as the imposition of civil penalties. By legislative provision and the so-called Parker Order, OSM was required to collect civil penalties from coal companies not in compliance with the regulations.[77] By 1986, more than $181 million in civil penalties had been assessed by OSM; only $14.4 million, roughly 8 percent, had been collected. Moreover, testimony at congressional hearings suggested that penalties were not assessed for all observed violations and that thousands of outstanding violations may require additional penalties, the amount of which was conjecture at the time of the hearing.[78]

By the mid-1980s, several factors indicated that OSM was readjusting its enforcement orientation and entering a new phase of regulatory realignment. New leadership in the Department of the Interior, as well as OSM, reduced the pro-industry tenor of OSM.[79] James Harris resigned as director in 1984 and was replaced by Jed D. Christensen in 1985. Among other issues, Christensen sought to improve OSM management, address delinquent penalty collections, and maintain consistency in enforcement to protect the environment. By 1989, the agency's objective, as stated in the 1989 budget justification report, was "to assure that the mining's economic benefits are not achieved at a cost of long term environmental degradation."[80] This appears to be more closely in conformance with the initial posture of OSM, but with less attention paid to citing every violation.

This period also included technological improvements to implementing SMCRA—chief among these is the Applicant Violator System (AVS). This computerized system identifies coal firms across the country with outstanding violations and subsequently prevents them from receiving mining permits in other locations. AVS, which was required by court order, may have the potential to track violators and increase the collection of civil penalties. Perhaps the most potent element of AVS is its ability to stop new mining permits from going to companies that have failed to reclaim previous mine sites.[81]

Other signs, however, suggest that OSM directors of the 1990s and early 2000s are clearly not of the same cloth as the first administrators at OSM. For one thing, the OSM directorship is a political appointment that requires the approval of the Senate. As a political appointee, the director is beholden to the ideological persuasion of the secretary of the interior as well as the president. For another, OSM administrators do not stay around long enough for an especially strong philosophy to permeate the organization. During the 1980s, the average tenure of OSM directors was less than two years—hardly long enough to inculcate a particular policy philosophy.[82] This trend continued into the 1990s and early 2000s—with four OSM directors between 1997 and 2002.

While the official OSM oversight policy has vacillated, and the number of inspections has steadily decreased, many of the same OSM inspectors have remained on the job during at least one of these transitional periods. This has created apparent confusion within the agency, especially between the field office and OSM headquarters staff. Interviews with OSM officials outside Washington suggest that they have not recovered from the internal dissension created in the early 1980s. One OSM field director complained: "We were muzzled early by [James] Watt. The leadership in the agency has been so bad. We don't have a mission; OSM has no goals. Ask anyone—no one [in the agency] could tell you what it is [agency mission]."[83]

In short, OSM's enforcement style, like a pendulum, moved from enforced compliance and limited state discretion during its early years to an accommodative posture minimizing federal intervention in the 1980s. Its style moderated between these two positions from the late 1980s through most of the 1990s. However, perhaps the most dramatic change in its oversight philosophy since its inception nearly two decades ago began in 1996, when it revealed a strategy of "shared commitment."

Getting Away from the "Gotcha" Syndrome

Like EPA, OSM has embraced a new philosophy of federal–state relations that permeates its oversight duties and official orientation toward primacy states, as was described in chapter 1. Its 1995 and subsequent annual reports sport the slogan, "Protecting the environment: a shared commitment." OSM director Robert J. Uram referred to the agency as the "new" Office of Surface Mining, and suggested that OSM has "re-engineered oversight from a process-driven to a results-oriented system."[84] Further reflecting this new orientation was the agency's "remolding" of the contentious TDN process to "truly respect state judgments" and to "end intrusive federal second-guessing" of state inspectors.[85]

The new oversight policy is the product of an OSM–state oversight team that began a dialogue on state–federal interactions in 1994. The new policy, known as the REG 8 Directive, began with the 1996 fiscal year. As was discussed in chapter 1, among the major changes in oversight approach is the development of performance agreements that evaluate states on the basis of "on-the-ground results" rather than number of inspections or citations issued.[86]

Figure 6.4 illustrates the new OSM oversight approach. In looking at this flowchart, it appears that a primacy state's programs should be afforded greater opportunities for positive evaluations, as evidenced by the three directives to "report it" (meaning report a positive evaluation for the primacy state). For example, if the OSM evaluator believes that even though the state did not achieve the targets established in the performance agreement and failed to address off-site effects but subsequently took action to address the problem, he or she should report the state's performance as adequate. OSM should take corrective action only upon reaching the bottom of the flowchart. Thus, OSM

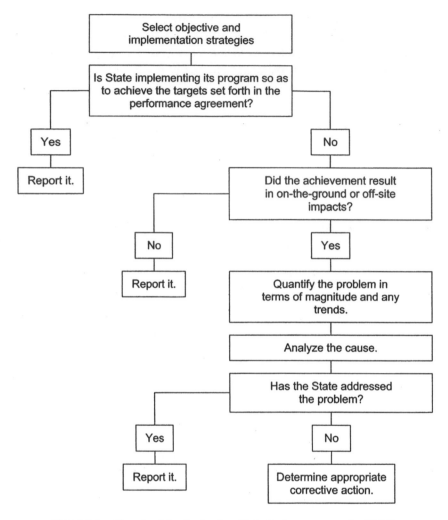

Figure 6.4. Flowchart for Evaluating State Performance under REG 8

Source: U.S. Department of the Interior, Office of Surface Mining, *REG 8 Directive: Oversight of Regulatory Programs* (Washington, D.C.: Office of Surface Mining, January 30, 1996), 7.

would most likely exercise its TDN and NOV authority only in situations that are not corrected by the state and have the potential to affect reclamation success, health, or safety or cause off-site damage—certainly a far cry from the agency's initial posture to cite every violation.

What is not yet resolved, however, is how to determine when situations call for OSM backup enforcement. For example, when a citizen complains to OSM about a coal mining operation, does the OSM field office disregard that complaint or refer it to the state without follow-up? OSM director Uram observed the need for federal enforcement to be "strong and compelling," and added "many coalfield citizens tell us that OSM's presence in the coalfields is one of the most important benefits they get from the surface mining law." He promised that "OSM will act independently to protect the public interest."[87] Thus, the new philosophy of federal–state shared commitment and results-oriented oversight was not without limits, at least under Uram's watch.

Gone forever, at least in the eyes of the Oversight Team, is the perceived propensity of OSM inspectors to engage in detailed oversight of state inspection staff. In the past, according to OSM Western Regional Office officials, OSM field office inspectors spent too much time trying to find fault with state inspections. Good oversight was measured by the number of "gotchas"—that is, the number of times the OSM staff could catch an omission of the state inspection or enforcement effort. The Oversight Team recognized the "gotcha" syndrome of OSM field offices as a particular sore spot.

This renewed attention to federal–state "shared commitment" came at a time of turmoil for OSM, not unlike the regulatory retrenchment period of the early 1980s. In the past six years, the agency has reorganized, cut its regulations in half, and reduced staff.[88] In November 1995, OSM lost 182 FTE employees through a reduction in force—more than 15 percent of its staff. Between 1996 and 2003, three directors and three acting directors led OSM, about one a year.[89] The current director, Jeffrey Jarrett, a former executive with Cravat Coal and Drummond Coal who was confirmed by the Senate in 2002, has come under attack from environmental groups who view him as overly friendly to the coal industry. J. Steven Griles, who was OSM's assistant director from 1981 to 1983, now serves as deputy secretary of the interior. The chapter now turns to the perceptions of state officials regarding working relationships and SMCRA implementation.

Perceptions of State Surface Mining Officials

The following comments and observations come from two mailed surveys and from e-mail and telephone conversations. State surface mining officials in the twenty-four coal-producing states received surveys in 1995. Of twenty-eight surveys sent (some states list multiple officials), twenty-four were returned, for a response rate of 86 percent.[90] In 2002, twenty-four surveys were sent and nineteen were returned, for a response rate of 79 percent. Eight phone interviews with state officials, six with OSM officials, and four with environmental group staff in 2003 complement the survey data.

Many of the state surface mining regulatory programs predate SMCRA, with half of the programs being more than twenty-five years old. State surface

Table 6.3. Factors That Hinder SMCRA Implementation, as Ranked by State Officials, 2002

Factor	Percentage identifying as an issue (N = 19)
Legal challenges	37
Bankruptcy or other challenges faced by small mining operations	32
OSM oversight, program administration, or policy changes	32
Insufficient or fluctuating resources; 50 percent match	26
Changes in interpretation of regulations or the law	26
Lack of coordination among federal agencies; multiple laws	21
Citizen or environmental activists, complaints about mining	21
Staffing issues (inability to fill positions with trained personnel)	16
Insufficient fines and/or sanctions	10

Note: SMCRA = Surface Mining Control and Reclamation Act; OSM = U.S. Department of the Interior, Office of Surface Mining.

mining programs tend to be larger than the other programs reviewed. The largest state program in terms of personnel is Kentucky's, with 302 FTE personnel involved in the regulatory program and 82 FTE involved in AML. Conversely, Wyoming has only 28 FTE in the regulatory program and 15 FTE in the AML.

When asked to identify the greatest struggle in implementing state coal mining programs, state officials point to various concerns, as are shown in table 6.3. A third of state officials responding to the survey's open-ended question commented on legal challenges, issues with small mine operators, and inconsistent OSM policies as recent stumbling blocks to implementation.

Legal challenges come from both directions: Environmental groups challenge OSM and state enforcement of SMCRA; mining companies challenge new regulations. Litigation has not slowed appreciably since the early days of SMCRA. For some Appalachian states, issues such as adequate bonding, mountaintop removal, and subsidence are "hot button" legal issues. "Challenges by one or two operators on program statute and rules have taken a lot of energy and staff time. They are a distraction," commented one official. "Challenges [appeals] to permit issuance are a struggle. This [SMCRA] and other laws can be manipulated to prevent mining." Another suggested that legal staff should be included as part of the state agency: "Currently all legal assistance is provided through a separate office. This situation results in numerous logistical problems in the enforcement program."

State officials must deal with the evolving nature of the surface mining industry. Many noted the competitive pressures on mine operators, especially related to the seemingly limitless Wyoming coal. "Dealing with Chapter 7 and

11 bankruptcies of several coal producers and the financial failure of several major insurance companies with surety reclamation bonds is our greatest struggle. Ensuring that the interests of the state are addressed in dealing with struggling companies is resource intensive." Another official commented, "The Title V program has suffered from the closing of mines due to being able to compete with large Western coal mines." As one official noted, "Our coal communities are always facing high unemployment rates—the unemployment rate for the state is less than 6 percent, but coal mining counties have unemployment rates three to four times as high."

State officials who see changes in OSM policy or regulations as an implementation challenge often point to interpretations of reclamation standards. One state official observed, "Clarifying and defining requirements and standards to be met for revegetation and postmine land use to facilitate the release of reclamation bonds has been one of our greatest struggles." Another agreed: "Meeting the legal criteria for revegetation success or failure is one of the biggest questions to be answered." "We need to continue to accommodate permitting while revisiting laws," commented another official.

Some state officials responding to the survey view environmental groups and citizen activism as obstacles to implementation. One official described his greatest struggles as "repetitive attacks from activist groups using the courts to snarl administrative proceedings." He noted that these activities "drain time and manpower resources better spent in addressing true problems." Another agreed: "Activists who lack technical expertise and are unethical, [represent one of our greatest struggles] because of the time and resources they take away from real issues." Other officials, however, find value in public participation. "The greatest accomplishment is that the program has expanded the involvement of the public in the entire SMCRA program."

No doubt, grassroots environmental groups are active in implementing the law. As was mentioned in previous sections, SMCRA provides many opportunities for citizen involvement, from permit approval to bond release. Environmental groups such as the Ohio Valley Environmental Coalition, the West Virginia Highlands Conservancy, the Kentucky Resources Council, and the Citizens Coal Council (a coalition of 48 grassroots groups) have lobbied and litigated what they view as failures in surface mining law (figure 6.5).

In comparison with the other environmental programs, state officials responsible for SMCRA generally perceive higher levels of political attention to their program. Respondents are likely to believe that state administrators, legislators, and citizens are concerned about the surface mining program (in 1995, respectively 86, 67, and 62 percent). Yet the political attention that state officials perceive to be directed toward their program does not necessarily improve implementation performance. This attention may serve to constrain the

Figure 6.5.   Citizens March toward the West Virginia Capitol Building in
Charleston, October 28, 2000

Photograph by Deana Steiner Smith; used by permission.

regulatory choices made by inspection personnel, as evidenced by this comment: "One of the major problems in administering a reclamation program is the lack of uniformity of mission between state regulators who are charged with obtaining good reclamation and elected officials who desire only to get reelected."

It is also evident from the survey data and interviews with state personnel that state inspectors are more likely to embrace a more accommodative orientation toward coal operators. One state inspector observed that the state agency embraces "compliance through education" and that it does little good to cite a violation or assess a fine if the operator was unaware of the regulation or if the violation is minor (i.e., does not harm the environment). As is shown in table 6.4, only 21 percent of state respondents in 1995 and 33 percent in 2002 link strong enforcement to citing all violations, and 60 percent disagree that such a connection exists.

However, state officials applaud the implementation of Title IV. More than three-fourths of state officials agree (with 67 percent strongly agreeing) that abandoned mines are being reclaimed with money from the AML fund. "Successfully reclaimed abandoned mines, watershed programs, and the Clean Stream Initiatives are among the state's greatest accomplishments under SMCRA. The AML program has greatly improved relationships with citizens," commented one official.

Table 6.4. Perceptions of State Surface Mining Officials about State Programs
(percentage indicating that they strongly agree or agree), 1995 and 2002

Perception	1995 (N = 24)	2002 (N = 19)
State has been able to reclaim abandoned mines	n.a.	78
Coal is a top environmental priority	n.a.	72
Top-level administrators are supportive	86	72
Program is stronger than three years ago	75	67
Reclamation efforts of coal companies are better	n.a.	61
Program is adequately funded	70	56
Need a stronger state program, decrease OSM role	63	33
Strong enforcement depends upon citing all violations	21	33
Environmental problems are more serious	0	0

Note: n.a. = not available; OSM = U.S. Department of the Interior, Office of Surface Mining.

When asked whether environmental problems associated with coal mining are more serious than in the past, state officials are of one voice. No one feels that the problems are worse today. Indeed, 61 percent believe that the reclamation efforts of coal companies have improved, and 67 percent (75 percent in 1995) agree that the state program is stronger.

In sum, when state-level implementation variables are considered, state officials have positive perceptions about the way they operate the regulatory program, the accomplishments of the program, and the ability of their staff to continue to implement SMCRA under primacy. They are much more likely to agree (when compared with state officials in other environmental programs) that their program is adequately funded and supported by state legislators and top-level administrators.

One of the more remarkable findings of this study is that state officials appear to have a more cordial working relationship with OSM than six years ago, as is shown in table 6.5. Though the survey is limited, it does appear that the reorientation of oversight policy through the REG 8 Directive and other OSM policies has been effective in changing federal–state working relationships. State officials are much more likely to perceive flexible oversight (78 percent in 2002, compared with only 24 percent in 1995), and they are more likely to agree that OSM evaluates the state program fairly (61 percent, compared with 29 percent). Moreover, OSM is much more "hands-on" in overseeing state programs than are its counterparts in the other programs reviewed. About 80 percent of state officials agree that OSM keeps in frequent contact with them.

When asked about OSM's oversight role in 1995, many state officials expressed criticism. One official suggested that OSM should "eliminate the

Table 6.5. Perceptions of State Surface Mining Officials about Working Relationships with OSM (percentage indicating that they strongly agree or agree), 1995 and 2002

Perception	1995 (N = 44)	2002 (N = 30)
OSM keeps in frequent contact with me	76	83
OSM is concerned about controlling environmental damage	65	83
Oversight is flexible	24	78
I have a positive relationship with OSM enforcement staff	57	72
OSM program is adequately funded	55	61
OSM inspectors have a high degree of technical expertise	25	61
OSM evaluates the state program fairly	29	61
OSM program is working effectively	11	55
State–OSM relationships have improved since REG 8	n.a.	50
Reporting requirements are reasonable	14	38
OSM has been consistent in establishing requirements for state	35	27
Field Office and headquarters officials view program similarly	20	22
Without OSM, the state would not be as serious about running a surface mining program	19	17

Note: n.a. = not available; OSM = U.S. Department of the Interior, Office of Surface Mining.

second-guessing of state actions," while another commented that the agency is "too intrusive and mistrusting of states. . . . OSM believes a bold allegation from a citizen before they believe a state [official]." Other state officials noted what they perceived to be a tendency of OSM field office staff to look for small violations—evidence of the "gotcha" syndrome: "The OSM [staff] is too rigid in their enforcement procedures. They do it by the book whether or not it makes sense in a particular situation." A Coal Program Supervisor in a Western state put it this way: "Instead of assuming that state programs would not be as strong without federal oversight, I believe that most state programs would remain strong and be more efficient without an OSM presence. In many instances, OSM's oversight role has ebbed and flowed based on factors outside of state efforts. Meanwhile, we keep doing what we've been doing for fourteen years—running a sound program and protecting the environment."

When asked about working relationships, 57 percent of state program officials in 1995 agreed that their working relationships with OSM were positive (compared with 72 percent in 2002). No doubt, working relationships seem smoother. Half of the state officials agree that the REG 8 change prompted better relations. Still, working relationships are not perfect.

Of the state officials who did not believe working relationships were positive in 1995, comments most frequently point to a micromanagement of their program by OSM field office staff. As one put it, "We do not receive support from our OSM field office. They continually attempt to disparage and frustrate our efforts. They refuse to acknowledge that we are both working toward the same goal. They continually choose to substitute their judgment for ours. OSM dictates how the program is to be run, frequently changes directives with no notice, and constantly finds fault with minor details of our program." Other comments from 1995 and 1996 interviews reveal the frustration of state directors: "OSM focuses on dotting the "i's" and crossing the "t's" and does not focus on whether the environment is ultimately protected." And "the true measure of our program should be the extent to which we mitigate environmental harm, not how many violations we cite, how many reports are on time, how many signs are upright, and whether or not every map is stamped by a registered engineer." In 2002, some state officials reached a similar conclusion: "Change OSM's approach from 'Imperial dictum' to cooperation and collaboration of equals." "Many OSM field staff continue to view their job as finding something wrong rather than solving problems and improving reclamation."

Also evident from the survey data and interviews are perceptions that OSM's reporting requirements are overly burdensome. Only 14 percent of state officials in 1995 and 38 percent in 2002 believe that reporting requirements are reasonable. Moreover, some officials perceive unfair treatment: "Our state receives a disproportionate number of inspections when compared to other states." Another pointed to OSM's slow decision-making process: "The OSM review process for approval or disapproval of state program amendments can take years!"

State officials do not believe OSM oversight encourages implementation. Indeed, more than two-thirds of state officials strongly disagree with the necessity of OSM oversight, a level over twice as high as in other state environmental programs. Less than 20 percent of officials responding to either survey agree that without OSM the state would not be as serious about running a surface mining program.

Conclusions

The conceptual framework of extrinsic and intrinsic factors that influence implementation seems useful in evaluating this program, because virtually every element in the framework has added its own part to the story of implementing

SMCRA. Constraints on SMCRA implementation are found less in the lack of financial resources to operate the program and more in the politicization of the regulatory program within states. The changing nature of the target group, the geology and geography of coal mining, and changes in presidential administration all affect implementation progress.

Twenty-five years after its creation, OSM remains an agency in transition that continues to be battered or used by national political forces. Presidential administrations and Congress have been eager to be on both sides of the issue: protecting the environment and supporting coal production, while simultaneously supporting states' rights and strong enforcement.

The legislative language is as interesting for what was left out as what was eventually retained in SMCRA. For example, underground mining of coal was protected (SMCRA regulates only the surface effects of coal mining), and hard rock mining of copper, gold, and other metals was totally excluded. Regulatory requirements are challenged by states for being overly prescriptive and not allowing sufficient discretion. Potent political forces capture the ear of the solons in Congress and in state capitals with continued challenges to existing SMCRA provisions and OSM regulations. Meanwhile, active environmental groups engage OSM and states in battles over the appropriate interpretation of the law.

Evolving OSM oversight philosophies, frequent changes in structure, and the agency's revolving door of new leadership have further complicated SMCRA implementation. The legacy of organizational upheaval continues to affect the ability of agency headquarters and field office staff to move collectively toward the same goal. Reductions in force amounting to nearly 28 percent of OSM's personnel will likely not do much to instill a sense of mission and high morale. However, OSM officials point to stronger enforcement techniques (e.g., AVS) and a renewed commitment to establishing better working relationships with state implementers as reasons for optimism.

The REG 8 Directive as well as the more accommodating role orientations of recent top-level OSM officials appears to have made it easier for federal and state implementers to work together. Grassroots groups would argue that these changes have not been positive. They fear that state and federal regulators now are more likely to act in concert in bowing to the demands of King Coal. Students of federal–state relations, however, would applaud the shift from the very contentious intergovernmental relationships that have existed since the passage of SMCRA toward a more harmonious federal–state interaction. When considered in light of the working-relationship typology, this federal–state relationship seems to have shifted from a position in the "coming apart and contentious" quadrant toward a more synergistic position.

Notes

1. Public Law 95-87, Sec. 102.

2. Public Law 95-87, Sec. 503(a): 1–7.

3. Eugene Bardach and Robert A. Kagan, *Going by the Book: The Problem of Regulatory Unreasonableness* (Philadelphia: Temple University Press, 1982).

4. Patricia McGee Crotty, "The New Federalism Game: Primacy Implementation of Environmental Policy," *Publius: The Journal of Federalism* 17 (1987): 53–67.

5. U.S. Department of Energy, Energy Information Administration, "Total U.S. Coal Statistics, 1990, 1995–1999," www.eia.doe.gov/cneaf/coal/statepro/imagemap /us1p1html (March 16, 2003). A short ton is a unit of weight equal to 2,000 pounds.

6. U.S. Department of Energy, Energy Information Administration, "Coal Resources, Reserves and Mine Sizes, U.S. Total," www.eia.doe.gov/cneaf/coal/statepro /imagemap/us4p1html (March 16, 2003).

7. U.S. Department of Energy, Energy Information Administration, *Coal Data: A Reference* (Washington, D.C.: Energy Information Administration, 1989), 7.

8. U.S. Department of Energy, Energy Information Administration, "Energy in the United States: 1635–2000," www.eia/doe/gov/emeu/aer/eh/coal.html (March 4, 2003).

9. Robert C. Milici, "Production Trends of Major U.S. Coal Producing Regions," in *Proceedings of the Pittsburgh Coal Conference*, U.S. Geological Survey, June 15, 2001, http://energy.er.usgs.gov/products/Papers/PCC_96/production.htm (March 16, 2003).

10. Damon Franz, "Last Year's Production Could Be a Record—EIA," *Greenwire*, E&E Publishing, January 23, 2002, www.eenews.net/Greenwire/searcharchive/ (March 4, 2003).

11. Energy Information Administration, *Coal Data*, 15.

12. Energy Information Administration, "Energy in the United States."

13. U.S. Department of the Interior, Office of Surface Mining, *1989 Annual Report* (Washington, D.C.: U.S. Department of the Interior, 1990), 6.

14. Energy Information Administration, *Coal Data*, 22.

15. For a discussion of the regional impact of the Clean Air Act on the coal industry, see Bruce A. Ackerman and William T. Hassler, *Clean Coal, Dirty Air* (New Haven, Conn.: Yale University Press, 1980).

16. Richard Bonskowski, "The U.S. Coal Industry in the 1990's: Low Prices and Record Production," Energy Information Administration, September 1999, www.eia.doe.gov/cneaf/coal/special/coalfeat.htm (March 4, 2003), 11.

17. U.S. Department of Energy, Energy Information Administration, "Major U.S. Coal Mines, 2001," January 22, 2003, www.eia.doe.gov/cneaf/coal/page/acr/table10.html (March 4, 2003); U.S. Department of Energy, Energy Information Administration, "Coal Production and Number of Mines by State and Mine Type, 2001–2000," www.eia .doe.gov/cneaf/coal/page/acr/table1.html (March 4, 2003).

18. Bonskowski, "U.S. Coal Industry in the 1990's," 14.

19. Ohio Valley Environmental Coalition, "Mountain Top Removal," www.ohvec .org/old_site/mountains03.htm (March 15, 2003).

20. Milici, "Production Trends of Major U.S. Coal Producing Regions."

21. U.S. Department of Energy, Energy Information Administration, "Coal Production by State and Mine Type, 2000," www.eia.doe.gov/cneaf/coal/cia/html/tb1/tb103p01p1.html (March 4, 2003).

22. U.S. Department of Energy, Energy Information Administration, *Longwall Mining*, DOE/EIA-TR-0588 (Washington, D.C.: U.S. Government Printing Office, 1995), 3.

23. U.S. Department of Energy, Energy Information Administration, *Longwall Mining*, vii.

24. Jacob Messer, "Victims Salvage What They Can: Small Logan Town Ravaged When Pond Overflows," *Charleston* [West Virginia] *Daily News*, July 20, 2002 www.dailymail.com/news/News/200207202/ (March 4, 2003).

25. U.S. Congress. House Committee on Interior and Insular Affairs, Subcommittee on Energy and the Environment, "Tenth Anniversary of SMCRA of 1977," Serial No. 100-26 (August 3, 1987), 2.

26. Kenneth Hechler, telephone conversation, March 15, 2003.

27. U.S. Congress, House Committee on Interior and Insular Affairs, Hearing before the Subcommittee on Energy and the Environment, "Surface Mining Veto Justification Briefing," 94th Cong., 1st sess. (94-23, June 3, 1975), 15.

28. House Committee on Interior and Insular Affairs, "Veto Justification," 17.

29. House Committee on Interior and Insular Affairs, "Veto Justification," 14–15.

30. See Richard Harris, *Coal Firms under the New Social Regulation* (Durham, N.C.: Duke University Press, 1985), for a discussion of how coal firms would be affected by federal regulations.

31. For a discussion of the position of Appalachian coal companies, see Neal Shover, Donald A. Clelland, and John Lynxwiler, *Enforcement or Negotiation: Constructing a Regulatory Bureaucracy* (Albany: State University of New York Press, 1986).

32. Environmentalists initially focused attention on Appalachian coal mining. An early report on surface mining, issued in 1967 (and before the concern over foreign oil dominated administrative thought) by secretary of the interior Stewart Udall, made policymakers aware of the dire ecological results of coal mining in the Appalachia and provided ample political fodder for environmental organizations. Attention was subsequently directed to Western mining, as environmentalists urged Congress to avoid a "second Appalachia."

33. The concern over union jobs in Appalachia prompted an alliance between grassroots citizen groups and local chapters of the UMW. For example, the Virginia Citizens for Better Reclamation efforts were formally endorsed by the Virginia UMW Association, and several members of that group were UMW members. See U.S. Congress, Senate Committee on Energy and National Resources, Surface Mining Reclamation and Control Act of 1977, 95th Cong., 2d sess. (Public Law 95-32, 1977), 557–58.

34. *Washington Post*, "UMW Shifts Stand on Strip Mining" September 30, 1976.

35. U.S. Congress, Senate Committee on Energy and Natural Resources, "State Surface Mining Laws: A Comparison with the Proposed Federal Legislation and Background Information" (Report by the Congressional Research Service, 95-25, June 1977), 14.

36. For a discussion of the inadequacy of state programs, see U.S. Congress, Senate Committee on Energy and Natural Resources, Subcommittee on Public Lands and Resources, "Surface Mining Control and Reclamation Act," 95th Cong., 2d. sess. (March 1–3, 1977). For a general discussion, see Morris Udall, "The Enactment of the Surface Mining Control and Reclamation Act of 1977 in Retrospect," *West Virginia Law Review* 81 (1979): 4.

37. U.S. Congress, Senate Committee on Energy and Natural Resources, "Surface Mining Control and Reclamation Act," 20.

38. Quoted in K. W. James Rochow, "The Far Side of Paradox: State Regulation of the Environmental Effects of Coal Mining," *West Virginia Law Review* 81 (1979): 585.

39. SMCRA, Public Law 95-87, Sec. 101(b) [30 USC 1201]: 1.

40. On this point see, Hamlet J. Barry III, "The Surface Mining Control and Reclamation Act of 1977 and the Office of Surface Mining: Moving Target or Immovable Object?" *Rocky Mountain Mineral Law Institute* 27 (1982): 169–337.

41. U.S. Department of Interior, Office of Surface Mining, *1987–1988 Annual Report* (Washington, D.C.: U.S. Department of the Interior, 1989).

42. U.S. Department of the Interior, Office of Surface Mining, Abandoned Mine Land Fund Status, January 29, 2003, www.osmre.gov/fundstat.htm (March 18, 2003).

43. The Abandoned Mine Reclamation Act of 1990 (Public Law 101-508) extended fee-collection authority for OSM through September 30, 1995. The Energy Policy Act (Public Law 102-468) subsequently extended fee collection authority until September 30, 2004.

44. Joel Brinkley, "Death Toll Rises but Money in Mine Fund Goes Unspent," *New York Times*, September 26, 2002, www.nytimes.com/2002/09/26/politics/26MINE.html (September 26, 2002).

45. Wyoming Department of Environmental Quality, Abandoned Mine Land Fund, http://deq.state.wy.us/aml/index.asp?pageid=23 (March 18, 2003).

46. Brinkley, "Death Toll Rises."

47. Brinkley, "Death Toll Rises."

48. SMCRA [USC 1251], Sec. 501(b).

49. The reclamation bond provision is found at 30 USC 1259, Sec. 509(a). The amount of reclamation bonds required is often judged insufficient to fully reclaim the land; see U.S. General Accounting Office, *Surface Mining: Cost and Availability of Reclamation Bonds*, PEMD-88-17 (Washington, D.C.: U.S. General Accounting Office, 1988).

50. Ken Ward, "Lawsuit Seeks Action to Fund Mine Reclamation," *Charleston* [West Virginia] *Gazette*, November 15, 2000.

51. SMCRA [30 USC 1265 and 1266].

52. SMCRA, Sec. 522(e)(1).

53. U.S. Department of the Interior, Office of Surface Mining, *On-the-Ground Success: 2001 Annual and Financial Accountability Report* (Washington, D.C.: U.S. Department of the Interior, 2001), 23.

54. SMCRA [30 USC 1267], Sec. 517 and 518.

55. U.S. General Accounting Office, *Surface Mining: Interior Department and States Could Improve Inspection Programs*, GAO/RCED-87-40 (Washington, D.C.: U.S. General Accounting Office, 1986), 9.

56. U.S. Congress, Senate Committee on Interior and Insular Affairs, "Legislative Proposals Concerning Surface Mining of Coal," 92nd Cong., 1st sess. (1971), 129.

57. U.S. Department of the Interior, Office of Surface Mining, "Citizen Complaints Received by OSM, Report Period from 10/01/2001 to 9/30/2002," Inspection and Enforcement Monthly Reports, October 17, 2002, www.osmre.gov/i&eindex.htm (March 3, 2003).

58. "Bush Asks Judge to Suspend Mountaintop Mining Decision," *Greenwire*, May 14, 2002, www.eenews.net/greenwire/search archive (March 4, 2003).

59. Office of Surface Mining, *On-the-Ground Success*, 22.

60. States, theoretically at least, must run a regulatory program in accordance with SMCRA provisions. A state that fails to do so may face program revocation, and OSM reassumes regulatory control. Loss of primacy also means loss of AML funds, as well as loss of regulatory control. Nevertheless, in practice, OSM has been reluctant to take over state programs, only reassuming regulatory authority in Tennessee after that state's legislature repealed its state surface mining law, and temporarily assuming the inspection and enforcement (I/E) program in Oklahoma. Typically, OSM relies on less drastic oversight measures.

61. In 1988, in response to state criticism, OSM lengthened state response time from ten to up to twenty days, plus mailing time, according to an OSM official.

62. See *National Coal Association v. Christensen*, Civ. No. 87-2076 (DDC July 27, 1987); *Clinchfield Coal Co. v. Department of the Interior*, 802 F.2d 102, 17 ELR 20240 (4th Cir. 1986); *Annaco, Inc. v. Interior Dept.*, 27 Envt. Rep. Cas. (BNA) (1140 E.D.Ky. 1987).

63. Although this section is based upon the author's review of OSM annual reports and other information, see Donald C. Menzel, "Creating a Regulatory Agency: Profile of the Office of Surface Mining," in *Moving the Earth: Cooperative Federalism and Implementation of the Surface Mining Act*, ed. Uday Desai (Westport, Conn.: Greenwood Press, 1993), 31–45.

64. U.S. Department of Interior, Office of Surface Mining, "Chronology of the Office of Surface Mining and the Surface Mining Law Implementation," February 13, 2003, www.osmre.gov/history.htm (March 18, 2003).

65. Performance standards require a regulated industry to meet certain requirements but allow the industry discretion in achieving the standard. Design standards, in contrast, require that the industry also employ specific technologies in meeting the performance standards.

66. Many scholars have noted OSM's changing orientation, e.g., Donald C. Menzel, "Redirecting the Implementation of a Law: The Reagan Administration and Coal Surface Mining Regulation," *Public Administration Review* 43, no. 3 (1983): 411–20.

67. This is based on the author's conversation with an OSM inspector in the Big Stone Gap Field Office in June 1991.

68. Menzel, "Creating a Regulatory Agency," 34.

69. Menzel, "Creating a Regulatory Agency," 35.

70. U.S. Department of the Interior, Office of Surface Mining, *Annual Report for Fiscal Year 1981* (Washington, D.C.: Office of Surface Mining, 1982), 4.

71. U.S. Department of the Interior, Office of Surface Mining, *Annual Report for Fiscal Year 1983* (Washington, D.C.: Office of Surface Mining, 1984), 3.

72. U.S. Department of the Interior, Office of Surface Mining, *Annual Report for Fiscal Year 1982* (Washington, D.C.: Office of Surface Mining, 1983), 3; Office of Surface Mining, *Annual Report for Fiscal Year 1983*, 3.

73. Office of Surface Mining, Directives System, "Revision of Inspection and Enforcement Policy," INE-13, April 11, 1983.

74. Office of Surface Mining, *Annual Report for Fiscal Year 1981*, 2.

75. Office of Surface Mining, *Annual Report for Fiscal Year 1983*, 2.

76. Office of Surface Mining, *Annual Report for Fiscal Year 1982*, 51.

77. The "Parker-Gash Order" issued in December 1982, required OSM to assess and collect civil penalties against coal mine operators who failed to abate strip-mining violations when notified. It also required OSM to conduct a timely assessment of its penalties and not issue new permits to individual or corporate violators. This order implicitly applied to all primacy states.

78. U.S. Congress, House Committee on Government Operations, "Surface Mining Law: A Promise Yet to be Fulfilled," 100th Cong., 2d. sess. (H.R. No. 183, 1987).

79. James Watt resigned in 1983; James Harris resigned in 1984.

80. U.S. Department of the Interior, Office of Surface Mining, "Budget Justification Report for 1989" (unpublished document, 1989), 2.

81. Michael Lipske, "Cracking Down on Mining Pollution," *National Wildlife* 33, no. 4 (1995): 20–24, at 24.

82. This is based on a review of annual reports for the Office of Surface Mining from 1981 to 1987.

83. This is based on personal interviews with OSM field officers on April 19,1989, and on April 6,1990.

84. Office of Surface Mining, *A Shared Commitment: 1995 Annual Report* (Washington, D.C.: Office of Surface Mining, 1996), 3.

85. Office of Surface Mining, *Shared Commitment*, 3.

86. Office of Surface Mining, "Surface Mining Director Proposes New Oversight Policy" (press release, November 1, 1994); Office of Surface Mining, "New Surface Mine Oversight Directive Focuses on Results" (press release, January 31, 1996).

87. U.S. Department of the Interior, Office of Surface Mining, "Federal–State Shared Commitment to Reclamation Remains Strong Despite Lack of Consensus on Federal Enforcement" (press release, March 14, 1996).

88. Office of Surface Mining, "Chronology of the Office of Surface Mining and the Surface Mining Law Implementation," February 3, 2003, www.osmrc.gov/history.htm (May 5, 2003).

89. Office of Surface Mining, "OSM Directors," April 18, 2003, www.osmre.gov /directors.htm (September 15, 2003).

90. The 1995 surveys were sent when state officials were aware of the new OSM oversight policy. However, the new OSM philosophy was not put in place until 1996.

· 7 ·

Conclusions about Implementation
and Working Relationships

This book is about implementing environmental programs. By exploring the asbestos, radon, drinking water, and surface mining programs, one can see the implementation story unfold and get a sense of what life is like inside the program. The book started with two premises. The first—that working relationships matter, and matter a lot, in explaining how environmental programs work—was explored in each program chapter as well as in the introductory chapter. The second is that the implementation of each environmental law is a fascinating story, filled with a remarkable cast of characters employing strategies to influence the rate, timing, and degree to which policies unfold. The framing of the story is accomplished by using the lens of the conceptual framework presented in chapter 2. If only one conclusion should be drawn from the study, it is this: To take a law at face value, without exploring the rich detail of the policy story and its implementation through the states and federal regional offices, is to ignore a fundamental reality of the policy process. The remaining pages explore and extend these premises.

Pulling Together, Coming Apart, or
Somewhere in Between?

Are state and federal officials in regional and headquarters offices cooperatively "pulling together" to make environmental programs work, or are these relationships "coming apart" because these actors are responding to different political cues, have different expectations for performance, and hold different views about how performance should be evaluated? This study suggests that both of these attributes of pulling together and coming apart are occurring among the four environmental programs, although they differ by the type of program reviewed.

This section begins by distinguishing federal regional from federal headquarters personnel, and examining how such distinctions contribute to an understanding of federal–state working relationships. The next section presents

Table 7.1. Summary of Perceptions of State Officials about Federal–State Relationships (percentage of officials agreeing), 2002–3 and 1995–96 (1995–96 in parentheses)

Perception	Asbestos	Radon	Drinking Water	Coal
Oversight is flexible	64 (69)	73 (90)	36 (19)	78 (24)
Relationship is positive (region)	80 (86)	83 (88)	91 (86)	72 (57)
Relationship is positive (headquarters)	52 (39)	43 (58)	45 (30)	n.a.
EPA or OSM region is adequately funded	8 (25)	23 (48)	27 (12)	61 (55)
Communication is clear	24 (19)	40 (44)	18 (21)	n.a. (35)
Regional and headquarters views are similar	12 (28)	10 (42)	0 (0)	22 (20)
Without federal oversight, states not as serious about implementation	16 (16)	43 (44)	18 (30)	17 (19)
Reporting requirements are reasonable	n.a. (56)	n.a. (65)	0 (9)	38 (14)
N, 2002 (1995)	25 (37)	30 (44)	11(43)	19 (24)

Note: EPA = U.S. Environmental Protect Agency; n.a. = not available; OSM = U.S. Department of the Interior, Office of Surface Mining.

common observations of state program directors and regional program officials. It also explores how perceptions have changed between 1996 and 2003. The last section revisits the typology of working relationships and framework for policy implementation developed in chapters 1 and 2, and it offers suggestions for moving toward working relationships that pull together, in light of the National Environmental Performance Partnership System (NEPPS) and the REG 8 Directive.

Working Relationships among Headquarters, Regional, and State Officials

Table 7.1 presents the collected perceptions of state officials responding to surveys during the 1995–96 and 2002–3 studies. Though one must use caution in taking too much from the table, the figures do provide clues to working relationships.

Miles's Law, suggesting "Where you stand depends upon where you sit," is clearly operating among federal and state personnel. One of the remarkable findings from the 1995–96 and 2002–3 studies shown in table 7.1 is that state officials continue to view regional and headquarters staff quite differently. Similarly, state officials have very different relationships with federal headquarters staff than they do with federal regional staff. For the three programs reviewed that are overseen by the U.S. Environmental Protection Agency

(EPA)—asbestos, radon, and drinking water—nearly twice as many state officials agree that they have positive working relationships with their EPA regional
counterparts than agree that relationships are positive with EPA headquarters
staff. This is not very surprising, given the proximity of the EPA regional project officer to state officials. State officials believe that headquarters staff fail
to appreciate the difficulties of achieving on-the-ground performance.

Another observation gleaned from the study is that state officials operating
regulatory programs strongly believe that the federal oversight does not influence the level of attention paid to running an effective program. Fewer than
20 percent of state officials in drinking water, asbestos, or surface mining
agreed that without their federal "gorilla" they would not be as serious about
implementation. That changes, however, for the nonregulatory radon program, for which about 40 percent of state officials agreed that serious state efforts need federal involvement. This is likely due to the tenuous nature of state
radon programs. Many state radon officials wondered aloud in conversations
whether their program would continue to exist if EPA stopped funding it.

State officials continue to believe that funding for regional EPA programs
is inadequate. This is especially true for the asbestos and radon programs, for
which only 8 percent of state officials agree that the EPA regional offices have
enough funding to operate an effective program. A review of the story of asbestos policy and implementing the Asbestos Hazard and Emergency Response
Act suggests that state officials have reached the right conclusion (see chapter 3). Surface mining officials tend to believe that their federal counterparts
have enough funding to operate, even though the Office of Surface Mining
(OSM) had a significant reduction in force in 1995.

Perhaps the most remarkable observation from the study is the apparent
change in federal–state working relationships in the surface mining program.
State officials responding to the survey in 2002 were three times more likely
to agree that oversight is flexible and that reporting requirements are reasonable than those that responded to the 1995 survey. They were 50 percent more
likely to find positive relationships. Though state officials in surface mining
were still not as likely as other state officials to find positive relationships, the
change is dramatic. Several factors most likely account for the improved relationships. First, the REG 8 Directive described in chapters 1 and 6 has worked.
More than half of the state respondents agreed that intergovernmental life had
improved after REG 8. As one OSM official put it, "OSM's approach to oversight is now more focused on end results than process. This approach lessens
the feeling that many states had that OSM was second guessing every move
they made and merely counting the number of violations they missed or the
number of errors they made. Oversight [in the past] was more directed at identifying problems instead of solving them."

Second, the agency has established a culture of "shared commitment" with state regulators that appears to have recently taken hold in the field offices as well as headquarters. Some of the "old guard" inspectors who had a strict, go-by-the-book enforcement philosophy have retired or left the agency. As was noted in chapter 6, OSM has undergone numerous changes in top-level administrators, with a new director about every two years. However, the most recent director, Kathy Karpan, and the current director, Jeff Jarrett, have both consistently expressed allegiance to the philosophy of shared commitment. Third, in 1996, OSM cut the number of regulations in half at the same time that it undertook a reduction in force.

In contrast, the NEPPS program does not capture the attention of state radon, asbestos, or drinking water officials. Moreover, it appears that most of the regional staff interviewed for this study do not wholeheartedly embrace NEPPS. To be fair, OSM covers only one environmental program (surface mining), whereas EPA must address multiple programs. This makes implementing NEPPS far more complex. Only a few state officials interviewed expressed the opinion that Performance Partnership Agreements (PPAs) had improved the way they interact with their EPA project officers. When they mentioned NEPPS at all, officials expressed concern over two things: first, that the Performance Partnership Grants (PPGs) had shifted or might shift scarce resources out of their program; second, that the PPAs had actually caused them to double reporting, because they had to respond to requirements under the program as well as the PPA.

What is surprising is that so few state officials in any program are likely to agree that EPA regional and headquarters officials view their program similarly. This is especially true for the drinking water program, for which not a single state official in either 1995 or 2002 agreed that regional and headquarters staffs were of the same mindset. What this suggests is that not only are relationships more positive between regional and state officials but that state officials also tend to appreciate the viewpoint of EPA regional staff. One reason offered for a lower evaluation of the headquarters relationship was a lack of communication. State directors are sometimes frustrated by what they view as inadequate communication from the EPA headquarters staff, but many remain in close communication with their regional counterparts. Several state directors expressed concern about the EPA headquarter staff's inability or unwillingness to establish relatively simple communication connections with state personnel—even to the extent of returning telephone calls. Many more state officials pointed to other communication problems, including untimely notification of major policy changes, short time periods for feedback and comments on pending changes, and, insufficient attention paid by headquarters staff to state-level suggestions.

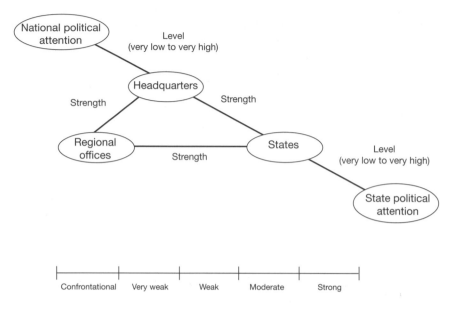

Figure 7.1.   Model of Federal–State Interactions

A Tripartite Model

Figure 7.1 suggests one way of viewing the tripartite nature of federal–state relationships within programs. For most national environmental programs, federal–state relationships are comprised of three interactions: interactions between state and federal regional personnel; interactions between state and federal headquarters personnel; and interactions between federal regional and headquarters personnel. Varying levels of state and national political attention structure the context for these interactions. Thus, the model is comprised of five parts: the three governmental units involved in policy implementation, and the national and state political arenas.

In turn, each interaction can be described on a continuum that ranges from confrontational to very weak, weak, moderate, or strong. Stronger relationships are brought about by the attention that is paid to them by the actors in each bureaucratic unit. In general, the more frequent the personal contact, the more positive the communication; and the more headquarters, regional, and state staffs are "on the same wavelength," the stronger the relationship.

The political environment also influences interactions between these three sets of actors. State environmental programs operate in political arenas that provide opportunities for very low to very high levels of political attention to the state program. Most often, this is interpreted as the nature of relationships that exist between state program personnel and top-level agency officials, state administrators, and state legislators. This connection between state political actors and state implementers of environmental programs is noted in the lower right corner of the figure.

Similarly, the level of national political attention influencing interactions among federal headquarters, regional, and state officials is shown in the upper left part of the model. If Congress, the courts, or the administration is putting the collective feet of the agency to the fire to accomplish legislative goals, the attention of headquarters officials is first directed outside the organization (and to the external actor or actors) and then focused on interactions with state and regional personnel.

The political context surrounding this tripartite group produces two possible effects. First, high levels of state or national political attention may work to make relationships stronger as pressure is put on both federal and state agencies to "do something" about the problem. Second, high levels of state or national political attention may work in the opposite direction; political attention directed toward policy implementation may fragment working relationships as different actors (national headquarters officials or state officials) respond to external demands. Both the drinking water and the surface mining programs operate in political environments that tend to frustrate cooperative interaction.

For the same reason, when administrators and legislators are not very interested in a particular environmental program, the relationships between state and federal actors may grow stronger. Like "picket fence" federalism—which suggests that federal, state, and local bureaucrats develop close relationships because of the expertise that is required to operate the program—officials of these programs may develop a kind of "survival" federalism.[1] A lack of state political attention to these specialized functional programs opens the window for increased federal–state staff activity, as federal and state actors become less concerned about the political examination of their program. The radon program is a case in point. However, though the picket fence model suggests that bureaucrats tend to amass political power, the survival model makes no such prediction. Indeed, it may well be that state and federal officials in a specialized program such as asbestos become allies simply to survive bureaucratic competition from more visible environmental programs.

In sum, the message of figure 7.1 is simple: One must be sensitive to interactions that occur among all three actors involved in making a program work. To fail to consider the headquarters staff is to neglect the importance of national implementation constraints in the political arena, as well as to perhaps miss the physical and psychological distance between headquarters personnel and other intergovernmental policy actors. To forget the regional staff—or, worse yet, to lump them together with headquarters personnel—is to miss an opportunity to get a view from the middle of the process from people who have the ear of both federal headquarters and the states. Finally, states as ultimate policy implementers react to federal headquarters program requirements and to shifts in operation and guidance. States interact with regional personnel in matters of oversight, grant administration, and program performance. States interact with and respond to the cues of both headquarters and regional personnel, so both units are important to any systematic review of public programs.

An additional lesson from the model is that the political arenas in which policy is implemented—which include not only the national arena but also the politics within each state—change the nature of the interactions among the three units. Proximity to Congress and the administration, combined with the distance from many states, mitigates against strong interactions between federal headquarters and the states, whereas regional offices are more likely to appreciate the nature of political forces in individual states.

The challenge now becomes how to strengthen interactions, moving from weak to strong in the model, without decreasing the legitimate oversight roles of the national actors. In other words, are there areas within federal–state relationships that could be improved while simultaneously increasing implementation performance? Is win–win possible—whereby working relationships *and* policy outcomes are both improved? Before answering this question, it is appropriate to review what the data from the study suggest that state officials and regional staff want from working relationships.

State "Wish Lists" for the Future

Even in instances where working relationships are positive, state officials identify common elements of concern, and the same suggestions for implementation improvement emerge in all five programs, to greater and lesser degrees. Similarly, federal regional staffs have common perceptions about program implementation and their own wish lists for change. Each viewpoint is considered in turn.

The interview and survey data from the directors of these environmental programs suggest two general observations. First, cooperative intergovernmental relations seem, for the most part, to describe the relationship between federal regional and state officials, signifying that state directors and EPA regional officials have their oars rowing together, to return to the rowboat metaphor used in chapter 1. Most state officials agree that the EPA regional staff is supportive of their programs. Fewer than half of the respondents want to remove the national involvement from state programs.

However, if state environmental directors had a "wish list" for improving working relationships, several items would appear. As is suggested by table 7.2,

Table 7.2. Summary of Common Perceptions among State Environmental
Program Staffs

State officials perceive:
- Need for national law, program, and federal funding
- A tendency of federal oversight personnel to micromanage programs, especially program and reporting requirements
- Poor communication of national program goals and requirements
- Support from EPA regional project officers and OSM field staff
- That federal headquarters personnel are too remote to know how things work "on the ground"
- Less effective federal programs than state programs
- That EPA regional offices are financially strained

State officials want:
- Adequately funded mandates (no increase in requirements without commensurate increase in funding)
- More flexibility in operating their programs, including funding flexibility
- No double reporting under PPAs and programs
- Less reliance on quantitative evaluation measures of state performance ("bean counting")
- Need for more technical support
- Clarification and anticipation of national goals
- EPA headquarters staff to understand on-the-ground issues
- Ability to set own priorities for the program

Note: EPA = U.S. Environmental Protection Agency; OSM = U.S. Department of the Interior, Office of Surface Mining; PPAs = Performance Partnership Agreements.

state directors want more flexibility in program development, as well as more flexibility in tailoring federal funds to state priorities. A common trend identified in the implementation case studies presented in the previous chapters is for EPA or OSM to increase demands for state performance under cooperative agreements without commensurate increases in federal funding. Thus, states resent what they believe to be an overly prescriptive federal orientation toward state programs, especially in light of stable or decreasing grant awards. As was mentioned above and in chapter 1, it does not appear that PPAs have significantly decreased either reporting requirements or programmatic flexibility, at least in the programs reviewed.

Conversely, state officials and regional project officers are wary of the effect that PPGs may have on funding for their program. The move toward a block grant approach to funding state environmental programs puts low-priority programs in precarious positions. The ultimate in funding flexibility, then, is not necessary what officials working in specific programs want. Flexibility in reporting requirements and flexibility in programmatic activities are desired by state personnel, but not necessarily when accompanied by the ability of top-level state administrators to make funding choices among programs.

Along with state concerns about EPA headquarters' predilection to prescribe program requirements without commensurately increasing funding (or the possibility of increasing competition for funding within the state), states are concerned that national goals for the programs are not clearly communicated. Poor goal clarification by EPA or OSM headquarters complicates state programs. When this happens, federal agencies become both *inflexible* regarding grant requirements and *vague* about the larger picture of desired policy outcomes. Often, EPA and OSM are similarly constrained by legislative or executive political whims. As summarized by one state program director, "EPA stands on political quicksand, responding to the shifting mood in Washington. Goals shift, and we wonder what the next 'priority de jour' will be. That wreaks havoc on our ability to plan a successful program."

Implicit in state directors' concerns about federal "bean counting" and inflexible requirements is the larger issue of trust. State directors feel adequately prepared to meet many of the implementation challenge inherent in their programs; however, they often feel that the institutions of EPA or OSM have little or no regard for state programmatic innovation or similar dedication to the fundamental goals of the policy.

This study suggests that though some national efforts to redirect environmental policy are nicely aligned with state officials concerns, others are not. The movement toward increasing state flexibility and devolving environmental programs to the states correlates with state officials' concerns about reporting requirements. States being seen as "customers" of the federal agencies and recent efforts to improve these federal–state relationships are warranted. PPGs or increasing the involvement of local governments or national associations, however, may not improve federal–state relationships at the program level, if state program officials feel that their program's funding is vulnerable. In addition, no initiative can replace the simple but effective efforts of state and federal officials to keep in contact and to appreciate the conditions under which each one operates.

Regional "Wish Lists" for the Future

Regional and field office personnel generally believe they are in that most maligned of positions, between a rock and a hard place. Agency regional staff feels they have tough job assignments. Their burden is guaranteeing programmatic performance—but they often shoulder the responsibility for on-

Table 7.3. Summary of Common Perceptions among Federal Regional Environmental Program Staffs

EPA Regional and OSM Field Office staff perceive:
- Less effective federal programs
- Political constraints on state program directors
- Need for cooperative relationships between regions and states
- Political constraints on headquarters staff
- Multiple, sometimes conflicting, objectives set by headquarters staff
- Capable state agencies and technical personnel
- Inadequate funding for regional and state activities

EPA Regional and OSM Field Office staff want:
- Recognition of their expertise by headquarters
- Consistent messages about program requirements from headquarters staff
- Greater input into policy decisions
- Greater political support for their program
- An appreciation by headquarters staff of their perspective

Note: EPA = U.S. Environmental Protection Agency; OSM = U.S. Department of the Interior, Office of Surface Mining

the-ground results with inadequate funding, a perceived lack of empathy from the national office, and no strong political base of support for their work from state or national actors (table 7.3).

A second observation is a corollary to the first one. That is, given the difficulty of their tasks, regional staffs commonly expresses the desire for their headquarters colleagues to spend some time with them, to talk personally to state officials, to encounter the challenges of being the federal "conduit" for policy implementation. Many regional staff members in these programs often feel they are the "Rodney Dangerfields" of federal–state working relationships—they get no respect from headquarters staff or from state officials. To return to Miles's Law, regional staff often express the desire that headquarters personnel come and sit where they do for a while.

Implicit in these findings is the conclusion that many regional staff members are a little discouraged with their job assignments. Although looking at agency morale was not the purpose of this study, it is troubling that regional personnel frequently have less than positive views of the operation of their national environmental programs. Interview and survey comments suggest the need to develop greater levels of support for regional personnel.

What regional staff put on their wish list for improved working relationships and policy implementation (besides more funding) is a desire to be recognized by headquarters staff for their substantive expertise, to be more a part of the front end of the implementation process, and to increase the awareness of headquarters staff of on-the-ground implementation obstacles. In short, regional staff seek many of the same things as state officials: recognition for the unique constraints on their work, the opportunity for more input into policy decisions, higher levels of trust on the part of headquarters staff, and more consistent work requirements.

Suggestions for Getting to Relationships That "Pull Together"

Chapter 1 presented a typology that characterized federal–state working relationships on the basis of two dimensions: levels of trust and levels of involvement. Two observations are worth noting. First, the dimensions of trust and involvement seem useful in predicting when participants will positively perceive intergovernmental relationships. Granted, trust is a slippery concept that is often measured by the participants themselves. What I looked for in interviews and survey responses and explored in documents was some evidence that federal and state officials were of one mind about their programs. Trust also meant that they had confidence in their intergovernmental colleagues and took as a matter of faith that their federal or state counterparts was as interested in protecting public health or the environment as they were. Furthermore, state officials wanted their federal colleagues to be involved in implementing state programs—not to look over the state's shoulder but rather to provide technical support and advice, and in rare instances serve as a backup enforcer.

Second, working relationships in programs are not static. Relationships can change, as is evident in the surface mining program. As the result of more than a hundred interviews that started with my first look at surface mining in 1991, and continued in subsequent studies that included other environmental programs, I have gleaned some pearls of wisdom from state and regional officials on how to achieve relationships that "pull together."

Figure 7.2 presents an ideal case: a situation in which suboptimal relationships become more synergistic and cooperative. In other words, participants start to pull together. Depending on where the program is located in the typology, participants need to increase levels of trust, levels of the right kind of involvement, or both.

Suggestions for increasing involvement include encouraging personal contacts, opening and using multiple communication channels, regularly sharing information and new knowledge, promoting organizational and interagency learning, communicating in a timely manner with opportunities for all

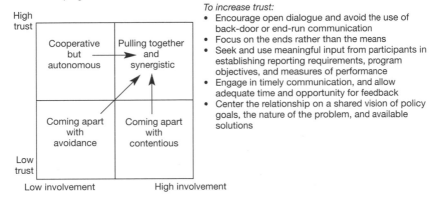

To increase involvement:
- Increase the use of face-to-face, on-site, informal communication among participants
- Regularly share information and new knowledge
- Promote inter- and intra-agency learning
- Use multiple ways of communicating information to increase the connections among federal Headquarts and regional, and state staff
- Keep participants aware of anticipated changes for the program

To increase trust:
- Encourage open dialogue and avoid the use of back-door or end-run communication
- Focus on the ends rather than the means
- Seek and use meaningful input from participants in establishing reporting requirements, program objectives, and measures of performance
- Engage in timely communication, and allow adequate time and opportunity for feedback
- Center the relationship on a shared vision of policy goals, the nature of the problem, and available solutions

Figure 7.2. Getting to Relationships That "Pull Together"

participants to have feedback, and keeping participants in the loop. Regional offices of federal bureaucracies are more than just mouthpieces for headquarters' initiatives. Some amount of translation and interpretation occurs within the message within an agency before it is delivered to state implementers. Strategic relationships develop between federal regional staff and state program officials. For example, it is not uncommon for regional staff to seek the opinions of state officials about new policy initiatives, public information tools, or similar outputs from agency headquarters and then to include those state comments with their own.

Meanwhile, EPA or OSM headquarters staffs are also communicating with state officials. Sometimes, communication is two ways and direct, such as when state officials are invited by headquarters staff to comment during a rule-making procedure. State officials are also contacted to participate in program reviews, appear before congressional oversight committees, and to help develop new regulations. More often, the communication is one way and indirect, with headquarters alerting regional offices of new requirements and the regional offices, in turn, passing that information on to states.

When this happens, national-level implementers lose the opportunity for meaningful feedback. Richard Stillman views feedback processes as an integral

Table 7.4. Techniques for Improving Communication and Establishing Better Working
Relationships

---

1. Minimize the social, geographic, and status distance between communicators.
2. Increase the use of face-to-face, on-site, informal communication among intergovernmental policy implementers.
3. Establish a climate of mutual trust and open communication channels that are in harmony.
4. Develop a shared perception about the nature of the problem and the best solutions available among implementers.
5. Allow adequate time to send, receive, rework, and resend new messages.
6. Avoid institutional or personal censorship of the message and allow for freedom in communication, and avoid the use ofback-door, end-run communication of new program requirements.

Source: Adapted from Richard J. Stillman, *The American Bureaucracy: The Core of Modern Government,*
2d ed. (Chicago: Nelson-Hall, 1996), 269.

part of maximizing bureaucratic outputs.[2] Feedback helps participants get involved in assessing the program. Accurate assessment, in turn, maximizes the outputs of agencies when it is immediate, supportive and clear, and it contains adequate information for program improvement, as is shown in table 7.4.

A clearer understanding of the different perspectives of state, regional, and headquarters implementers is more likely when participants can meet in person. Comments from both state and regional staffs often pointed to the need to have their vantage point understood by other participants—not necessarily to have other participants adopt that position, but more to understand why people feel the way they do about a particular element of the program.

It is not easy to increase levels of trust, if only because of the oversight orientations and responsibilities of federal headquarters and regional staffs. Suggestions for increasing trust within federal–state working relationships include encouraging open dialogue and avoiding the use of back-door or end-run communication tactics; focusing on the ends and not the means; establishing mechanisms for meaningful input by all participants; centering the relationship on shared visions about policy goals, problem dimensions, and available solutions; and increasing the connections within the tripartite relationship.

Many of these suggestions focus on the inherent strengths of intergovernmental relationships. For example, participants typically agree on the wisdom of the policy goal, which is, after all, the hoped-for "ends" of public policy. To the extent that federal overseers can avoid micromanaging while all participants focus on the desired future state, trust can be increased. Similarly, state officials, in turn, may need to increase their receptiveness to the legitimate national interests in running effective on-the-ground environmental programs.

Implementing Environmental Laws and the Conceptual Framework

The conceptual framework given in chapter 2 suggested that both extrinsic and intrinsic factors affect the ability of state agencies to implement public policy. The extrinsic factors—including political arrangements, the role orientations of the federal oversight agency, the nature of the problem, resource allocation, statutory and regulatory language, judicial interpretations, refocusing events, and the demand for change—either facilitated or hindered state implementation performance in varying degrees in all four programs reviewed. The intrinsic factors—such as working relationships, agency capacity, and the relationship of the implementing agency to the target group in the state—were equally important.

Extrinsic Factors

Politics plays a powerful role in implementing the environmental programs reviewed. In the asbestos program, the political fallout from school districts removing asbestos (rather than managing it in place) has, in part, resulted in reduced federal funding for asbestos, angry and litigious publics, and little implementation of the Asbestos Hazard and Emergency Response Act (AHERA) by EPA regional staff. For the surface mining program, the political histories of state and federal conflicts, combined with political pressure from coal companies at the state and national levels, explain more of the implementation story than a lack of available state staff or funding. Thorny issues, such as mountaintop removal and bonding, loom large on the political horizons and continue to divide environmental groups and state and OSM officials. The result is a continuing legal battle over SMCRA implementation. As one environmental group member put it, "Our only recourse is to sue, sue, sue."

Conversely, state politicians are simply not very interested in radon programs. Radon in homes is an individual concern, and few people care about mitigating existing housing stock. Radon is a known carcinogen and the second leading cause of lung cancer, but people are willing to take the risk of elevated radon levels. Little or no political pressure is exerted at the national, regional, or state levels.

If political pressure to reduce radon levels is missing, political forces seeking to implement AHERA had virtually disappeared. In the mid-1990s, EPA emerged badly bruised from its guidance on the management of asbestos-containing materials in schools. Public school officials and members of Congress took turns chastising the agency for its seeming encouragement to remove asbestos. In early 2000, EPA cut the AHERA program significantly as other pollutants, most notably lead, captured the attention of the public and top officials in the enforcement program for the Toxic Substances Control Act. AHERA might have faded into virtual organizational oblivion but for two refocusing events: the vermiculite problem in Libby, Montana, and the collapse of the twin towers of the World Trade Center. Suddenly, asbestos was in the news. Also in the news was the rapid rise of asbestos liability litigation. Asbestos proved to be a very extraordinary implementation story indeed.

It is also useful to look at the nature of the environmental problem. One way to view the nature of the problem is to look at the heterogeneity of the target group. Two implementation stories, that of coal mining and drinking water, illustrate this factor well. In the case of coal mining, the existence of gargantuan low-sulfur coal seams in the West had already doomed many small Appalachian operations. Coal mining employment has decreased at the same time coal production has reached record levels. Moreover, the remaining mining operations are politically very powerful and have the ear of the Bush administration. Public water suppliers are a very heterogeneous target group, as was detailed in chapter 5. Small water system suppliers simply cannot afford to pass costs of compliance onto their customers, not to mention the already heavy financial burden of infrastructure repair and replacement.

Promulgating "safe" levels of drinking water contaminants presents a regulatory nightmare for EPA, which was only partially alleviated by the 1996 amendments to the Safe Drinking Water Act (SDWA). The standard for radon in water is still not final, and most people in EPA and state agencies hopes it remains in a draft form, for the reasons described in chapter 4. They are not likely to get their wish, however, because Congress required EPA to promulgate the radon standard, and it prescribed the approach the agency must take, when it amended the drinking water law. The arsenic standard also represents high-stakes politics, pitting the State of Nebraska against EPA and the constitutionality of the drinking water law itself.

The 1986 amendments to SDWA, which required the promulgation of national standards for eighty-three new contaminants, not only impeded the implementation of the drinking water program but also threw the agency into turmoil and the states into a fervor. Political revolts, led by the battle cry of "unfunded mandates," were started by local governments that viewed the costs associated with compliance as enormous or even overwhelming for small public water system suppliers. Clearly, the statutory language of both the 1986 and 1996 amendments is affecting the implementation of the drinking water program.

The role orientations of agency staff are important, as is illustrated especially by the policy history of the surface mining program. The different approaches to citing violations taken by OSM field office personnel have evolved during the twenty-six-year history of the agency, influencing both the nature of working relationships but also the pace of implementation. For many years, the "gotcha syndrome" permeating OSM's culture and contributed to a confrontational state–federal working relationship that frustrated state inspectors. One state coal program supervisor described it this way in 1995:

> We do not receive support from our OSM field office. They continually attempt to disparage and frustrate our efforts. They refuse to acknowledge that they and we are working toward the same goal. They continually choose to substitute their own judgment for ours. Washington is too removed to appreciate Western concerns and is overwhelmed with mining problems in the east. OSM dictates how the program is to be run, frequently changes directives with no notice, and constantly finds fault with minor details of our program. They report every failing and few of our successes.

Judicial interpretations have played a major role in implementing both SMCRA and SDWA. Every drinking water standard set by EPA has been challenged. SMCRA's implementation has been peppered with lawsuits from environmental groups, mining associations, and states. Most recently, a court decision to prohibit mines from filling up valleys with overburden was overturned, prompting a coalition of environmental groups to file an intent to sue under the Endangered Species Act. This judicial event illustrates the increasingly important connections among environmental laws. This intersection may be helpful, or it may work at cross-purposes.

Finally, the demand for change is illustrated by several cases. Demands to change an unworkable law brought Congress back to the drawing board to pass amendments to SDWA. The demand for change has pressed EPA to rethink its asbestos policy, as evidenced by the nationwide task force and upcoming development of a national asbestos strategy. Equally important, however, is the absence of any demand for change. Radon has been relegated to just another indoor pollutant, and as such, it continues to struggle to get the attention of the public and of policymakers. Without another Watras event, as described in chapter 4, no push to protect people from radon is likely.

Intrinsic Factors

Intergovernmental relationships are important in all the programs and occupy much of the space in this book. If anything, reviewing different programs and looking at these programs over time has illustrated the need for more scholarly attention to be paid to this component of environmental policy implementation, especially to address the nature of working relationships, levels of trust, and interactions among participants.

The role orientations of staff inside the implementing agency are essential determinants of policy implementation. Survey and interview comments suggest that most state staffs are dedicated to the ultimate goal of their programs. Perhaps the biggest difference in role orientation between state and federal personnel is that state inspectors are most likely to adopt a consultative approach to enforcing environmental laws, as is illustrated by this comment: "I would prefer to perceive formal enforcement action as one of many tools available to ensure compliance. . . . However, the OSM forces us to take action against companies for infractions as minor as a fallen sign, or a report a week late." Another clear example of different role orientations between state and federal officials comes from the drinking water program. Not a single drinking water administrator responding to the survey believes that EPA understands the needs of small water system suppliers.

States are clearly pinched for funding. Although available resources are an issue, however, other measures of agency capacity are strong. State officials believe they run effective programs with staff who are adequately trained. A lack of available staff in the program is partially overcome by the enthusiasm and dedication of implementation energizers. This study revealed several such people. In the asbestos program, one official refused to go along with EPA's disinvestment from AHERA. The radon program, though minuscule in staff in many states, operated more effectively than anticipated because of the motivation of one or two key people, as is illustrated by this comment: "We can't wait for the EPA or the Office of Management and Budget to decide what to do and how to do it. I've got high levels [of radon] in my state and I'm going to do what I can with the resources I have."

The relationship between the implementing agency and the target group often influences implementation, especially as described in the surface mining and drinking water programs. The level of state political support also influences the implementation process, as mentioned above.

Finally, agency outputs do appear to differ from policy outcomes. Activities undertaken by state agencies may or may not result in the achievement of desired policy goals. As was mentioned earlier in the chapter, a number of state and regional staff commented that some program requirements were "make-work" activities, which detracted from the ultimate goal of making the living environment a safer place. Similarly, policy outcomes are happening without the direct intervention of implementers—as when schools act to eliminate asbestos exposure.

In sum, the implementation factors in the framework presented in chapter 2 seem to make sense, at least when looking at these environmental programs. Studies of policy implementation that fail to consider federal–state interactions paint too simple a picture of a very complex web of relationships. Interactions between people matter; mutual respect is important. There is little evidence that changing orientations at the top of the intergovernmental chain produce more effective approaches in state implementation; nor is there evidence that state directors desire OSM- or EPA-dictated priorities.

This study is only a beginning, however. Additional regulatory and non-regulatory programs should be studied to be more confident that the data in this study reflect a common orientation of state directors and regional EPA staff. In addition, systematic study of national office staff is needed to better explain federal perceptions of state programs and individual role orientations.

Demands for the integration of environmental programs, devolving regulatory authority, and ecosystem management make understanding working relationships and implementation dynamics even more crucial. Strategies for coping with changes in agency culture, role orientations, and organizational commitments will be paramount. Agencies are in the midst of nonincremental changes in implementing environmental programs. The challenge is to continue working to fulfill the vision of environmental and public health protection in cooperation with other participants and stakeholders and with more sensitivity to the important role that each plays in the implementation story.

Notes

1. Terry Sanford, *Storm over the States* (New York: McGraw-Hill, 1967), 80. For a discussion of models of federalism and intergovernmental relations, see David C. Nice and Patricia Fredericksen, *The Politics of Intergovernmental Relations*, 2d ed. (Chicago: Nelson-Hall, 1995); and Deil S. Wright, *Understanding Intergovernmental Relations*, 2d ed. (Monterey, Calif.: Brooks/Cole, 1982).

2. Richard J. Stillman, *The American Bureaucracy: The Core of Modern Government*, 2d ed. (Chicago: Nelson-Hall, 1996), 269.

Appendix: Research Sources and Methods

The research for this project was conducted in 2002 and 2003. The book also incorporates some of the results from an earlier study conducted in 1995–96, which included 85 interviews and 230 returned surveys.

During the course of eight months in 2002 and 2003, 73 interviews were conducted with administrators of state asbestos, radon, drinking water, and surface mining programs, EPA and OSM officials, environmental group executive directors, and executive directors of three professional associations. Interviews were conducted on the telephone and averaged 45 minutes per conversation. In many cases, follow-up e-mail or telephone conversations occurred. Former U.S. representative Ken Hechler (W. Va.) also agreed to be interviewed regarding the early history of SMCRA implementation.

In 2002, 138 surveys were sent to state officials listed on EPA and OSM websites as having primary responsibility for directing the radon, asbestos, and surface mining programs. No EPA listing of drinking water administrators was available on the agency's website or by phone or mail. Instead, a partial list of drinking water administrators was collected from the websites of the Association of State Drinking Water Administrators and of state environmental agencies. An additional 10 surveys were sent to EPA Regional NEPPS coordinators by using contact information on the EPA website. Eighty-five of the 138 surveys sent to state program directors were returned, for a response rate of 62 percent. Five of the 10 surveys sent to NEPPS coordinators were returned, for a response rate of 50 percent. The response rates for individual programs are noted in the text of each chapter.

Extensive reviews of government and other professional documents were conducted for this project. When possible, additional sources of information—including unpublished correspondence, websites of professional associations, newspapers, and scholarly journals—provided additional material for the study.

Index

A

Abandoned Mine Reclamation Act (1990), 189n43

Abandoned Mine Reclamation Fund, 168–69

Abelson, Phillip H., 123n45

Ackerman, Bruce, 187n15

Adams, Stephen, 12

Advertising Council, 101, 102f4.1, 110

Adler, Jonathan H., 28n23

Alabama, 66, 161

Alaska, 138, 140

Albuquerque (N.M.), 132

Alliance (Neb.), 133

American Association of Radon Scientists and Technologists, 100

American Lung Association, 110

Anton, Thomas, 7

Applicant Violator System (AVS), 176, 186. *See also* Surface Mining Control and Reclamation Act (1977); surface mining program

Arizona, 13

Army Corps of Engineers, 172

arsenic, 130, 132–33, 136, 149

asbestos, 56; diseases associated with, 56–58, 60; government response to, 59–64; history of, 56; lawsuits related to, 61, 66, 67, 75; occupational exposure to, 58–59, 60; use of during World War II, 56, 59–60

asbestosis, 58, 60

asbestos-containing materials (ACMs), 55, 59, 62, 63, 73, 81, 86; EPA attempted ban of, 65; EPA standard for, 73. *See also* asbestos; asbestos program

Asbestos Hazard and Emergency Response Act (AHERA) (1986), 9, 55, 61–62, 97, 125, 205; compared to radon law, 104, 106; funding for, 68, 77, 78t3.1, 81; guidance for Lower Manhattan clean-up, 72–74; implementation of, current years, 68–70, 71–76, 84, 86; implementation of, early years, 66–68; state waivers under, 63, 76. *See also* asbestos program

asbestos program, 52, 69, 154, 155; characteristics of state programs, 76–83, 140; costs of, 67, 77; criticisms of asbestos removal, 66–67; funding of, 76–77, 78t3.1, 81; implementation of, 64–66, 68, 71–76, 79–83, 205–6; model accreditation plans of, 63; requirements for schools, 62–63, 64–65, 67, 70, 82; requirements for states, 63; state officials' perceptions of, 76–83, 194; working relationships within, 83–87. *See also* Asbestos Hazard and Emergency Response Act (1986)

Asbestos in Schools Act (1982), 62

Asbestos in Schools Rule, 65

Asbestos School Hazard Abatement Act (1984), 62, 67

Asbestos School Hazard and Detection Act (1980), 62

B

Bardach, Eugene, 37, 39, 45

Barry III, Hamlet J., 189n40

Berkeley Wellness Letter, 106

Berks County (Pa.), 96

Berkshire Hathaway, 61